Best of the Best from the

Great Lakes

Cookbook

Selected Recipes from the
Favorite Cookbooks of
MICHIGAN, MINNESOTA, and WISCONSIN

Big Sable Point Lighthouse, located at Ludington State Park on the eastern shore of Lake Michigan, is one of the few Michigan lights with a tower reaching 100 feet. Michigan is bounded by four of the five Great Lakes (Lake Erie, Lake Huron, Lake Michigan, and Lake Superior) with well over 100 lighthouses on its shoreline, including more than 60 that are still active.

Best of the Best from the
Great Lakes
Cookbook

Selected Recipes from the
Favorite Cookbooks of
MICHIGAN, MINNESOTA, and WISCONSIN

EDITED BY

Gwen McKee

AND

Barbara Moseley

QUAIL RIDGE PRESS
Preserving America's Food Heritage

Library of Congress Cataloging-in-Publication Data
Best of the best from the Great Lakes cookbook : selected recipes from the favorite
    cookbooks of Michigan, Minnesota, and Wisconsin / edited by Gwen McKee
    and Barbara Moseley. — 1st ed.
      p. cm..— (Best of the best cookbook series)
    ISBN-13: 978-1-934193-35-8
    ISBN-10: 1-934193-35-6
      1. Cookery, American. 2. Cookery—Michigan. 3. Cookery—Minnesota.
    4. Cookery—Wisconsin. I. McKee, Gwen. II. Moseley, Barbara.
    TX715.B4856154 2010
    641.5977—dc22   2010008174

ISBN-13: 978-1-934193-35-8 • ISBN-10: 1-934193-35-6

Book design by Cyndi Clark
Cover photo by Greg Campbell • Illustrated by Tupper England

Printed in Canada
First edition, November 2010
On the cover: Cherry Cheese Brownie Bars, page 239

QUAIL RIDGE PRESS
P. O. Box 123 • Brandon, MS 39043
info@quailridge.com • www.quailridge.com

Contents

The Great Lakes Aquarium in Duluth, Minnesota, is the only aquarium in the United States that focuses on freshwater exhibits. All of the main exhibits of the aquarium are based upon actual habitats in the Lake Superior basin. Shown here with another major landmark in the port city, the Aerial Lift Bridge, in the background.

Quest for the Best Regional Cooking

*T*he cuisines of Minnesota, Wisconsin, and Michigan have similarities because of their their proximity to the Great Lakes, and of course because of their ancestry. Many of the recipes originated from natives who were fishermen and hunters and farmers who learned to turn their bounty into everything from humble meals to magnificent feasts. The European immigration of Swedes, Germans, French Canadians, and Norwegians introduced their cuisines to the area, bringing flat breads, streusels, kringles, and the like. The pasty (pronounced *pass tee*), a kind of meat turnover originally brought to the region by Cornish miners, is popular among locals and tourists alike. Wild rice grows beautifully in many parts of this region, as well as cherries and an assortment of berries; hops to make beer; cheese and beer and brats, and so many creative ways to cook fish and meat, and to turn dairy products and cherries and berries into delicious desserts.

Traveling to every state in the United States in search of the best cookbooks and recipes took Barbara Moseley and me the better part of 27 years. What started in our home state of Mississippi with one cookbook, grew to include our neighboring states, then as each one neared completion, we reached out farther and farther away from home to explore the cuisines of states far and wide. The experience has been one that has enabled us to bring home each new state's recipes to become ours forever.

But nothing seems so special and dear as when you share it with others who you know will enjoy it as much as you do. Our BEST OF THE BEST STATE COOKBOOKS feature chosen favorite recipes that we are proud to have brought from each state home to you, wherever you are. I wish we could introduce you to the many people we have met in every state who were proud of their cooking heritage and eager to show us just how good their recipes were, and are! Sometimes

it was a particular local ingredient, or the way they kneaded the dough, or browned the flour, or marinated the meat, or maybe a secret method they used to make something particularly unique to their way of cooking. It has truly been a delicious experience!

Treat yourself to a smorgasbord of delicious food from the beautiful Great Lakes region of our country.

Gwen McKee

Gwen McKee and Barbara Moseley, editors of
BEST OF THE BEST STATE COOKBOOK SERIES

Beverages and Appetizers

The Apostle Islands National Lakeshore consists of 21 islands and 12 miles of pristine Lake Superior shoreline on the northern tip of Wisconsin's peninsula. The lakeshore consists of soft sand beaches, rocky cliffs, and mystical sea caves. Kayaking has become a popular way to travel among the Apostle Islands, and camping is available on 18 of the lakeshore's 21 islands.

Simply Cherry Smoothie

2 cups frozen tart cherries
1 ripe banana
1 cup cherry juice blend

Strawberries or cherries for
garnish

Combine frozen cherries, banana, and cherry juice in a blender or food processor. Purée until smooth. Pour into individual serving glasses. Garnish with fresh strawberry or cherry.

Cherry Home Companion (Michigan)

Spicy Warm Cider

1 gallon apple cider
1 (6-ounce) can frozen
** concentrate orange juice**

7 cinnamon sticks
1½ teaspoons whole cloves
1 teaspoon whole allspice

Combine cider and frozen orange juice in small soup pot. Place cinnamon sticks, cloves, and allspice in a double layer of cheesecloth, and tie with kitchen string. Lower the bag into the juice. Simmer mixture, covered, for 1 hour over low heat. Strain, if not using a cheesecloth bag. Serve cider warm (it can be reheated). Serves 30.

Heart Smart Cookbook II (Michigan)

Red Wine Punch

3 cups red wine
2 cups fresh tea
½ cup rum

1¾ cup sugar
Juice of 2 lemons

Mix together wine, tea, rum, and sugar. Heat to boiling. Add lemon juice. Serve hot or cold. Serves 6–8.

History from the Hearth (Michigan)

Slush

Make Slush two days in advance so it has time to freeze.

1½ quarts cran-raspberry juice
1 (12-ounce) can frozen lemonade concentrate

1 (12-ounce) frozen orange juice concentrate
4 cups 7-Up
2 cups vodka

Mix these ingredients and freeze. To serve, fill glass ²/₃ full with slush and ¹/₃ 7-Up.

Marketplace Recipes Volume I (Wisconsin)

Mango Salsa

3 tablespoons minced red onion
2 cups diced pineapple
1½ cups diced mangoes
1½ tablespoons fresh lime juice

1½ tablespoons seeded, minced jalapeño pepper
¼ teaspoon salt
3 tablespoons chopped cilantro

Mix all ingredients except cilantro. Refrigerate. Add cilantro just before serving. Makes about 5 cups.

Taste of Clarkston: Tried & True Recipes (Michigan)

Minnesota is famous for its many beautiful lakes and rivers. In fact, the state got its nickname, "Land of 10,000 Lakes" because it has 11,842 named lakes larger than ten acres. When including unnamed lakes over ten acres, the number for Minnesota jumps to 15,291. Estimates suggest that if Minnesota included five-acre lakes, the number could approach or exceed 20,000. Only one of the state's 87 counties, Rock County, doesn't have a natural lake.

Chili Cheese Dip

CHILI MEAT SAUCE:

½ pound lean ground beef or lean ground turkey

⅛ teaspoon each: salt and ground black pepper, or to taste

½ teaspoon chili powder

½ teaspoon ground cumin

¼ cup tomato sauce

½ small jalapeño pepper, diced fine

2 tablespoons finely diced onion

Crumble meat into a medium frying pan over medium heat and add salt, pepper, chili powder, and cumin; cook until meat is well done. Pour off accumulated grease, if any. Stir in tomato sauce, jalapeño pepper, and onion. Makes about 1 cup.

DIP:

1 (8-ounce) package cream cheese, softened

1 cup Chili Meat Sauce

4 green onions, sliced fine

½ cup grated Monterey Jack cheese

½ cup grated Cheddar cheese

Preheat oven broiler. Spray a 9-inch pie plate with nonstick cooking spray and spread bottom with cream cheese. Layer on Chili Meat Sauce, green onions, Jack cheese, and Cheddar cheese. Place under oven broiler until cheese melts. Serves 6 or more.

Reduced-Fat and Calorie Variation: Make Chili Meat Sauce with lean ground turkey, substitute reduced-fat cream cheese for regular, reduced-fat mozzarella for Monterey Jack, and reduced-fat Cheddar for regular.

Recipes from Joan's Kitchen (Michigan)

BLT Dip

1 cup chopped tomatoes

1 cup chopped lettuce

1 cup sour cream

1 cup Miracle Whip

1 cup bacon bits

Mix together and serve with crunchy snack bread or bagels.

Dr. Martin Luther Church 100th Anniversary Cookbook (Wisconsin)

Artichoke Dip

Assemble ahead; put in oven just before guests arrive.

2 (8½-ounce) cans artichoke
   hearts
1 cup fresh grated Parmesan
   cheese

1 cup mayonnaise
8 ounces shredded mozzarella
   cheese
Pinch of garlic

Mix. Put in casserole dish. Bake at 350° for 25–30 minutes. Serve with crackers.

Variation: Omit mozzarella cheese and garlic. Or substitute 2 tablespoons no-fat sour cream and ³⁄₄ cup no-fat yogurt (room temperature) for mayonnaise and add 4 drops hot sauce.

Sharing our Best to Help the Rest (Minnesota)

Warm Artichoke Dip

An excellent sandwich spread, good with a grilled veggie sandwich; on baked potatoes instead of sour cream; or in grilled mushroom caps.

1 teaspoon olive oil
1 medium onion, diced
3 cloves garlic, minced
1 (9-ounce) package frozen
   artichoke hearts, or
   2 (15-ounce) cans
1 (8-ounce) package fat-free
   cream cheese

⅓ cup freshly grated
   Parmesan cheese
Dash of hot sauce
¼ teaspoon salt, or to taste
¼ cup chopped fresh basil
Dash of paprika

Heat oil in skillet; saute onion and garlic over medium heat till soft, about 3 minutes. Add artichoke heart and cover. Reduce heat to low and cook 5 minutes. Transfer mixture to food processor. Add cream cheese and Parmesan; pulse ingredients to combine. Add hot sauce, salt, and basil. Pulse to combine. Serve warm, sprinkled lightly with paprika. Makes 10 servings.

High Fit–Low Fat Vegetarian (Michigan)

Italian Crabmeat Dip

1 (8-ounce) and 1 (3-ounce)
 package cream cheese,
 softened
2 tablespoons mayonnaise
Dash of garlic powder
Dash of Worcestershire

Dash of lemon juice
1 (12-ounce) jar chili sauce
Diced onion to taste
1 (6-ounce) can crabmeat,
 drained
Green parsley for garnish

In blender add cream cheese, mayonnaise, garlic powder, Worcestershire, and lemon juice; blend till smooth. Spread onto a 14-inch pizza pan. Spread chili sauce on top of mixture. Top with diced onion, crabmeat, and parsley. Serve with assorted crackers.

Just Inn Time for Breakfast (Michigan)

Crispy Pita Triangles

Delicious with savory dips and spread as an alternative to fat-free crackers.

5 whole-wheat pita bread
 pockets
Vegetable cooking spray

¼ cup shredded Parmesan
 cheese

Preheat oven to 375°. Separate each pita pocket into 2 equal pieces. Stack pieces on top of each other and cut in half, then cut each half into 4 to make 16 wedges altogether. Separate wedges and place on a cookie sheet (lightly sprayed with vegetable cooking spray) in a single layer. Lightly spray the pita wedges with vegetable cooking spray, then sprinkle with Parmesan cheese.

   Place in a preheated oven to bake till crispy and lightly golden in color, 7–10 minutes. Watch carefully to avoid burning. Will keep fresh for several weeks. Makes 20 servings (4 triangles each).

High Fit–Low Fat Vegetarian (Wisconsin)

Herbed Pita Bites

¾ cup butter or margarine,
  softened
2 tablespoons minced
  fresh parsley
2 tablespoons snipped chives

1 large clove garlic, minced
1 tablespoon lemon juice
Salt and pepper to taste
4 pita breads, halved into
  rounds

Cream butter, parsley, chives, garlic, lemon juice, salt and pepper. Spread on pita bread halves and broil just before serving. Cut each into 8 wedges. Makes 32 pieces. Fat 4.5 grams per serving.

Minnesota Heritage Cookbook II (Minnesota)

Jacquie Cater's Nutty Cherry Gorgonzola Balls

2 tablespoons butter
¾ cup finely chopped
  walnuts
1 (8-ounce) package cream
  cheese, softened

4 ounces Gorgonzola cheese,
  crumbled
½ cup dried cherries

Melt butter in a sauté pan over medium-high heat. Sauté walnuts until lightly browned and fragrant. Place cream cheese, Gorgonzola, and cherries in the bowl of your food processor and process until the mixture is creamy and the cherries are finely chopped. Transfer mixture into a bowl and place in freezer for 30 minutes.

Remove chilled mixture from freezer and scoop and mold into walnut-size balls. Roll balls of cheese in butter-toasted walnuts until covered. Place mini cheese balls in a container and chill at least 4 hours to blend flavors.

When ready to serve, cut balls in half with a serrated knife, using a sawing motion. Serve on crackers or toasted baguettes, or with apple or pear slices. Serves 8–12.

Cherry Home Companion (Michigan)

Cranberry Glazed Brie

3 cups cranberries
¾ cup brown sugar
⅓ cup dried currants
⅓ cup water
⅛ teaspoon dry mustard

⅛ teaspoon ground allspice
⅛ teaspoon cardamom
⅛ teaspoon cloves
⅛ teaspoon ginger
1 (2.2-pound) brie cheese wheel

In a saucepan, combine cranberries, brown sugar, currants, water, and spices. Cook over high heat for 5 minutes. Remove from heat to cool. Cover and refrigerate. (This may be made up to 3 days in advance.) Set brie on a heat-proof platter. Using a sharp knife, cut a circular top off rind, leaving ½-inch border. Spread cranberry marmalade over brie and refrigerate for 6 hours. Remove from refrigerator 2 hours before serving and bring to room temperature. Bake at 300° for 12 minutes. Serve with fresh fruit slices such as apples or pears, and/or crackers. Serves 12.

Recipes of Note for Entertaining (Minnesota)

Hot Cheese Cubes

1 (3-ounce) package cream
  cheese
¼ pound Cheddar cheese,
  cubed

½ pound butter
2 egg whites, stiffly beaten
1 pound bread, unsliced

In a double boiler, add the cream cheese, Cheddar cheese, and butter. Cook, stirring, until melted and fully blended. Let stand a few minutes. Fold in the stiffly beaten egg whites. Trim the crust from the bread and cut into 1-inch cubes. Dip each cube in the cheese mixture and place on a greased cookie sheet. Bake at 375° for 12–15 minutes. These can be made the night before and refrigerated and reheated in the oven or microwave. Makes 36 cubes.

Recipes from Minnesota with Love (Minnesota)

Stuffed Michigan Morels

Michiganians are fortunate to have access to 3 native varieties of fresh morels in early May each year.

25 large morels
½ cup butter
1 cup chopped onion
1 cup chopped celery
1 teaspoon salt
½ teaspoon black pepper

½ teaspoon paprika
5 cups dry bread crumbs
1½ cups coarsely chopped
    pecans
Beaten eggs
½–1 cup butter, melted

Select large, preferably white, morels. Rinse thoroughly; trim off stems; set morels aside and chop stems. Heat butter in large, heavy skillet and saute* onion, celery, and chopped mushroom stems till tender and transparent. Stir in seasonings, bread crumbs, and pecans. Stir in enough beaten eggs to moisten mixture. Spoon filling in pastry bag fitted with a serrated metal tip, and stuff morels. Set stuffed morels, points up, on a buttered baking sheet. Drizzle with melted butter and bake at 350° for 20–30 minutes. Serve upright on chopped parsley or other greens. Serves 10–12.

Cranbrook Reflections (Michigan)

Pepperoni Appetizer

3 cups milk
3 eggs, beaten
3 cups all-purpose flour
1½ cups shredded Muenster
   cheese

1 teaspoon salt
Dash of pepper and oregano
1 large stick pepperoni, sliced
   thin (1½ cups)

Combine milk and eggs. Mix in flour with mixer until smooth (blender works well). Add remaining ingredients and stir to incorporate well. Bake in greased 9x13-inch pan at 425° for about 40 minutes. Cut into bite-size pieces. Serve warm.

Feeding the Flock (Minnesota)

Greek Mini Pizzas

4 pita breads, split
¼ cup olive oil
4 cloves garlic, minced
2 tomatoes, chopped
1 bunch scallions, chopped

¾ cup chopped Greek olives
1½ teaspoons oregano
1 cup crumbled feta cheese
1 cup shredded provolone
  cheese

Brush pita with olive oil. Sprinkle with garlic, tomatoes, scallions, and olives. Add oregano, feta, and top with shredded provolone. Can refrigerate several hours. Bake at 350° for 10–12 minutes. Cut each round in fourths and serve warm. Yields 32 appetizers.

Something Special (Michigan)

Puff Pastry Prosciutto Pinwheels

Impressive looking and not hard to make!

1 sheet puff pastry
3 tablespoons honey mustard
¼ pound thinly sliced
  prosciutto, chopped
1 cup grated Parmesan cheese

1 egg
Water
Parchment paper
Pam cooking spray

Preheat oven to 400°. Place puff pastry on lightly floured surface and roll out to 12x18 inches; spread mustard on top of pastry. Arrange prosciutto evenly to cover all the pastry; sprinkle with cheese. Lightly press cheese into prosciutto with a rolling pin.

Starting at one long edge, roll up the pastry like a jellyroll just to the middle of the dough (approximately 3 times); roll up the other side in the same way. Where the 2 rolls meet in the center, use a small amount of water to seal seam.

Cut the rolls into ½-inch slices using a serrated knife. Place slices on cookie sheet lined with parchment sprayed with Pam; flatten slightly with spatula. Refrigerate at least 15 minutes or till ready to bake.

Beat egg with 2 tablespoons water; brush each pinwheel with egg wash. Bake 10 minutes, till lightly golden. Turn pinwheels over; bake 5 minutes more. Serve warm. Makes 2 dozen.

The Bountiful Arbor (Michigan)

Creamy Horseradish Ham Roll-Ups

This appetizer looks great when served with deviled eggs.

1 (8-ounce) package cream
  cheese, softened
2 tablespoons prepared
  horseradish
2 tablespoons mayonnaise

1 teaspoon Worcestershire
⅛ teaspoon salt
⅛ teaspoon pepper
1 pound baked deli ham

Blend all ingredients except ham. Spread on ham slices and roll up lengthwise. Refrigerate until time of serving. Slice into 1-inch pieces. Serve on lettuce leaves.

Wisconsin's Best (Wisconsin)

Ham Meatballs

1 pound ham, ground
1 pound veal or pork, ground
2 cups soft bread crumbs
  (8 slices)
1 cup milk
2 eggs

¼ cup minced onion
1 teaspoon dry mustard
⅓–½ cup ground almonds
  or walnuts
½ teaspoon garlic powder

Mix all well and roll into small balls, about ½ inch. Brown in pan or oven at 350° for 20 minutes. Shake pan from time to time to keep balls round. Put into Cranberry Glaze.

CRANBERRY GLAZE:

1 (16-ounce) can jellied
  cranberry sauce
3 tablespoons wine vinegar
3 tablespoons apricot preserves
2 tablespoons brown sugar
1 teaspoon lemon juice

2 tablespoons currants
½ teaspoon Worcestershire
¼ cup water (optional)
1 teaspoon orange juice
1 teaspoon dry mustard
8 teaspoons cinnamon

Combine all ingredients in saucepan; heat and stir till blended. Put meatballs into Glaze. Makes 100 meatballs.

Allen Park Garden Club Recipe Book (Michigan)

Crab Cake Appetizers

These crab cakes are simple to prepare and are very tasty. They work well as a first course to a meal or are great with cocktails.

2 ounces uncooked angel
  hair pasta
6 ounces crabmeat, well
  drained
2 tablespoons minced celery
2 tablespoons minced
  green onion
½ cup bread crumbs

1 tablespoon minced green bell
  pepper
1 teaspoon Worcestershire
2 tablespoons Miracle Whip
1 egg
Vegetable oil for frying
2 lemons, garnish

Break uncooked pasta into 1–1½-inch lengths. Cook, drain well, and cool. Combine next 7 ingredients in medium-size bowl. Beat egg well and add to mixture. Add cooled pasta, mix well, and refrigerate 2 hours or overnight.

    Pour oil in deep fryer or place ¾-inch oil in heavy skillet; heat oil to 350°. Form mixture into small mounds and flatten to ¾-inch-thick cakes or form into small balls. Deep-fry 3–4 minutes or until golden brown and crisp. Keep warm in 200° oven until serving. Cut lemons into wedges and use as garnish. Yields 12–14 appetizer servings.

Recipe by Polecat & Lace, Minocqua
Our Best Cookbook 2 (Wisconsin)

Crab-N-Cream Cheese Won Tons

2 (8-ounce) packages
  cream cheese
1 package mock crabmeat
3 tablespoons minced garlic

1 package won ton skins
Cooking oil for wok/fryer/
  frying pan (preferably
  peanut oil for flavor)

Mix cream cheese, crab, and garlic. Place spoonful of mixture in the middle of won ton skin. Dip finger in bowl of water and wet adjacent 2 sides of won ton skin. Fold opposite side of skin over to meet corner to corner, making a triangle. Press sides down firmly together. Drop into fryer/wok/frying pan of hot oil. Flip when browned. Remove. Drain on paper towel or rack. Serve with hot mustard and sweet-n-sour sauce.

Mt. Carmel's "Cooking with the Oldies" (Wisconsin)

Crabmeat Quesadillas

1½ cups shredded Cheddar cheese
¼ cup mayonnaise
⅓ cup sour cream
8 ounces cooked crabmeat, chopped

2 tablespoons finely chopped green onion
2 tablespoons chopped chiles, drained
10 (8-ounce) flour tortillas
2 tablespoons butter, melted

In large mixing bowl, combine all ingredients, except tortillas and butter. Refrigerate till ready to complete. Spread about 3 tablespoons filling on each tortilla. Fold in half. Brush both sides of tortillas with butter. Place on baking sheet. Bake at 375° for 10–15 minutes. Cut each quesadilla into 3 wedges. Yields 30 appetizers.

Something Special (Michigan)

WIKIPEDIA IMAGE BY DAVID BALL

The Grand Hotel is a historic lodging facility located on Mackinac Island, Michigan. Constructed in the late 19th century, the hotel's front porch is purportedly the longest in the world at some 660 feet in length, overlooking a vast tea garden and the resort-scale Esther Williams swimming pool. The Grand Hotel is well known for a number of notable visitors, including five U.S. presidents, inventor Thomas Edison, and author Mark Twain.

Shrimp Marinated in Beer

2 pounds shrimp, shelled,
 deveined
1 tablespoon chopped chives
1 tablespoon chopped parsley
2 teaspoons dried basil
1 teaspoon finely chopped
 garlic
2 teaspoons dry mustard
½ teaspoon freshly ground
 black pepper
½ teaspoon celery salt
1 teaspoon salt
1 (12-ounce) can beer

Marinate shrimp in remaining ingredients 8 hours or more in refrigerator. Stir frequently. Drain. Place shrimp in preheated broiler pan 3 inches from heat. Broil for 5 minutes, turning once. Serves 8–10.

Eet Smakelijk (Michigan)

Pickled Fish

Fresh fish fillets
Salt
White vinegar to cover fish
1 cup white vinegar, for
 syrup
1 tablespoon mixed pickling
 spices
1¼ cups white sugar
4 ounces white port wine
Onion, thinly sliced

Place fish fillets in jar or crock in salt brine (one cup salt to one quart water) for 24 hours. Drain, and cover with white vinegar for 24 hours. Drain; cut in pieces.

Make a syrup from vinegar, mixed pickling spices, and white sugar. Boil for 5 minutes. Cool; add wine. Pack fish in layers with onion. Pour syrup over fish. May be eaten in 24 hours.

A Taste of Faith (Minnesota)

Appetizer Quiche

CRUST:

1½ cups all-purpose flour

1½ cups crushed Ritz Crackers

⅔ cup butter-flavored Crisco

½ cup water

Preheat oven to 400°. Combine flour and cracker crumbs. Cut in Crisco until mixture resembles cornmeal. Add water; press mixture into bottom of ungreased 10x15-inch pan. Prick with fork.

FILLING:

2 cups shredded Swiss cheese

⅔ cup each: chopped ham, crumbled cooked sausage, and diced pepperoni or crumbled cooked bacon

¾ cup chopped green onions

¼ cup snipped parsley

1 (4-ounce) jar diced pimentos

5 eggs

1 cup whipping cream

1 cup half-and-half

1 teaspoon salt

¼ teaspoon pepper

Sprinkle cheese, meats, onions, parsley, and pimentos evenly over Crust. Beat eggs, cream, half-and-half, salt, and pepper. Pour over filled Crust. Bake at 400° for 25–30 minutes. Cool 5–10 minutes. Cut into pieces and serve warm. Makes about 50 (1½x2-inch) appetizers. Or can be served as larger portions with a salad for a meal.

Dell & Barry's Holiday Delights for All Seasons (Michigan)

Eggroll

½ cup dry black mushrooms
1 bunch glass noodles
1 small onion, chopped
2 stalks celery, chopped
2 carrots, scraped, chopped
1 pound ground beef, chicken
 or pork

1 teaspoon salt
1 teaspoon garlic powder
1 teaspoon pepper
1 package eggroll wraps

Soak black mushrooms and glass noodles in warm water in 2 separate bowls. Take both of them out when you think they are soft enough, then chop into little pieces. Put everything together in large mixing bowl: ground meat, salt, garlic powder, pepper, glass noodles, black mushrooms, and chopped vegetables. Use your hands to mix well and roll in egg roll wrappers. Deep fry in a frying pan. Keep watching till eggrolls turn brown, then take out and serve. Serves 15–20.

A Century of Recipes Through the Windows of Time (Michigan)

Hot Ryes

1 cup shredded Swiss cheese
¼ cup crumbled crisp-cooked
 bacon
½ cup finely chopped onion
1 teaspoon Worcestershire

¼ teaspoon salt
¼ cup mayonnaise
1 loaf cocktail rye bread or rye
 crackers

Combine cheese, bacon, onion, Worcestershire, salt, and mayonnaise in a bowl. Spread cheese mixture on bread and arrange on a greased baking sheet. Bake at 300° for 15 minutes. Serves 20.

Between the Lakes (Michigan)

Teddy Bear Snack Mix

3 cups teddy bear-shaped
  graham snacks
1 cup raisins
1 cup chopped dried apples

1 cup honey nut round toasted
  oat cereal
¼ cup candy-coated chocolate
  pieces (M&M type)

In a large bowl, mix graham snacks, raisins, dried apples, honey nut round oat cereal, and M&M's. Store snack mix in sealed plastic bag or airtight container at room temperature up to 5 days. Makes 12 (¹/₂-cup) servings.

Heart Smart Kids Cookbook (Michigan)

Tijuana Tidbits

4 cups tortilla chips, broken
3 cups Crispix cereal
1 bag microwave popcorn,
  popped
1 (12-ounce) can mixed nuts
½ cup light corn syrup

½ cup butter or margarine
½ cup brown sugar
1 tablespoon chili powder
⅛ teaspoon cinnamon
⅛–¼ teaspoon ground
  red pepper

Combine first 4 ingredients in large pan. Combine syrup, butter, sugar, and seasonings in small saucepan. Heat to boiling. Pour over cereal mixture in pan, stirring. Spread on jellyroll pan sprayed with Pam. Bake at 250° for one hour, stirring every 20 minutes. Remove from oven and turn onto waxed paper to cool. Store in airtight container up to 2 weeks. Makes 18 cups.

St. Charles Parish Cookbook (Wisconsin)

Wisconsin has the most Native American tribes east of the Mississippi, with more than a half million acres of beautiful landscape. It is home to eleven Native American tribes, and fifteen Native American casinos, the largest being Potawatomi Bingo Casino. Located in the Menomonee Valley just south of downtown Milwaukee, it offers guests an array of gaming options, including blackjack, craps, roulette, Let-It-Ride bonus poker, bingo, and over 1500 slot machines.

Mango Chutney

2 pounds green mangoes,
 sliced
1 pound dried apricots,
 soaked, chopped
2 pounds dark brown sugar
1 cup malt vinegar
4 cloves garlic, chopped

2 heaping teaspoons grated
 ginger
½ pound raisins or currants
1 teaspoon whole cloves
 (or less powdered)
½ teaspoon cayenne

Bring all ingredients to a boil in a large pot. Turn down to simmer till thick and brown and mangoes are tender. Be careful not to let it stick and burn or get too thick. It will thicken when refrigerated.

This makes enough to give some away and have enough left for yourself. It's good on fresh bread and cheese, or homemade mayonnaise. Keeps several months.

Tasteful Art (Michigan)

Bread and Breakfast

© TRAVEL MICHIGAN BY BRIAN WALTERS

The Mackinac Bridge is one of the longest suspension bridges in the world. The five-mile-long bridge connects the Upper and Lower Peninsulas of Michigan over the Straits of Mackinac, which is where Lake Michigan and Lake Huron meet. The "Mighty Mac" was opened to traffic in 1957.

Quick & Moist Beer Bread

5 cups unsifted self-rising
  flour
5 tablespoons sugar
1½ cups sour cream

1 (12-ounce) can beer, room
  temperature
Melted butter to coat bread

In large bowl, combine flour and sugar. Add sour cream and beer alternately; mix well. Pour batter into greased 2-quart round baking dish. Bake 45 minutes at 350°. Remove from oven and brush top of bread with butter. Return to oven and bake for 15–20 minutes or until done. Cool slightly. Serve warm. Can toast. Makes one loaf.

Cooking with Grace (Wisconsin)

Herb Bread Sticks

3 cups all-purpose flour
1 envelope rapid-rise dry
  yeast
1 tablespoon salt
¼ cup chopped fresh parsley
1 bunch fresh chives,
  chopped

2 tablespoons chopped fresh
  dill
7 tablespoons olive oil
6 tablespoons very warm
  water (130°)
Cornmeal

In a large bowl, mix flour, yeast, salt, and herbs. Add olive oil and water, and mix until a dough is formed. On a floured surface, knead dough until smooth and elastic, about 5 minutes. Place dough in an oiled bowl, cover with a towel, and set in a warm place to rise. When dough has doubled in size, about 30 minutes, punch it down and divide it into 16 pieces. Roll each piece into a 12-inch "snake."

Sprinkle 2 sheet pans with cornmeal. Transfer bread sticks to the sheet pans, cover with dish towels, and leave in a warm place to rise for about 20 minutes. Preheat oven to 400°. Bake until lightly browned, 15–20 minutes. Makes 16 bread sticks.

Growing & Using Herbs (Wisconsin)

Focaccia

Serve with any Italian meal.

1 package dry yeast	**2 teaspoons salt**
1 cup warm water (105–115°)	**3 cups flour**
3 tablespoons rosemary	**Olive oil**
3 tablespoons olive oil	**Freshly grated Parmesan cheese**

Dissolve yeast in warm water in large bowl. Stir in rosemary, oil, salt, and 2$\frac{1}{2}$ cups flour. Knead dough on lightly floured surface, adding flour as needed. When smooth and elastic, place in greased bowl. Brush with oil and cover. Let rise until double (about one hour). Punch down and press in oiled 12-inch pizza pan. Brush with olive oil and sprinkle with cheese. Let rise another 30 minutes. Bake in preheated 400° oven for 20–25 minutes.

Herbs in a Minnesota Kitchen (Minnesota)

Lefse

Won first prize.

5 cups riced or mashed potatoes	**3 tablespoons melted butter**
$\frac{1}{2}$ cup cream	**2$\frac{1}{2}$ cups flour**
	Salt to taste

Mix potatoes and cream. Mix well. Add melted butter, flour, and salt; mix well. Roll out a small piece at a time into a circle as thin as possible. Fry until lightly browned; turn and brown other side.

The Ultimate Potato Cookbook (Minnesota)

Lefse is a soft Norwegian flatbread traditionally served as an accompaniment to lutefisk. The fish is often rolled up in the lefse, but now it is more common to butter a pie-shaped wedge and sprinkle it with cinnamon sugar and eat it rolled or folded.

Spinach-Cheese Bread

1 package J.B. Dough Classic
   White Bread Mix
2 tablespoons butter
1 clove garlic, finely chopped
1 (10-ounce) package frozen
   spinach, cooked, drained
⅓ cup grated Parmesan cheese

½ teaspoon onion powder
¼ teaspoon basil
1 egg, beaten
1 tablespoon water
Grated Parmesan cheese
   to taste

Prepare bread mix following package instructions. Set your machine on dough mode or on manual setting. Remove dough from bread machine. Roll into rectangle on lightly floured surface.

Microwave butter and garlic in microwave-safe dish 30 seconds or till butter melts. Drizzle butter mixture over dough. Spread with mixture of spinach and Parmesan cheese; sprinkle with onion powder and basil. Roll as for jellyroll, sealing edge. Cut roll lengthwise with sharp knife or scissors forming 2 strips; turn filling-side-up. Twist strips together loosely.

Coil strip into circle, turning end under. Transfer with spatula to greased springform pan, dough does not touch edge of pan. Brush with mixture of egg and water; sprinkle with Parmesan cheese. Let rise in warm place for 1 hour. Bake at 350° for 30 minutes or till brown. Makes one loaf.

In the Dough (Michigan)

Cheddar Jalapeño Cornbread

1 cup yellow cornmeal
½ cup flour
1½ teaspoons baking powder
¾ teaspoon baking soda
¾ teaspoon salt
2 eggs, lightly beaten

1 cup buttermilk
¼ cup melted butter
½–1 cup grated Cheddar cheese
1–2 jalapeño peppers, seeded
   and chopped

Combine cornmeal, flour, baking powder, baking soda, and salt. Add eggs, buttermilk, and butter. Stir until moistened. Fold in cheese and pepper. Pour into a greased 8x8-inch baking dish. Bake at 350° for 25–30 minutes, or until toothpick tests clean.

Marquette University High School Mother's Guild Cookbook (Wisconsin)

Detroit Cornbread

1 cup all-purpose flour
¾ cup cornmeal
3 tablespoons sugar
1 tablespoon baking powder

1 teaspoon salt
1 egg
⅔ cup milk
6 tablespoons butter, melted

Grease a 8x8-inch baking pan. In a bowl, mix first 5 ingredients. In a small bowl, beat egg, milk, and melted butter. Stir egg mixture into flour mixture just till blended. Spread batter in pan. Bake at 425° for 25 minutes. Cut into squares; serve warm. Makes 9 servings.

Cook Book: The Best of Michigan (Michigan)

©JAMES MARVIN PHELPS

Detroit is the largest city in Michigan. It is the hometown of the American automobile industry and an important source of popular music—legacies celebrated by the city's two familiar nicknames, Motor City and Motown. Other nicknames emerged in the twentieth century, including Rock City, Arsenal of Democracy (during World War II), The 3-1-3 (its area code), The D, and D-Town. Located north of Windsor, Ontario, Detroit is a geographical oddity as the only U.S. city that looks south to Canada.

Cranberry Pecan Bread

1½ cups all-purpose flour
⅔ cup sugar
1 teaspoon baking powder
⅔ teaspoon salt
⅓ teaspoon baking soda
3 tablespoons margarine, melted

⅔ cup orange juice
3 tablespoons water
1 egg, well beaten
1 cup chopped cranberries
⅔ cup coarsely ground pecans
2 teaspoons grated orange rind

Sift together first 5 ingredients. Make a well in the center. Combine next 4 ingredients. Pour into well and stir just until moistened. Fold in last 3 ingredients. Pour into greased 5x9-inch loaf pan. Bake 1 hour at 350°. Cool completely before removing from pan. Cut into ¹/₂-inch slices. Makes 15 slices.

McManus Family Recipes Volume 2 (Michigan)

Banana Nut Bread

¾ cup butter, softened
1½ cups sugar
2 eggs, well beaten
1 teaspoon vanilla
2 cups all-purpose flour
1 teaspoon baking soda

¼ teaspoon salt
4 good-size ripe bananas, mashed
½ cup buttermilk
¾ cup chopped nuts

Cream butter and sugar. Blend in eggs and vanilla. Sift flour, baking soda, and salt together. Mix bananas and creamed mixture together. Stir flour mixture alternately with buttermilk; mix in nuts. Pour into 2 greased loaf pans and bake at 325° for an hour and 15 minutes or until done. Makes 2 loaves.

Taste of Clarkston: Tried & True Recipes (Michigan)

Rhubarb Bread

⅔ cup salad oil
1½ cups brown sugar
1 cup sour milk or (1 teaspoon
  vinegar and 1 cup milk)
1 egg
1 teaspoon salt

1 teaspoon vanilla
1 teaspoon baking soda
2½ cups flour
1½ cups rhubarb, chopped
½ cup chopped nuts

TOPPING:

½ cup granulated sugar

1 teaspoon melted butter

Combine salad oil and brown sugar. Add milk and egg. Beat well. Add in salt, vanilla, baking soda, and flour. Mix until smooth. Add in rhubarb and nuts. Pour into greased loaf pans. Mix topping ingredients. Sprinkle onto batter. Yields 2 medium loaves.

Anoka County 4H Cook Book (Minnesota)

Almond Poppy Seed Bread

3 eggs
1½ cups milk
1⅛ cups oil
2½ cups sugar
1½ teaspoons salt

3 cups all-purpose flour
1½ teaspoons baking powder
1½ tablespoons poppy seeds
1½ teaspoons each: vanilla,
  butter, and almond flavorings

Combine eggs, milk, oil, sugar, and salt. Sift flour with baking powder and add to egg mixture gradually. Add poppy seeds and flavorings; mix well. Pour into 2 greased and floured loaf pans. Bake at 350° for 1 hour.

GLAZE:

¼ cup orange juice
¾ cup powdered sugar

½ teaspoon each: vanilla,
  butter, and almond flavorings

Combine and mix all ingredients. While bread is still warm, poke holes into top of bread with fork and drizzle Glaze slowly over top so it runs into the bread. This bread can be frozen for up to several months.

Blissfield Preschool Cookbook (Michigan)

Blueberry Lemon Bread

⅓ cup butter
1 cup sugar
3 tablespoons lemon juice
2 tablespoons lemon rind
2 eggs
1½ cups flour
1 teaspoon baking powder

1 teaspoon salt
½ cup milk
1 cup blueberries, coated with flour
½ cup walnuts or almonds, chopped

Mix butter, sugar, lemon juice, and rind. Beat in eggs. In separate bowl mix flour, baking powder, and salt. Alternately add flour mixture and milk. Fold in blueberries and nuts. Pour into 2 (9x5x3-inch) loaf pans and bake at 350° for 60 minutes.

Cooks Extraordinaires (Wisconsin)

Michigan Blueberry Muffins

Holland has acres and acres of blueberry fields.

1¼ cups sugar, divided
½ cup margarine, softened, divided
2 eggs
2⅓ cups all-purpose flour, divided

2 teaspoons baking powder
¼ teaspoon salt
½ cup milk
2 cups fresh blueberries
½ teaspoon cinnamon

Cream ³⁄₄ cup sugar and ¹⁄₄ cup margarine in a mixer bowl till light and fluffy. Bean in eggs, one at a time. Mix 2 cups flour, baking powder, and salt together. Add to creamed mixture alternately with milk, beating well after each addition. Fold in blueberries. Line muffin cups with paper liners. Fill muffin cups ³⁄₄ full.

Mix remaining ¹⁄₄ cup margarine, ¹⁄₂ cup sugar, ¹⁄₃ cup flour, and the cinnamon together in a bowl. Sprinkle over muffin batter. Bake at 350° for 18–20 minutes or till muffins test done. Serve warm. Yields 12 muffins.

Dawn to Dusk (Michigan)

Cherry Muffins

4 cups flour
1 cup sugar
2 tablespoons baking powder
1 teaspoon cinnamon
3 cups tart cherries, rinsed
  and drained

1 cup butter or margarine,
  melted
1 cup milk
4 eggs
1 teaspoon vanilla

In a large bowl, sift together flour, sugar, baking powder, and cinnamon. Put cherries in another bowl; add one tablespoon of flour mixture and toss into cherries. In another bowl, mix together butter, milk, eggs, and vanilla; stir this into dry ingredients and fold in cherries. Spoon into greased muffin tins to ³/₄ full.

TOPPING:

1 cup flour
½ cup sugar

½ teaspoon cinnamon
⅓ cup butter, softened

To make topping, mix together flour, sugar, and cinnamon in a small bowl. Cut in butter with a pastry blender or fork until uniformly crumbly. Sprinkle topping over muffins. Bake at 425° for 15–20 minutes. Makes 2 dozen.

Seasons of a Farm Family (Wisconsin)

WWW.WIKIPEDIA.ORG

Michigan produces about 75 percent of the nation's tart cherries. That makes Michigan the nation's number one cherry-producing state. Traverse City is the self-proclaimed Cherry Capital of the World. Every year more than 500,000 attendees enjoy its National Cherry Festival, now in its 82nd year. Families can enjoy many kinds of activities from cherry pit spitting and pie eating contests, to the Grand Royale Parade in which the newly crowned Cherry Queen greets the crowds. Originally held in mid-to-late July to coincide with the cherry harvest, the Festival was moved to early July to take advantage of the July 4th weekend. During the harvest, approximately 200,000,000 pounds of tart (Montmorency) cherries are harvested. Other cherries, including sweet cherries and Balaton cherries are also harvested.

Orange Raisin Scones with Orange Butter

Scones are a great alternative to muffins for breakfast. These are particularly popular, and the orange butter enhances the flavor of the scones.

1¾ cups flour	⅓ cup butter
3 tablespoons sugar	½ cup golden raisins
2½ teaspoons baking powder	2 eggs
2 teaspoons grated orange peel	4–6 tablespoons half-and-half

Preheat oven to 400°. In medium bowl, combine flour, sugar, baking powder, and orange peel. Cut in butter until crumbly. Stir in raisins, one egg, lightly beaten, and enough half-and-half to just moisten mixture.

Turn dough onto lightly floured surface; knead lightly 10 times. Roll into 9-inch circle. Cut into 8–12 wedges. Place on cookie sheet one inch apart. Brush with remaining egg, beaten. Bake 10–12 minutes or until golden brown. Immediately remove from cookie sheet.

ORANGE BUTTER:

½ cup butter, softened	2 tablespoons orange marmalade

Make Orange Butter by mixing together butter and marmalade until combined. Serve with warm scones. Makes 8–12 scones.

Recipe from Courthouse Square Bed & Breakfast, Crandon
Have Breakfast with Us . . . Again (Wisconsin)

Sweet Cream Scones

2 cups flour
1 tablespoon baking powder
2 tablespoons sugar
¾ teaspoon salt
6 tablespoons (¾ stick)
   unsalted chilled butter

½ cup currants
1 egg
½ cup cream
½ cup milk

Combine flour, baking powder, sugar, and salt in a bowl. Cut chilled butter in small pieces. Cut in butter with pastry blender until mixture resembles coarse crumbs. Add currants. Set aside.

In small bowl beat egg with fork; add cream and milk. Stir egg mixture into flour mixture until just blended. Turn out onto floured board; put some flour on top. This is soft dough.

Pat out to ¾-inch high. Cut with biscuit cutter. Place about 1-inch apart on sprayed cookie sheet. Bake at 375° for 12 minutes or until golden brown. Serve hot or reheat in the microwave a few seconds or your regular oven a few minutes at 250°. They freeze well, too. Makes 12 scones.

Chickadee Cottage Cookbook (Minnesota)

The Chippewa National Forest is the oldest natural forest in the United States. The forest contains an area known as the "Lost Forty"; this area (actually 144 acres) was accidentally mapped as part of Coddington Lake when the original maps of the region were laid out in 1882. As a result of this mapping error, the Lost Forty was never logged. This area has become some of the oldest forest in the state, with some trees over 350 years old. Less than two percent of Minnesota's forested land today is old growth, never logged forest. In 2005, the State of Minnesota became the largest public land manager in the United States to certify its lands under the Sustainable Forestry Initiative. Over one million white pine seedlings are being planted in Minnesota each year. On average more than 30 white pine trees are being planted for every tree harvested.

Raspberry Cream Cheese Coffeecake

2¼ cups flour
¾ cup sugar
¾ cup margarine
½ teaspoon baking powder
½ teaspoon baking soda
¼ teaspoon salt
¾ cup sour cream
1 egg

1 teaspoon almond extract
1 (8-ounce) package cream
  cheese
¼ cup sugar
1 egg
½–¾ cup raspberry preserves
½ cup sliced almonds

Heat oven to 350°. Grease and flour bottom and sides of a 9-or 10-inch springform pan. In large bowl, combine flour and ¾ cup sugar. Using pastry blender, cut in margarine until mixture resembles crumbs. Reserve one cup. To remaining crumb mixture, add baking powder, baking soda, salt, sour cream, egg, and almond extract. Blend well. Spread batter over bottom and 2 inches up sides. In small bowl, combine cream cheese, ¼ cup sugar, and egg; blend well. Pour over batter in pan. Carefully spoon on preserves. Sprinkle reserved crumbs and almonds over top. Bake 45–55 minutes, or longer. Cool 15 minutes. Remove sides. Refrigerate.

Great Cooks of Zion Church (Minnesota)

Chocolate-Sour Cream Coffee Cake

CAKE:

1 cup butter or margarine, softened

2 cups sugar

2 eggs

1½ cups cake flour

1½ teaspoons baking powder

½ teaspoon salt

1 cup sour cream

½ teaspoon vanilla

Preheat oven to 350°. Cream butter and sugar in a large bowl until fluffy. Add eggs, beating until smooth. In a medium bowl, sift together flour, baking powder, and salt. Gradually add dry ingredients to creamed mixture, blending well. Gently fold in the sour cream and vanilla.

TOPPING:

1 cup chopped pecans

2 tablespoons sugar

1 teaspoon cinnamon

Combine ingredients in a small bowl.

CHOCOLATE GLAZE:

¼ cup butter or margarine

½ cup semisweet chocolate chips

Melt butter and chocolate chips in a small saucepan over low heat, stirring until smooth. Sprinkle 2 tablespoons Topping in bottom of greased and floured 9-inch tube pan. Spoon ½ cake batter into pan. Sprinkle 4 tablespoons Topping over batter and drizzle ½ cup Glaze over Topping. Spoon remaining batter into pan and sprinkle with remaining Topping. Reserve remaining Glaze. Bake 1 hour to 1 hour 15 minutes or until a toothpick inserted in center comes out clean. Cool 10 minutes in pan. Turn onto serving plate. Drizzle remaining Glaze over top of warm cake. Yields about 20 servings.

Favorite Recipes from Our Kitchens to Yours (Michigan)

Kimberly's Strawberry Coffee Cake

Every cook has one of those "whip-it-up-in-a-jiffy" company cakes. It looks like you really fussed, and they'll never believe how easy it was!

1 cup flour	**1 egg**
½ cup sugar	**1 teaspoon vanilla**
2 teaspoons baking powder	**2 tablespoons butter, melted**
½ teaspoon salt	**1½ cups fresh strawberries,**
½ cup milk	** sliced**

In large bowl, mix flour, sugar, baking powder, and salt. Add milk, egg, vanilla, and butter. Stir until well blended. Pour into greased and floured 8-inch springform pan. Top with berries.

STREUSEL:

½ cup flour	**¼ cup butter, softened**
½ cup sugar	

Make streusel by combining flour, sugar, and butter; sprinkle over berries. Bake at 375° for 30 minutes, or until golden brown and toothpick inserted in cake comes out clean. Slice into 8 wedges and serve. Serves 8.

Variations: Add sliced plums and nutmeg, sugar and streusel ...the list goes on. Top the warm cake with frozen yogurt, ice cream, or whipped cream for a terrific dessert.

Have Breakfast with Us . . . Again (Wisconsin)

Battle Creek, Michigan, known as the "Cereal City," is the world headquarters of Kellogg Company, founded by brothers Dr. John Harvey Kellogg and William Keith Kellogg in 1906. The Kellogg brothers developed the concept of a cold breakfast cereal as an alternative to the traditional meat-based breakfast. Battle Creek is also home to Post Cereals, which was part of General Foods Corporation and is now part of Kraft Foods.

Aunt Mary Ellen's Swedish Kringle

BASE:

½ cup butter   2 tablespoon water
1 cup flour

Cut butter into flour. Add water and mix well with a fork. Divide in half and shape into balls. On a cookie sheet, shape dough into two strips 3 inches wide and 15 inches long.

FILLING:

1 cup water   3 eggs
½ cup butter   ½ teaspoon vanilla extract
1 cup flour   ½ teaspoon almond extract
1 teaspoon sugar

Bring butter and water to a rolling boil. Add flour and sugar all at once. Stir vigorously until mixture forms a ball that does not separate. Remove from heat and cool slightly. Add eggs, one at a time, with extracts. Beat vigorously after each addition. Spread evenly over pastry. Bake at 350° for 60 minutes.

FROSTING:

1 cup powdered sugar   ¼ teaspoon vanilla extract
1 tablespoon cream   Chopped almonds or pecans
¼ teaspoon almond extract

While still warm, drizzle with frosting made by combining sugar with cream and extracts. Sprinkle with chopped nuts. Yields 2 kringles.

All in Good Taste I (Wisconsin)

 The "World's Longest Breakfast Table," is an annual event held in downtown Battle Creek in June. Over 300 tables are set-up to serve cereal, Pop Tarts, donut holes, and bananas free of charge to 60,000 visitors.

Nutty Cinnamon Ring

⅓ cup chopped pecans
¾ cup sugar
1½ teaspoons cinnamon

2 (8-ounces) cans refrigerated
  buttermilk biscuits
⅓ cup butter, melted

Heat oven to 350°. Sprinkle half the nuts into a 9-inch ring mold. Combine sugar and cinnamon. Dip each biscuit in melted butter, then in sugar mixture. Place biscuits in ring mold. Sprinkle with the remaining nuts. Top with remaining coated biscuits. Bake for 25–30 minutes; turn onto serving plate, and let pan remain there for a few minutes to allow syrup to run over biscuits.

Kitchen Keepsakes (Minnesota)

Orange Sticky Buns

½ stick margarine or butter,
  softened
¼ cup packed brown sugar
½ cup flaked coconut
¼ cup sliced or slivered
  almonds

½ cup orange marmalade
¼–½ teaspoon grated
  gingerroot
1 (10-ounce) can refrigerated
  flaky biscuits

Combine margarine, brown sugar, coconut, and almonds in mixing bowl. Spoon into a 5x9-inch loaf pan. Heat in 375° oven until margarine melts. Remove from oven. Spread mixture evenly on bottom of pan. Combine marmalade and gingerroot in a small bowl and set aside. Separate dough into 10 biscuits. Spread about 2 teaspoons marmalade mixture on 1 side of each biscuit. Stand biscuits on edge slightly overlapping in 2 rows of 5 biscuits each in the pan. Bake at 375° for 25–30 minutes or until deep golden brown, covering pan with foil during last 15 minutes of baking to prevent overbaking. Cool 4 minutes. Run a knife around edges to loosen. Invert onto a serving plate. Serves 10.

Between the Lakes (Michigan)

Wisconsin French Toast

4 eggs
⅔ cup orange juice
⅓ cup milk
¼ cup sugar
¼ teaspoon nutmeg
½ teaspoon vanilla extract

½ loaf Italian bread (cut in
   1-inch slices)
⅓ cup butter, melted
Ground orange peel to taste
¾ cup pecan pieces

Using a wire whisk, beat together eggs, juice, milk, sugar, nutmeg, and vanilla in a large bowl. Place bread, edges touching, in a single layer in a large baking dish. Pour milk mixture over bread; cover and refrigerate overnight, turning once. When ready to cook, preheat oven to 400°. Pour melted butter on a jellyroll pan, spreading evenly. Arrange soaked bread slices in a single layer on pan. Sprinkle evenly with orange peel and pecans. Bake until golden, 20–25 minutes. Check slices during last 5 minutes to avoid burning. Serve with maple syrup and butter. Yields 4 servings.

Green Thumbs in the Kitchen (Wisconsin)

Michigan Baked Oatmeal

This is more like a pudding and the ingredients are as surprising to our guests as the cooking method.

2 cups old-fashioned oats
4 cups milk
½ teaspoon almond flavoring
¼ cup brown sugar

½ cup sliced almonds
½ cup dried cherries
1 large apple, unpeeled, grated

Preheat oven to 400°. Coat a 3-quart casserole or baking pan with cooking spray. In mixing bowl, combine all ingredients. Transfer to baking dish. Sprinkle top with additional almonds. Bake uncovered for 45 minutes. Serve hot. Yields 6–8 servings.

Variation: Omit almonds, almond flavoring, and cherries. Add 1 tablespoon cinnamon, ½ cup raisins, and ½ cup chopped peanuts.

Best of Breakfast Menus & Recipes (Michigan)

Potato Pancakes

These pancakes are delicious served with barbecued ribs.

1½ quarts peeled, grated
  raw potatoes
4 eggs, beaten

1 tablespoon salt, or to taste
½ cup all-purpose flour
1 level teaspoon baking powder

Mix potatoes, eggs, and salt. In a small bowl, mix flour with baking powder, then add to potato mixture. Mix thoroughly and fry till brown on both sides on a very hot griddle with plenty of oil to get crispy edges. Serve hot with butter and applesauce.

Wild Game Recipes from the Heart of the U.P. (Michigan)

Norwegian Sour Cream Waffles with Apple Pecan Topping

2 cups sour cream
2 fresh eggs
1 cup unbleached flour
1 teaspoon baking powder
½ teaspoon baking soda

½ teaspoon salt
2 tablespoons sugar
½ teaspoon ground cardamom
3 tablespoons water

In large bowl beat sour cream until fluffy. In separate bowl beat eggs until light; combine with sour cream and beat again. Sift dry ingredients; fold into sour cream/egg mixture; add water. Bake according to wafflemaker directions. Serve with maple syrup and Apple Pecan Topping.

APPLE PECAN TOPPING:
2 tablespoons butter
¼ cup brown sugar
2 large apples, cored and
  sliced

½ teaspoon cinnamon
¼ cup chopped pecans

In skillet melt butter and brown sugar. Add apples, cinnamon, and pecans. Cook until apples are tender; about 3–4 minutes. Keep warm. Serves 4.

From The Mustard Seed Bed and Breakfast
Have Breakfast with Us II (Wisconsin)

Eggs Monterey

1½ cups cubed ham
8 ounces bacon, crisp-fried,
   crumbled
12 eggs
1 teaspoon seasoned salt
½ teaspoon pepper

1 (4-ounce) can green chiles
1½ cups shredded Monterey
   Jack cheese
1 avocado, peeled, thinly sliced
1 tomato, thinly sliced

Spread ham and bacon in bottom of a greased 2-quart casserole. Beat eggs, seasoned salt, pepper, and chiles in a bowl. Pour over ham and bacon. Bake at 325° for 30 minutes or until set. Sprinkle Monterey Jack cheese over top of baked layers. Arrange avocado and tomato slices on top of cheese. Place under the broiler and broil until cheese is melted. Yields 6–8 servings.

Dawn to Dusk (Michigan)

Milwaukee Breakfast

1 small potato
2 eggs
1 small tomato, diced
1 small piece green pepper,
   diced

1 small piece onion, diced
2 button mushrooms, diced
1–2 pats butter

Cook potato in microwave on HIGH for 3–4 minutes, until you can get a fork in easily. Peel and dice potato into ¼-inch pieces. Beat eggs until smooth. Combine all ingredients and add to scrambled eggs. Cook on HIGH for one minute, stir, cook for one more minute, stir. If eggs are a little wet, let sit for about 10 seconds and then stir again. Do not overcook unless you like it dry.

Taste and See (Wisconsin)

Potato/Sausage Casserole

1 (32-ounce) package hash
   browns, thawed
1 package brown and serve
   sausage, smoky links, or
   smoked sausage, cut into
   bite-size pieces
½ cup margarine, melted
1 teaspoon salt

⅛ teaspoon pepper
1 (10¾-ounce) can cream of
   celery soup
1 soup can warm water
1 (3½-ounce) can Durkee
   onion rings
1 cup shredded Parmesan cheese

Mix together potatoes, sausage, margarine, salt, and pepper. In separate bowl, mix together sour and water. Add ³/₄ of soup mixture to other ingredients; blend. Place in 9x13-inch (sprayed) or several smaller bowls (ramekins). Pour remainder of soup across top. On top of soup spread onion rings and Parmesan cheese. Bake at 350° about 30 minutes, till bubbly. Serve hot. This can be refrigerated or frozen till the day it is needed. Can also be rewarmed in microwave. Makes 10–12 servings.

Just Inn Time for Breakfast (Michigan)

Spicy Pears in Cranberry Sauce

This aroma of cinnamon and nutmeg mixed with fruit is tantalizing. It is also very simple to make.

1 (16-ounce) can whole-berry
   cranberry sauce
½ cup sugar
1 tablespoon lemon juice

¼ teaspoon ground cinnamon
¼ teaspoon ground ginger
6 medium pears, peeled, sliced

Combine cranberry sauce, sugar, lemon juice, cinnamon, and ginger in heavy saucepan. Bring mixture to a boil over medium heat, stirring often. Remove from heat. Combine pears in 2½-quart casserole. Pour cranberry mixture over fruit. Cover and bake at 350° for 40 minutes or until pears are tender.

   Serve warm from casserole with slotted spoon, or can be chilled and served cold, with vanilla yogurt or granola. Yields 8 servings.

Best of Breakfast Menus & Recipes (Michigan)

Cinnamon Breakfast Apples

The perfect fall comfort food . . . apples simmered with cinnamon and nutmeg. A splash of cream makes it a real treat.

1 cup sugar	**2 tablespoons water**
1 teaspoon cinnamon	**¼ cup butter**
¼ teaspoon nutmeg	
4 or 5 large cooking apples	
(about 1½ pounds)	

Combine sugar, cinnamon, and nutmeg. Peel and core apples. Chop apples into bite-size pieces and layer in 4-cup measure alternately with sugar mixture. When there are 4 cups, put apples, water, and butter into medium saucepan. Cover and cook over low to medium heat, stirring once or twice, for 15–20 minutes or until apples are tender. Serve as a side dish or as a topping for pancakes or waffles. Yields 4 servings.

Best of Breakfast Menus & Recipes (Michigan)

Rhubarb Blueberry Jam

5 cups rhubarb, diced	**1 cup blueberry pie filling**
1 cup water	**1 package raspberry Jell-O**
5 cups sugar	

Cook rhubarb in water over medium heat until tender. Add sugar and boil for 2 minutes. Stir in pie filling and cool for about 10 minutes. Add Jell-O and mix well. Pour into hot jars; process 15 minutes in boiling water or freeze. Yields 12 servings.

RHUBARB-PINEAPPLE VARIATION:

5 cups rhubarb, diced	**2 small boxes raspberry or**
4 cups sugar	**strawberry Jell-O**
1 small can crushed pine-	
apple, including juice	

Boil rhubarb and sugar with pineapple and juice for 10 minutes. Remove from heat and add Jell-O. Stir well. Put in jars; cover with lids; let cool and freeze. Yields 8 small jars.

Green Thumbs in the Kitchen (Wisconsin)

Egg Salad Sandwiches

2 (8-ounce) cartons
　Egg Beaters
2 tablespoons Dijon mustard
½ cup Kraft fat-free
　mayonnaise
¼ cup chopped celery

¼ cup chopped red pepper
2 tablespoons chopped
　scallions
12 slices whole-wheat bread
6 lettuce leaves

In a large non-stick skillet, pour Egg Beaters in and cover tightly, cooking over a very low heat for 10 minutes or until just set. Remove from skillet and cool completely. Chop into fine pieces.

In a bowl, combine hard-cooked Egg Beaters that have been chopped, Dijon mustard, mayonnaise, celery, red peppers, and scallions. Divide and spread on 6 bread slices. Top with lettuce and remaining bread. Serve immediately. Serves 6.

Per Serving: Cal 233 (9.1% from fat); Fat 3.4g (SAT 0.6g); Chol 1.7mg; Fiber 5.4g; Sod 897mg. Diabetic Exchange: 2½ starch + 1 lean meat.

Here's to Your Heart: Cooking Smart (Wisconsin)

Soups, Chilis, and Stews

WWW.WIKIPEDIA.ORG

Mayo Clinic, the first and largest integrated, not-for-profit group practice in the world, was founded in Rochester, Minnesota, as a single, small outpatient facility. It is one of the top-ranked hospitals in the United States with campuses in Minnesota, Florida, and Arizona, as well as community-based providers in more than 70 locations in Minnesota, Wisconsin, and Iowa. A bronze statue of the clinic's founders, the Mayo brothers, "Dr. Will" and "Dr. Charlie," is situated in front of the Minnesota campus' Gonda Building.

Cream of Asparagus Soup

Early Spring and buying just-picked asparagus at a Farmer's Market . . . what fun! This is a basic cream soup. Other puréed vegetables such as carrots, cauliflower, or spinach can be substituted with equally satisfactory results. Try your favorite herb for additional flavor interest.

2 cups fresh asparagus
½ cup butter
¾ cup flour
4 cups fresh or canned
  chicken broth

2 cups coffee cream, evaporated
  milk or evaporated skim milk
Salt and white pepper to taste

Wash and cut asparagus in 1-inch pieces; cook in ¹/₂ cup water until tender, and purée in blender. Melt the butter in soup kettle. Whisk in the flour. Add the chicken broth, which preferably has been heated. Whisk vigorously. When the mixture is thickened and smooth, continue cooking over low heat for 10 minutes.

To puréed asparagus, add enough water to make 2 cups. Add it and the cream to the thickened broth and heat another 5 minutes. Season the soup to taste and remove from heat. Serve topped with a few crisp-cooked asparagus tips and croutons. Makes 6 main dish or 10 first-course servings.

Note: Use the top 4 inches of the fresh asparagus as a special vegetable course and the less tender bottoms to make a wonderful soup.

Chickadee Cottage Cookbook (Minnesota)

The Great Lakes are a collection of freshwater lakes located in eastern North America, on the Canada-United States border. Consisting of Lakes Superior, Michigan, Huron, Erie, and Ontario, they form the largest group of freshwater lakes on Earth by surface area. The Great Lakes hold 20% of the world's fresh water. Four of the five lakes form part of the Canada-United States border; the fifth, Lake Michigan, is contained entirely within the United States.

Asparagus Tomato Soup

Like so many good soups, this came about by gambling on what was in the larder. It has unusual but wonderful flavor . . . the touch of cloves is magical.

1 medium onion, coarsely
   chopped
1 carrot, coarsely chopped
2 tablespoons butter
2 tablespoons flour
2 cups canned tomatoes
5 cups chicken broth
½ teaspoon sugar
1 tablespoon chopped parsley

1 bay leaf
½ teaspoon thyme
⅛ teaspoon ground cloves
Salt and freshly ground pepper
   to taste
1½ pounds fresh asparagus
Garnish: sour cream and
   chopped chives or parsley

In a large, heavy saucepan, sauté onion and carrot in butter until soft. Sprinkle with flour, and cook another minute, stirring. Add remaining ingredients except asparagus and garnish. Simmer, covered, 10 minutes or so.

In the meantime, cook asparagus until fork-tender but still a pretty green. Drain, then cut stalks into thirds. Discard bay leaf. Purée tomato mixture and asparagus in an electric blender in several batches. Reheat to serve, garnishing each bowl with a dollop of sour cream and a sprinkling of chopped chives or parsley. Serves 8.

Hollyhocks & Radishes (Michigan)

Tomato Dill Soup

This is such a pretty soup, with a vivid red color and flecks of green herbs. We make it often because it seems to go with everything (and our customers are always asking for it). The rich taste and texture make it perfect as a first course to an important dinner. Don't worry about leftovers; it tastes even better the second day and freezes well.

7½ tablespoons butter, divided
½ cup flour
1 cup diced onions
1 large clove garlic, minced
4 cups chicken stock
1 (29-ounce) can tomato purée, or 2 (15-ounce) cans
1 (16-ounce) can whole peeled tomatoes, chopped, juices reserved
3 tablespoons honey
1 tablespoon dill weed
1 teaspoon basil
½ teaspoon ground black pepper
½ teaspoon chili powder
⅛ teaspoon ground red (cayenne) pepper
3 dashes of hot pepper sauce
Salt and pepper to taste

To make roux, melt 4½ tablespoons butter in small saucepan. Stir in flour until well blended. Cook over low heat, stirring often, for 3–5 minutes. Remove from heat and set aside. Melt remaining 3 tablespoons of butter in large, heavy pot. Add onions; cook gently 5 minutes. Add garlic, cook 2 minutes more. Add chicken stock, bring to a boil, and reduce to a simmer. Whisk in roux until stock is thickened and smooth. Add remaining ingredients, including juice from canned tomatoes. Simmer 30–45 minutes, stirring often to prevent scorching. This is a thick soup, but you may adjust to your taste by adding more chicken stock. Add salt and pepper to taste. Serves 8–10.

The Ovens of Brittany Cookbook (Wisconsin)

Roasted Garlic Soup

1 whole bulb garlic, peeled
1 leek, 2-inch large dice
½ cup 2-inch large dice onion
⅓ cup large dice scallions
7 cups chicken broth, divided
Salt and pepper to taste
1 cup heavy cream
1 cup croutons

Place garlic bulb, leek, onion, and scallions in a small roasting pan. Add 2 cups chicken broth and place in a preheated 350° oven. Roast mixture 1 hour, stirring occasionally until garlic is mushy. Remove from oven; add 1 cup broth, and purée the mixture. Strain mixture through a fine strainer and place in a saucepan. Add rest of chicken broth and heavy cream to saucepan. Bring to a boil and simmer on medium-low heat 45 minutes. Adjust seasoning.

Place in 8 bowls and garnish with croutons. Serves 8.

The Simply Great Cookbook II (Michigan)

Michigan French Onion Soup

3½ pounds onions
¼ cup olive oil
2 cups unpasteurized apple cider
3 cups beef broth
1 cup water
2 tablespoons brandy
Salt and pepper to taste
6 (½-inch-thick) slices Italian bread, toasted lightly
3 ounces Roquefort or mozzarella cheese, crumbled (about ¾ cup)

Halve the onions lengthwise and slice thin. In a heavy kettle, cook onions in oil over moderately-high heat, stirring occasionally about 1 hour, or till onions are golden brown. Stir in cider, broth, water, brandy, salt and pepper. Simmer soup, uncovered, 20 minutes. Arrange toast slices on a baking sheet; sprinkle with cheese, and broil croutons under a preheated broiler about 4 inches from heat till cheese begins to melt. Ladle soup into heated bowls and float a cheese crouton in each serving bowl. Makes about 7 cups. Freezes well.

Woman's National Farm and Garden Association–
Rochester Cookbook Volume II (Michigan)

French Onion Soup with Swiss Cheese Croutons

1 tablespoon extra virgin olive oil
½ medium onion, sliced thin
¼ teaspoon salt
¼ teaspoon pepper
3 (14-ounce) cans beef broth

1 teaspoon Worcestershire
1 bay leaf
3 teaspoons unbleached, all-purpose flour
3 tablespoons water

Heat olive oil in a saucepan on medium heat until hot. Add onion and cook and stir until tender and browned. Sprinkle on salt and pepper; add beef broth, Worcestershire, and bay leaf; bring to a boil. Reduce heat and simmer 10 minutes. Combine flour with water and whisk until smooth. Bring soup back to boiling and whisk in flour water and boil 1 minute. Float a crouton on each serving. Makes about 4 (1¼-cup) servings.

SWISS CHEESE CROUTONS:
2 slices whole-grain, low-carb bread
½ tablespoon Smart Balance margarine

2 (1-ounce) slices Swiss cheese

Preheat oven broiler to high. Toast bread in a toaster and spread with margarine. Top each slice of bread with a slice of cheese and place under the broiler until cheese is melted. Cool slightly and cut each toast on the diagonal making 4 triangular croutons.

Recipes from Joan's Kitchen (Michigan)

Lemony Basil Mushroom Soup

¼ cup margarine
1¼ cups chopped onions
2 celery stalks, sliced
1 pound fresh mushrooms,
  sliced
2 carrots, sliced
4 garlic cloves, minced
6 cups water
3 (10¾-ounce) cans
  condensed chicken broth

1 (10¾-ounce) can cream
  of chicken soup
½ cup chopped fresh basil
1 teaspoon fresh ground pepper
1 teaspoon lemon juice
½ cup uncooked wild rice
¼ cup uncooked regular rice
1 lemon, sliced
Grated Parmesan cheese

In 6-quart Dutch oven, melt margarine. Saute* onions, mushrooms, celery, carrots, and garlic in margarine about 5 minutes. Stir in water, chicken broth, chicken soup, basil, pepper, lemon juice, and wild and regular rice; cover and simmer over low heat till wild rice is tender, about 40 minutes. Serve garnished with lemon slices and Parmesan cheese. Makes 16 (1-cup) servings.

Home Cookin': Almont Elementary PTA (Michigan)

Mushroom Barley Soup

2 large yellow onions,
  chopped
3 medium carrots, sliced
2 stalks celery
½ pound mushrooms, sliced
  thin

4 cups beef broth
¼ cup chopped parsley
½ cup medium-size barley
¼ teaspoon pepper
Salt to taste

Place all ingredients in pan and boil for 4 minutes. Simmer partly covered for 40 minutes or until the barley is tender. Serves 4.

The Oke Family Cookbook (Minnesota)

Gatherer's Soup
(Morel and Barley with Wild Leek)

Wild leeks fill the woods around the same time as morels and are much less elusive. What I like about this soup is that even if the morel harvest has been meager, the abundant leeks make you feel successful in your gathering. A wide variety of mushrooms may be substituted, in part or whole, for the morels.

1 bunch wild leeks, chopped (1–1½ cups)
¼ cup butter
1 pound morel mushrooms, sliced
½ cup pearl barley
6 cups beef stock, divided
Salt, pepper, and Worcestershire to taste

Sauté leeks in butter until limp and translucent. Lower heat and add mushrooms, stirring occasionally until lightly browned and liquid has cooked away. Add barley, stirring to coat with mushroom mixture. Add about 2 cups stock and bring to a boil. Cover and cook until barley is tender, about 45 minutes. Add remaining stock. Season with salt and pepper as needed. Add Worcestershire as needed. Serves 8.

The Rustic Gourmet (Michigan)

Potato-Carrot Potage

2 cups diced onions
½ cup butter
1½ cups chopped celery
4 cups peeled, thinly sliced carrots
8 cups peeled, diced potatoes
2 quarts chicken broth, seasoned
1 cup heavy cream or sour cream for garnish
4 tablespoons chopped chives for garnish

In a 6-quart soup pot, sauté onions in hot butter for 3 minutes over medium heat. Add celery and continue to sauté 3 additional minutes. Add carrots, potatoes, and chicken broth. Bring to a boil, reduce temperature, and simmer 1 hour or till potatoes and carrots are very soft. Purée about ⅓ of soup in a blender or food processor. Return purée to soup pot to chicken broth. At serving time, pour 1 tablespoon heavy cream in each bowl, or add a dollop of sour cream and sprinkle with chopped chives. Serves 10–12.

Cranbrook Reflections (Michigan)

Swiss Peasant Bread Soup

This great, easy-to-prepare mountain dish can help get you through a dark winter's evening. It's peasant fare—stale bread, onions, and dried mushrooms gathered earlier in the year. To me, this soup is what "French onion soup" should be like, but here the cheese is a garnish, not a two-inch-thick topping as it so often is in restaurants. (This recipe is best right off the stove rather than cooled and reheated the next day, because the bread will break down and leave you with a texture akin to that of oatmeal.)

2½ cups boiling water
1 cup dried porcini mushrooms
2 tablespoons butter
1 large sweet onion (Vidalia,
   Walla Walla, Texas Sweet),
   coarsely chopped
1 garlic clove, minced
1 sprig fresh thyme

6 cups chicken broth
½ (¾-pound) loaf peasant bread,
   torn into 2-inch chunks
½ teaspoon coarse sea salt
1 teaspoon freshly ground
   black pepper
1½ cups freshly grated aged
   Gruyère cheese for serving

In a large heat-proof bowl, pour boiling water over mushrooms. Soak, covered, 20 minutes. Strain mushrooms, reserving liquid. Rinse and clean mushrooms, discarding any tough stems. Set aside.

In a large stockpot, melt butter over medium heat. Add onion, garlic, and thyme, and sauté until onion is translucent, about 7 minutes.

Add chicken broth and reserved mushroom-soaking liquid. Bring to a boil, then reduce heat to medium-low. Remove and discard thyme sprig. Stir in bread cubes and mushrooms. Simmer 10 minutes more, or until bread is incorporated into broth. Add salt and pepper and serve immediately in warm bowls with a generous amount of Gruyère grated on top. Serves 4–6.

Zingerman's Guide to Good Eating (Michigan)

Traditionally, peasant bread refers to bread prepared by rural peasants and used as an everyday bread. The breads usually contained simple ingredients and were made with whole-grains. The type of bread made depended on the types of grains commonly grown in a particular region. Peasant breads were often shaped into rounds or rectangles and baked as hearth breads. Today, the term still refers to rustic breads made with simple ingredients. Peasant breads often feature a thick, crusty exterior and a hearty, flavorful crumb. Types of breads that might be considered peasant bread include Irish soda bread and Italian Pane Rustica.

St. Nicholas Festival Borscht

2 quarts water
1 medium beef bone with
  meat
2 beets, chopped
2 medium carrots, chopped
1 green pepper, seeded
  (whole)
Salt and pepper to taste
1 small onion, chopped

2 medium potatoes, peeled
  and cubed
½ small head cabbage,
  chopped
1 small can tomatoes,
  or diced
2–3 tablespoons tomato sauce
1 clove garlic, minced (optional)

In 3-quart saucepan, bring water with meaty bone to a boil. Skim and simmer 2–3 hours. Remove meat and bone from broth. To liquid, add beets; cook 10 minutes, then add carrots and green pepper. Cook 10 minutes. Add salt, pepper, onion, potatoes, and cabbage. Cook until potatoes and cabbage are tender. Remove green pepper. Add tomatoes, tomato sauce, and garlic, if desired. Cook 10–15 minutes. Serves 6.

Note: May add dill weed and parsley. Serve with sour cream and rye bread, if desired.

Sunflowers & Samovars (Wisconsin)

Fresh Cabbage Soup

5 slices bacon, diced
1 pound cabbage, chopped
2 carrots, diced
2 potatoes, diced
1 stalk celery, sliced

1½ quarts water
2 tablespoons flour
2 tablespoons butter, softened
Salt and pepper to taste

Fry bacon till golden in large saucepan; drain fat. Add vegetables and water; bring to a boil, then simmer 20 minutes or till vegetables are tender. Blend flour into butter till smooth; stir into soup. Bring soup to a boil, stirring well. Shut off heat, add seasonings, stir and serve.

Historically Delicious (Michigan)

Simple Split Pea Soup

8 cups water
2 cups dry split peas
2 tablespoons olive oil
2 cups chopped onions
**2 cups chopped celery and/
  or carrots**

2 bay leaves
1½ tablespoons onion powder
1 teaspoon garlic powder
2 teaspoons salt

Put first 2 ingredients into pot. Bring to a boil, reduce heat, cover and simmer ½ hour. Add remaining ingredients and simmer covered for one hour. Remove cover and simmer 30 more minutes. Stir occasionally. Yields 8½ cups.

Country Life: Vegetarian Cookbook (Michigan)

Sharon's Broccoli and Cheese Soup

In a word: Excellent.

**4 cups fat-free broth, low
  sodium**
**2 cups frozen shredded hash
  brown potatoes**
1 cup chopped celery
1 cup chopped onions
1 cup chopped carrots

4 cups chopped broccoli
3 tablespoons all-purpose flour
2 cups skim milk
**8 ounces fat-free pasteurized
  cheese, cubed**
Salt and pepper to taste

Put broth and vegetables in a large stockpot and bring to a boil. Simmer till vegetables are tender, about 15 minutes. Blend flour with milk and add to vegetables, stirring constantly till soup thickens. Remove from heat. Add cheese cubes and stir till cheese is melted and smooth. Season to taste. Serves 8.

Options: Use more cheese, if you prefer a cheesier flavor. Sprinkle a bit of paprika on each bowl before serving. If you want your broccoli to remain bright green, put it in the soup about 5 minutes after the other vegetables.

"Life Tastes Better Than Steak" Cookbook (Michigan)

Wisconsin Beer Cheese Soup

An admirable rendition of one of Wisconsin's famous tourist attractions readily con-verts to a zesty cheese sauce. Reduce the water by one and a half cups and pour the sauce over baked potatoes, broccoli or cauliflower. Serve as a topping on crêpes, pasta or as a dip for chips and pretzels.

¾ cup butter (1½ sticks)
1 cup finely chopped onions
1 tablespoon minced garlic
½ cup finely chopped celery
½ cup finely chopped carrots
½ cup flour
¼ cup vegetarian chicken-
   flavored powder
3 cups hot water
½ cup Old Milwaukee Beer

2 teaspoons Worcestershire
2 cups whole milk
¼ cup heavy cream
2 tablespoons sugar
2 teaspoons dry mustard
½ teaspoon ground fennel
⅛ teaspoon cayenne
   pepper
5 cups grated Wisconsin
   Cheddar cheese

Heat butter in a heavy 5-quart soup pot and add onions and garlic. Sauté until onions are translucent and add celery and carrots. Cook 2–3 minutes and stir in flour. Dissolve vegetarian powder in hot water and add to pot. Bring to a boil over high heat. Add beer, Worcester-shire, milk, and cream.

   Reduce heat to low, simmer 5 minutes and add sugar, mustard, fen-nel, and cayenne. Cook one minute longer and add cheeses, stirring constantly until cheese is melted and soup begins to bubble.

   If soup seems a little too thick, add additional vegetarian broth or warm milk as desired. Remove from heat and serve garnished with a sprinkle of paprika. Yields 2½ quarts.

Vegetarian International Cuisine (Wisconsin)

Cheese Soup

½ cup butter
½ cup flour
4 cups milk
½ cup grated carrots
¼ cup finely chopped onions

1 stalk celery, chopped
¼ cup finely diced green pepper
1 pint chicken broth
½ pound Cheddar cheese
Sherry (optional)

Melt the butter and blend in flour and then the milk. Cook until thickened while stirring constantly. Parboil the vegetables in the chicken broth. Melt the cheese in a double boiler or in the milk mixture. Combine all the ingredients and bring to boil. Add one tablespoon sherry to each bowl of soup when serving. Top each bowl of soup with a design cut from a slice of cheese and sprinkle parsley if desired. Garnish with popcorn. Makes 6–8 servings.

A Thyme for All Seasons (Minnesota)

Creamy Wild Rice Soup

6 tablespoons butter
4 tablespoons flour
2 cups half-and-half
3 cups chicken broth
1 cup chicken or turkey, diced
½ cup onion, chopped

½ cup thinly sliced celery
½ cup thinly sliced mushrooms
1½ cups cooked wild rice
½ cup white wine
Rosemary to taste
Thyme to taste

Melt butter and add flour. Cook 2 minutes, but do not brown. Add half-and-half and one cup of broth slowly; whisk constantly. Let come to a boil and cook 2 minutes. Add rest of ingredients. Simmer 30 minutes. Garnish with shredded blanched carrot.

Sharing Our Best/Home of the Good Shepherd (Minnesota)

Turkey Soup Continental

A hearty soup . . . a good main dish for a meal.

½ cup butter or margarine
1½ cups cooked turkey,
　cut up
3 tablespoons finely
　chopped onion
3 cups diced raw potatoes
1½ cups diced celery
3 cups turkey broth
1 (17-ounce) can cream-
　style corn

1½ (13-ounce) cans
　evaporated milk
3 tablespoons chopped parsley
1½ teaspoons salt
½ teaspoon ginger
½ teaspoon paprika
¼ teaspoon pepper or less

Melt butter over low heat. Add turkey and onion. Cook until onion is transparent. Add potatoes, celery, and broth. Stir and cook until mixture is well blended and slightly thick. Simmer until vegetables are done. Add corn, milk, and seasonings. Heat thoroughly, stirring occasionally. Serve hot. Garnish with parsley and serve with crackers, hard rolls, or toast.

Celebrating 150 Years of Faith and Food (Wisconsin)

Minestrone Soup

1 pound Italian sausage
　(cased)
1 tablespoon oil
1 cup onion, diced
1 clove garlic, minced
1 teaspoon basil
1 cup carrots, sliced

2 small zucchini, sliced
1 (16-ounce) can Italian tomatoes
7 cups beef broth
3 cups finely chopped cabbage
1 can Great Northern beans
Pepper to taste

Brown sliced sausage in oil. Add onion and garlic; cook 10 minutes. Add basil the last 5 minutes. Add carrots and zucchini. Chop tomatoes—do not drain; mix with the broth and add to soup with the cabbage. Simmer for 2 hours or longer. Add the undrained beans and pepper; simmer for 30–45 minutes.

Treasured Recipes from Treasured Friends (Minnesota)

Hearty Italian Soup

1 (28-ounce) can stewed
   tomatoes
1 (15-ounce) can tomato sauce
6 cups beef broth
1 cup sliced carrots
1 pound Italian sausage,
   mild or sweet
1 large onion, chopped
1 clove garlic, minced

1 cup sliced mushrooms
1 teaspoon sugar
1 teaspoon dried basil
1 teaspoon dried oregano
¼ cup fresh chopped parsley
   or 3 tablespoons dried
2 cups sliced zucchini
2 cups frozen tortellini
Parmesan cheese (optional)

Put tomatoes, tomato sauce, beef broth, and carrots in a large stock-pot; bring to a boil. Meanwhile remove casing from sausages and cook over medium heat in skillet, breaking into small pieces; fully cook. Drain; add to pot. In same skillet add onion, garlic, and mushrooms. Cook about 5 minutes. Add to pot along with seasonings. Cover, and cook about 30 minutes. Add zucchini, and cook 15–20 minutes. Add frozen tortellini, and cook about 5 minutes, until it floats. Top with grated Parmesan cheese, if desired. Serves 6–8.

Serving from the Heart (Michigan)

Autumn Soup

1½ pounds ground beef
1 cup chopped onion
4 cups water
1 cup carrots, cut up
1 cup celery, diced
1 cup potatoes, cubed

1 teaspoon seasoning salt
½ teaspoon Beau Monde
   seasoning
¼ teaspoon lemon pepper
½ teaspoon salt
6 fresh tomatoes, chopped

Cook and stir meat until brown. Cook and stir onion with meat until tender. Stir in remaining ingredients except fresh tomatoes. Heat to boiling, reduce heat, cook and simmer for 20 minutes. Add tomatoes. Cover and simmer for 10 minutes or until vegetables are tender. Serve. This soup can be frozen nicely.

Note: A 28-ounce can of tomatoes can be substituted for the 6 fresh tomatoes; use liquid and cut water to 3 cups.

The Crooked Lake Volunteer Fire Department Cookbook (Wisconsin)

Bavarian Liver Dumpling Soup

Soups with dumplings are very special to the Germans—almost required at most meals. And "liver dumpling soup is as good a soup as can be made."

2 slices calf or beef liver
   (about ¼ pound)
½ teaspoon salt
1 egg, slightly beaten
1 tablespoon soft butter
   or margarine
1 teaspoon finely minced
   parsley

1–2 teaspoons finely minced
   onion
2 slices dry bread
½ cup flour, approximately
Meat stock

Place liver on a chopping board and scrape to separate connective tissue. Combine with salt, egg, softened butter, chopped parsley, onion, and bread which has been softened in hot water and squeezed dry. Beat well to blend. Add flour to make a medium-stiff dough. Drop from a teaspoon into gently boiling meat stock. Cook, covered, for 20–25 minutes, depending on size of dumplings. Serve at once. Makes 14–16 dumplings.

Note: Avoid having mixture too thick. Test by dropping one dumpling into hot stock. If it does not hold together, add a little more flour. Serve liver dumplings in clear beef broth.

Recipe from Mader's German Restaurant, Milwaukee, owner Vic Mader
Wisconsin Cooks with Wisconsin Public Television (Wisconsin)

Sun-Kissed Soup

This is a late summer creation, to be done when fruit is very ripe, juicy, and abundant.

2 cups medium-dry white wine
½ cup honey
⅛ teaspoon cardamom
⅛ teaspoon ginger
Zest of large orange (colored part of peel)
4 cups chunks ripe melon (cantaloupe or other orange melon)
2 cups chunks ripe mangoes
2 cups chunks ripe peaches or nectarines
3 tablespoons fresh lime juice
Salt and white pepper to taste
1 pomegranate (seeds only), for garnish
Fresh lemon balm or mint, for garnish

In a medium saucepan, combine wine, honey, cardamom, ginger, and zest. Bring to a brisk simmer over medium heat, cooking until volume is reduced to 1½ cups. Cool to room temperature; discard zest. While cooling, purée melon, mangoes, and peaches in food processor (strain also, if you prefer). Stir together wine reduction, puréed fruit, and lime juice. Add a pinch of salt and white pepper as needed. Chill very well, preferably overnight.

Serve in pretty bowls, sprinkled with pomegranate seeds. Garnish with lemon balm or mint. Yields approximately 1 gallon.

The Rustic Gourmet (Michigan)

Weather can make navigating the Great Lakes a pleasure, a challenge, or a terror. Each season has its own weather problems. **Winter** navigation is severely restricted by ice and storms. Seaway shipping is usually at a stand-still from mid-December through early April. Fog is the principal navigation headache in **Spring**. Relatively warm air pumped over still cold lake waters creates an advection fog that plagues the mariner into the summer. While fog can hinder navigation, and an occasional low pressure system can bring a spell of bad weather, **Summer** is usually the most trouble free time. The principal threat is thunderstorms, which are most common from May through October. They can spring up quickly and generate strong winds and rough seas. **Autumn**'s clear, crisp days are often interrupted by rapidly intensifying low-pressure systems whose galeforce winds can whip tumultuous seas. Energy is supplied by the still warm waters, and contrasting air masses can spawn storms right over the Great Lakes Basin.

Quick Corn Chowder

2 cups chopped peeled
  potatoes
½ cup chopped carrot
½ cup chopped celery
¼ cup chopped onion
½ teaspoon pepper
2 cups water

¼ cup butter
¼ cup flour
2 cups milk
1 cup freshly grated Parmesan
  cheese
1 (8-ounce) can cream-style corn

Combine potatoes, carrot, celery, onion, pepper, and water in a saucepan. Bring to a boil; reduce heat. Simmer, covered, 10 minutes. Melt butter in a saucepan. Stir in flour and milk; mix well. Cook over medium heat until thick and bubbly, stirring constantly; cook 1 minute longer. Add cheese, stirring until melted. Add cheese mixture to vegetables; mix in corn. Cook until heated through, stirring constantly. Yields 4 servings.

Dawn to Dusk (Michigan)

White Chili

1 large onion, chopped
2 rounded teaspoons minced
  garlic
1 quart vegetable broth,
  divided
1 (4-ounce) can chopped
  green chiles, undrained
1 (48-ounce) can Great
  Northern beans, undrained
2 teaspoons ground cumin

1 teaspoon crumbled oregano
3–4 good dashes of Tabasco
Pinch of cayenne pepper
  (optional)
2 (19-ounce) cans chickpeas
Chopped parsley for garnish
Garnishes: Thinly sliced green
  onion tops, fat-free shredded
  cheese, sliced jalapeños, fat-
  free tortilla chips

In a large pot, cook onion and garlic in a few tablespoons vegetable broth. Add chiles and stir. Add beans (with liquid) and remaining vegetable broth. Mix in cumin, oregano, Tabasco, and cayenne, if desired. Bring to a boil and add chickpeas. Simmer, covered, for at least 30 minutes. Sprinkle with chopped parsley and garnishes as desired. Makes about 12 servings.

The Fruit of Her Hands (Michigan)

Goose Blind Chili

The Goose Blind Chili recipe featured here won the best spice award at the Wisconsin State Chili Cook-Off in 1991.

2½ pounds ground beef
1 large onion, diced
1 green pepper, diced
4 stalks celery, sliced
1 tablespoon oil
2 teaspoons crushed garlic
1 tablespoon chili powder
1 teaspoon black pepper
1 teaspoon crushed red pepper
  flakes

1 teaspoon cumin
1 teaspoon seasoned salt
Pinch of basil
Pinch of thyme
1 (28-ounce) can tomato pureé
1 (28-ounce) can diced
  tomatoes
1 (28-ounce) can kidney beans
1 (16-ounce) can tomato juice

In large stockpot, brown ground beef; drain. In separate pan, sauté vegetables in oil and seasonings. When vegetables are tender and onion is translucent, blend in with beef. Add canned items and allow to simmer at least one hour.

Optional: For hotter chili with a Southwestern twist, add a few tablespoons of diced jalapeños during the simmering process. Yields 12–15 servings.

Recipe from The Goose Blind, Green Lake, Wisconsin.
Our Best Cookbook 2 (Wisconsin)

Aunt "B's" White Chicken Chili

1 pound chicken pieces
¼ cup chopped onion
1 tablespoon olive oil
1 cup chicken broth or beer
1 can chopped green chiles
1 teaspoon garlic powder
1 teaspoon cumin
½ teaspoon oregano

½ teaspoon cilantro
¼ teaspoon cayenne pepper
1 can white kidney beans,
  undrained
1 can black beans, drained
Shredded Monterey Jack
  cheese, garnish
Sliced green onions, garnish

Cook chicken and onions in olive oil (break chicken into small pieces). Add remaining ingredients. Simmer 30 minutes. Garnish with the cheese and onions. Serve with flour tortillas, corn chips or corn bread. Serves 4.

Favorite Recipes of Lester Park & Rockridge Schools (Minnesota)

5-Hour Stew

2 pounds stew meat
Flour
1 cup chopped celery
1 pinch salt
Pepper
Basil
Parsley
1 tablespoon sugar
4–5 carrots, sliced
3–4 potatoes, cubed
1 quart stewed tomatoes
1 medium onion, chopped
¼ cup minute tapioca

Dredge meat in flour, Mix all together in a large covered casserole. Bake 5 hours at 250°. I have baked 6–8 hours at 200°, and it was great.

A Taste of Kennedy Cook Book (Minnesota)

Beef Stew

2 pounds stew meat
8 carrots, cubed
2 onions, quartered
6–8 potatoes, cubed
2 stalks celery, cut up
1 (15-ounce) can tomato sauce
¼ cup water
⅛ teaspoon garlic powder
1 teaspoon Worcestershire
2 teaspoons salt
½ teaspoon pepper
¼ cup all-purpose flour

Put meat and vegetables in crockpot. Combine remaining ingredients except flour and mix with meat and vegetables. Cook on LOW 9–11 hours or on HIGH 5–6 hours in crockpot. Mix flour with 2 teaspoons water and make into a paste. Turn crockpot on HIGH and add paste to stew. Cook another 15 minutes to thicken. Serves 4–6.

From Our Home to Yours (Michigan)

German Beef Stew

2 tablespoons flour
½ teaspoon celery salt
½ teaspoon ginger
¾ teaspoon salt
¼ teaspoon pepper
¼ teaspoon garlic powder
1½ pounds beef chuck,
   cut in 2-inch chunks
2 tablespoons salad oil

1½ cups sliced onion
1 (16-ounce) can tomatoes
¼ cup red wine vinegar
¼ cup dark molasses
½ cup water
5 carrots, peeled and cut into
   1-inch pieces
¼ cup dark raisins

Combine flour, celery salt, ginger, salt, pepper, and garlic powder. Coat beef on all sides with mixture. In large heavy pan or Dutch oven, heat oil, then add meat and brown on all sides, stirring frequently. Add onions and cook until lightly browned. Add tomatoes, vinegar, molasses, and $1/2$ cup water. Cover and simmer $1^1/2$ hours, stirring occasionally. Add carrots and raisins; simmer one hour. Serve over hot cooked noodles.

St. Frederick Parish Centennial Recipe Collection (Wisconsin)

Many of the foods of the Great Lakes region reflect the heritage of its ancestors. German bratwurst, sauerbraten and beer; Norwegian boiled codfish (Torsk, Lutefisk); Danish kringle; Cornish pasty; French Brie and Camembert cheese; Swiss cheese; Italian Provolone and Parmesan cheese; Czechoslovakian kolaches; and Belgian chicken booyah are a sampling of the ethnic foods that are enjoyed throughout this region.

Sweet and Sour Beef Stew with Dried Cherries

3 tablespoons all-purpose
 flour
1¼ teaspoons salt
½ teaspoon ground allspice
½ teaspoon ground cinnamon
½ teaspoon pepper
2 pounds boneless beef chuck,
 cut into 1-inch cubes
4 tablespoons vegetable oil,
 divided

2 large onions, thinly sliced
1 cup dried cherries
2 tablespoons sugar
2 tablespoons red wine vinegar
2 tablespoons water
1 cup dry red wine
1 cup beef stock or canned broth
½ pound button mushrooms,
 trimmed, quartered

Preheat oven to 350° with rack in center position. Combine flour, salt, allspice, cinnamon, and pepper in a large plastic bag. Add beef to bag and toss, coating pieces evenly with seasoned flour.

Heat 1 tablespoon oil in heavy skillet over medium-high heat. Add ¹/₃ beef and cook until brown, about 5 minutes. Transfer meat to Dutch oven, using a slotted spoon. Repeat with remaining meat in 2 batches, adding 1 tablespoon oil to skillet each time. Add remaining oil to same skillet. Stirring frequently, add onions and cherries, and cook until onions are soft and light brown, about 12 minutes. Mix in sugar, vinegar, and water. Increase heat to high and cook until brown, stirring frequently, about 8 minutes. Add onion mixture to beef in Dutch oven. Mix in wine, stock, and mushrooms; cover tightly and bake until beef is tender, about 2 hours 15 minutes, uncovering stew during last 2 minutes if liquid is too thin. Serve, or cover and refrigerate. Stew can be prepared 2 days ahead. Bring to room temperature first and reheat over low. Serves 6.

Cherry Home Companion (Michigan)

Salads

©WILLIAM I. HARTER, WWW.WIKIPEDIA.ORG

DOOR COUNTY

Door County, Wisconsin, the state's "thumb" extending into Lake Michigan, is unique in that it is located entirely on a peninsula. Therefore, the county has more shoreline than any other county in the United States—more than 250 miles. It is named after the strait between the Door Peninsula and Washington Island. The dangerous passage, scattered with shipwrecks, was known to early explorers as "Death's Door."

Leelanau Country Inn's Salad Leelanau

SALAD:

4 tablespoons chopped, toasted pecans

1 large head Bibb lettuce

1 large head red Boston Bibb lettuce

4 tablespoons Gorgonzola cheese

3 tablespoons dried cherries

½ cup Cherry Vinaigrette Dressing

Toast pecans under hot broiler for 2 minutes until golden brown. Chill large salad bowl. Wash and dry lettuce*. Hand-tear the lettuce into large salad bowl, and mix well. Sprinkle pecans, cheese, and dried cherries on lettuce. At the table, before serving, toss with Cherry Vinaigrette Dressing.

CHERRY VINAIGRETTE DRESSING:

1 cup cherry vinegar

2 cups canola oil

1 cup maple syrup

¼ cup country Dijon mustard

¼ cup chopped fresh basil

Mix all ingredients together well. May be stored, sealed under refrigeration for up to 1 month. It is always best to make dressing at least one day ahead of use to allow the flavors to marry. Cherry vinegar is available in most specialty shops. To make your own, combine 2 cups white vinegar and 2 cups red wine vinegar and add 3 cups halved tart cherries. Allow to stand for 36 hours. Then strain. Serves 4.

Note: Dressing will not stick to wet lettuce. Always be certain the lettuce is dry by draining for several hours or spinning dry, and carefully patting with a dry towel.

Cherry Home Companion (Michigan)

LEELANAU PENINSULA

The Leelanau Peninsula is located in the Northwest corner of Michigan's Lower Peninsula. Surrounded by water on three sides, the Leelanau Peninsula offers a wide variety of recreation, attractions and culture.

Caesar Salad

Most everyone loves a good Caesar salad, but concern over raw egg safety has made some cooks timid about serving this popular classic. Here's a version without the raw egg that my family has loved for years. Purists may blanch at the omission, but I believe your guests will appreciate your thoughtfulness.

2 anchovy fillets
2 medium cloves garlic, minced
1 teaspoon salt or to taste
6 tablespoons vegetable oil
2 tablespoons red wine
   vinegar
1 tablespoon fresh lemon
   juice, strained
½ teaspoon Worcestershire

1 teaspoon dry mustard
1 teaspoon freshly ground
   black pepper
2 large heads romaine lettuce,
   washed, drained, torn,
   and chilled
1 cup croutons
1 tablespoon freshly grated
   Parmesan cheese

Drain anchovies on paper towel, then put in small bowl and mash fine with fork. Place minced garlic in wooden or glass salad bowl. Add salt. Mash into paste with back of spoon. Add mashed anchovy fillets plus vegetable oil, vinegar, lemon juice, Worcestershire, dry mustard, and black pepper, and mix well.

Just before serving, add lettuce. Toss well to blend with dressing. Garnish with croutons and freshly grated Parmesan cheese. Makes 12 servings.

The Sunday Cook Collection (Wisconsin)

Chinese Tossed Salad

DRESSING:

½ cup Mazola oil

2 teaspoons salt

4 tablespoons Japanese rice vinegar, unseasoned

2 tablespoons toasted sesame seeds

4 teaspoons sugar

Mix all ingredients and refrigerate at least one day.

SALAD:

1 head lettuce

½ cup shredded cooked chicken

1–2 scallions, finely chopped

1 cup alfalfa sprouts

⅓ cup thinly sliced green bell pepper

2 tablespoons grated carrots

⅓ thinly sliced celery

¼ cup thinly sliced radishes

⅓ cup roasted peanuts

⅓ cup deep-fried wonton skins or 1 can LaChoy chow mein noodles

Wash and tear lettuce into bite-size pieces. Drain and refrigerate till ready to assemble. Just before serving, add chicken and vegetables. Pour on Dressing and add roasted peanuts and wonton skins, broken into small pieces. Serves 8–10.

Note: Can be prepared in advance.

The Bell Tower Cookbook (Michigan)

When a new road forced Henry Ford's beloved birthplace from its original location, Ford decided not only to move it, but to restore and refurnish it to match his boyhood recollections. The restoration received so much press that Ford was inundated with requests to save other buildings. Soon after, Greenfield Village was born. Nestled on 240 acres of land near Dearborn, Michigan, nearly one hundred historical buildings were moved to the property from their original locations and arranged in a village setting. Some of the most notable buildings include Henry Ford's prototype garage where he built the quadricycle; the Wright brothers' bicycle shop and home from Dayton, Ohio; Thomas Edison's Menlo Park laboratory from New Jersey; Noah Webster's house, and William Holmes McGuffey's birthplace.

Bev's Strawberry-Pecan Salad

SALAD:

½ head lettuce

1 head red Bibb lettuce

1 head romaine lettuce

1 quart fresh strawberries

1 cup roasted pecan halves

Toss together greens that have been coarsely sliced. Add strawberries, sliced from top to bottom, and roasted pecans.

DRESSING:

¾ cup sugar

⅓ cup white vinegar

1 teaspoon poppy seeds

1 teaspoon prepared mustard

1 teaspoon freshly grated onion

½ cup oil

Place all ingredients except oil in a saucepan. Bring to a boil to dissolve sugar. Chill. Place in blender with oil and blend 30–40 seconds or until well mixed. Put Dressing on Salad just before serving. Serves 6–8.

Treasures from Heaven (Michigan)

Replica of shop where Henry Ford built his first automobile, Greenfield Village, Dearborn, Michigan.

Spinach Salad with Sliced Apples

Looks and tastes as good as it sounds.

1 bunch spinach
1 apple, unpeeled
4 strips bacon, slivered, fried crisp

1 bunch green onions, chopped
2 ounces Amish or Jack cheese, cubed

Wash and dry spinach. Remove stems, then tear leaves into bite-size pieces. Cut apple in half lengthwise, then crosswise. Removing core, thinly slice. Place spinach and apple slices in salad bowl, along with bacon, chopped onions, and cheese.

DRESSING:

¼ cup olive oil
3 tablespoons white wine vinegar with tarragon
1 teaspoon sugar

½ teaspoon dry mustard
Garlic salt to taste
Freshly ground pepper

Whisk together above ingredients and pour over salad. Lightly toss. Serves 4–6.

Hollyhocks & Radishes (Michigan)

Warm Spinach Salad

A very pretty salad that doesn't try to overly impress you.

1¼ pounds fresh spinach
1 cup sliced fresh mushrooms
¾ cup finely chopped red onion
Salt and freshly ground pepper to taste

½ cup olive oil
¼ cup red wine vinegar
1 clove garlic, minced
1 teaspoon dried basil
2 eggs, hard-cooked, finely chopped

Wash and dry spinach. Trim, then tear into bite-size pieces. Place in salad bowl or heat-proof dish, and top with mushrooms and onion. Salt and pepper to taste. (This may be done in the morning, covered with plastic wrap, and refrigerated.)

In a small saucepan, heat oil over medium heat. Whisk in vinegar, garlic, and basil. Simmer ever so gently 5 minutes. Pour hot dressing over spinach and toss. Dress with finely chopped eggs and serve immediately. Serves 4–5.

Hollyhocks & Radishes (Michigan)

Summer Sunrise Melon and Spinach Salad

The bright, sunrise orange of cantaloupe and leafy green of spinach make this salad beautiful, while bits of scallions and toasty sesame seeds make it delicious. Serve it in August, when melons are at their market peak. (Or substitute fresh strawberries earlier in the summer.)

1½ pounds fresh spinach
2 tablespoons sesame seeds
⅓ cup red wine vinegar
2 tablespoons minced green onion
1 tablespoon sugar

1 teaspoon paprika
½ teaspoon Worcestershire
⅓ cup vegetable oil
2–3 cups cantaloupe chunks (or hulled strawberries)
Freshly ground black pepper

Wash spinach. Tear into bite-size pieces, removing stems. Dry in a salad spinner or clean towel. Chill spinach. Toast sesame seeds in a small, dry skillet over medium heat until golden, about 3–4 minutes. Do not scorch.

Mix vinegar, green onion, sugar, paprika, and Worcestershire in a bowl; whisk in oil in a thin stream. Just before serving, toss spinach, sesame seeds, dressing and fruit in a large glass bowl. Pass the pepper mill. Makes 6–8 large servings.

Fresh Market Wisconsin (Wisconsin)

Best-Ever Cole Slaw Dressing

1 cup sugar
1 cup salad oil
1 teaspoon salt
1 small onion, diced

½ cup vinegar
1 teaspoon celery seed
1 teaspoon dry mustard

Beat ingredients together until very creamy. Store in covered pint jar in refrigerator. Keeps very well.

Great Cooks of Zion Church (Minnesota)

Kozmo's Coleslaw

SALAD:
⅓–½ cup dried blueberries
   or cherries
⅓ cup chopped green onions
⅓ cup toasted sunflower seeds
3 carrots, chopped

1 (16-ounce) package coleslaw
   mix
1 (11-ounce) can Mandarin
   orange segments, reserve
   juice

DRESSING:
3 tablespoons firmly packed
   brown sugar
½ teaspoon pepper
¼ teaspoon salt
¼ teaspoon dried basil
   leaves
3 tablespoons white vinegar

1 tablespoon reserved
   Mandarin orange juice
1 beef-flavored packet from
   Ramen noodle soup (set
   noodles aside)
½ cup olive oil or vegetable oil

Mix Salad ingredients together. In a separate bowl, stir together Dressing ingredients with whisk, gradually adding oil. Refrigerate 1 hour. Pour Dressing over Salad; top with noodles.

a-MAIZE-ing Tailgating (Michigan)

Bleu Cheese Coleslaw

The bacon and bleu cheese give a face-lift to those tired old coleslaw recipes.

**2 tablespoons Mucky Duck
  mustard (sweet-tangy
  mustard)**
1 tablespoon chopped garlic
¼ cup white wine vinegar

¾ cup vegetable oil
4 slices bacon, coarsely chopped
1 head cabbage, shredded
4 ounces bleu cheese, crumbled
Freshly ground pepper to taste

Combine mustard, garlic, and vinegar in blender container. Add oil gradually, processing constantly. Process till thickened. Cook bacon in skillet till crisp; remove from heat. Stir dressing into bacon and drippings in skillet. Combine cabbage and bleu cheese in large bowl. Pour dressing over top; toss to mix. Season with pepper.

Mucky Duck Mustard Cookbook (Michigan)

Broccoli Supreme Salad

**1 large head broccoli, cut-up
  fine**
**1 large head cauliflower, cut
  up**
**3 cups red or green grapes,
  cut in half**

4 green onions, chopped
**½ pound bacon, cooked and
  crumbled (may use bacon
  bits)**
**¼ cup slivered almonds or
  sunflower seeds**

DRESSING:
1 cup mayonnaise
½ cup sugar

1 tablespoon vinegar
1 teaspoon lemon juice

Toss salad; marinate in refrigerator for 2 hours.

Variation: Use ³/₄ cup raisins instead of grapes.

Clinton's 110th Cookbook (Minnesota)

Zucchini & Corn Salad

Tired of hearing about foods you shouldn't eat? Don't count corn among them. It's very low in fat, high in complex carbohydrates, and loaded with fiber. This salad is an excellent way to use two vegetables that are abundant and affordable in mid-to-late summer.

2 small zucchini, washed, ends removed, sliced
1 (12-ounce) package frozen whole-kernel corn, defrosted
¼ cup chopped green onions
1 tablespoon vegetable oil
2 teaspoons cider vinegar

1 teaspoon lemon juice
1 clove garlic, peeled, ends removed, crushed
½ teaspoon chili powder
¼ teaspoon dry mustard
⅛ teaspoon ground cumin
⅛ teaspoon salt

In a medium-size bowl, combine zucchini, corn, and green onions; set aside. In a small bowl, combine oil, cider vinegar, lemon juice, garlic, chili powder, dry mustard, cumin, and salt. Whisk together until blended. Pour dressing over zucchini mixture and toss to coat. Cover and refrigerate, or serve immediately. Serves 4.

Heart Smart Cookbook II (Michigan)

Beet Salad

This recipe has no specific amounts for ingredients, it depends upon how much you want to make—just for yourself or for a crowd.

Beets, cooked, peeled, diced small
Raw onions, diced small

Salt and pepper to taste
Mayonnaise

Mix together beets, onions, salt and pepper. Add just enough mayonnaise to make it moist. Will keep in refrigerator approximately 3–4 days.

Crystal Clear Cooking (Michigan)

Asparagus Bundles

45–50 asparagus spears,
    trimmed to about 4 inches
10 small red tomatoes
¾ cup olive oil
2 teaspoons grated Parmesan
    cheese

½ cup lemon juice
1 teaspoon sugar
½ teaspoon oregano
1 teaspoon chopped garlic
⅛ teaspoon black pepper

Clean and cut tips off asparagus spears; blanch. Slice tomatoes and hollow out to make rings. Place 4–5 spears in each ring and cut ends to equal length. Beat remaining ingredients together and pour over bundles just before serving. Serves 10.

The Bountiful Arbor (Michigan)

Pea and Peanut Salad

1 (10-ounce) package frozen
    green peas (thawed)
2 cups Spanish peanuts
½ cup Miracle Whip

½ cup sour cream
2 tablespoons lemon juice
1 teaspoon Worcestershire

Mix uncooked peas and peanuts. Mix salad dressing, sour cream, lemon juice, and Worcestershire together and blend into peas and peanuts. Refrigerate covered with plastic wrap for 2 hours. Serves 8–10.

People Pleasers (Minnesota)

A misconception regarding the actual route of the Mississippi River during the signing of the 1783 Treaty of Paris created the "Northwest Angle," also known as the "chimney" of Minnesota. The parties did not suspect that the source of the Mississippi, Lake Itasca (then unknown to European explorers), was south of that point. The Northwest Angle cannot be reached by land from the rest of the United States without going through Canada; while remaining on U.S. territory it can be reached only by crossing the Lake of the Woods.

Wild Rice Salad

1 cup wild rice
3 cups water
1 teaspoon salt
2 cups diced turkey (ham or
 shrimp)
1 cup sliced water chestnuts

1 cup sliced fresh mushrooms
½ cup olives
1 cup mayonnaise
½ cup sour cream
½ teaspoon mustard
Pepper to taste

Cook rice in water and salt for 40 minutes until tender. Drain and add next 4 ingredients. Mix next 4 ingredients for dressing and add to wild rice mixture. Serves 12.

Martha Chapter #132 OES Cookbook (Minnesota)

Spring Salad

Great with ham, roast beef, lamb, or even barbecued chicken.

10–12 small red potatoes,
 unpeeled
1 pound fresh asparagus, cut
 into 1 to 2-inch lengths
5–6 carrots, peeled and thinly
 sliced
¾ cup canola oil
6 tablespoons red wine
 vinegar

1 tablespoon sugar
½ cup chopped parsley
1 tablespoon dried basil (or
 fresh basil if you have it)
2 cloves garlic, chopped fine
Salt and freshly ground pepper
4 tablespoons chopped green
 onion

Cook potatoes in salted water until tender; drain and set aside. Steam asparagus just until tender; drain and set aside. Cook carrots for 5 minutes, until tender; drain and set aside. Put all vegetables in a large bowl and chill. In a blender, combine oil, vinegar, sugar, parsley, basil, and garlic. Whirl until smooth. Add salt and pepper to taste. (Check flavor and add more vinegar, sugar, salt or pepper if you wish.) Add onions; toss with vegetables. Cover and chill. Serve cold or at room temperature. Yields 4–6 servings.

Recipes of Note for Entertaining (Minnesota)

Hot German Potato Salad

¾ cup diced bacon (6 slices)
½ cup chopped onion
2 teaspoons salt
1 teaspoon sugar
1 teaspoon flour
1 teaspoon mustard
⅛ teaspoon pepper
2 quarts cooked, sliced
   potatoes (2 pounds raw)
½ cup vinegar
½ cup boiling water
4 tablespoons chopped parsley

Fry bacon until slightly browned, then add onion and brown. Blend salt, sugar, flour, mustard, and pepper, and the onion and bacon. Add potatoes and then vinegar and water. Allow to heat through until moisture has been partly absorbed. Add parsley, and serve hot.

Celebrating 300 Years of Detroit Cooking (Michigan)

Bonnie's Potato Salad

2 pounds red potatoes
3 tablespoons onion, sliced
   paper thin
3 hard-boiled eggs, coarsely
   chopped
1 green pepper, seeded and
   finely chopped
2 stalks celery, chopped
2 tablespoons sliced ripe olives
2 tablespoons pimento, finely
   chopped
1 tablespoon finely chopped
   Italian parsley
2 tablespoons chives

Boil unpeeled potatoes in salted water for 25–30 minutes or until fork inserts easily. Slice into ¼-inch slices. Add onion to warm potatoes. Mix together eggs, pepper, celery, pimento, ripe olives, and parsley. Add to potatoes and onions. Add mayonnaise to moisten. Season to taste.

Herbs in a Minnesota Kitchen (Minnesota)

Tabbouleh Salad

½ cup medium burghul
  (bulgur) or cracked wheat
5 fresh ripe tomatoes, finely
  chopped
3 bunches fresh, crisp, curly
  parsley, finely chopped
1 bunch green onions or
  scallions, finely chopped
2–3 tablespoons crushed
  dried mint, or 1 cup finely
  chopped fresh peppermint

½ cup olive or vegetable oil
Juice of 1 lemon
Salt and freshly ground black
  pepper to taste
1 clove garlic, mashed
  (optional)
Fresh, crisp romaine lettuce
  leaves

Place burghul into a measuring cup and add warm water to cover; allow to soak and expand until soft, about 20 minutes. Drain and squeeze out excess water. Place into a large mixing bowl. Place chopped tomatoes over burghul to allow juice to absorb. Add remaining ingredients, except lettuce, and toss gently. Adjust seasonings. Serve well chilled with romaine lettuce or freshly picked, young tender grape leaves.

Note: Chopped, crisp green pepper or cucumbers may be added for added crunch.

What's Cooking at St. Stephens? (Michigan)

The Sault Locks (pronounced *Soo Locks*) allow ships to travel between Lake Superior and the lower Great Lakes. The locks are the busiest in the world, passing an average of 12,000 ships per year. This is achieved in spite of the locks being closed during the winter, from January through March, when ice shuts down shipping on the Great Lakes. The winter is used to inspect and maintain the locks.

Grilled Chicken Salad

HONEY MUSTARD DRESSING:

1 cup peanut oil
½ cup honey
4 tablespoons mustard
1 teaspoon minced garlic
¼ teaspoon paprika

1 tablespoon minced fresh
  gingerroot
2 tablespoons fresh lemon juice
3 tablespoons cider vinegar

Combine all ingredients in bowl. Whip together well for 3 minutes or until emulsified. Yields 4–6 servings.

4 (6-ounce) boneless, skinless
  chicken breasts
1 cup Honey Mustard Dressing
20 peeled orange sections
8 peeled cantaloupe wedges
8 tomato wedges
8 red leaf lettuce leaves

1 small bunch grapes (red or
  green, seedless)
1 apple, sliced, divided into 4
  servings
4 tablespoons walnuts,
  chopped

Marinate chicken breasts in Honey Mustard Dressing, covered, 2–4 hours. Grill chicken breasts until done on a preheated hot char grill. Refrigerate until cool.

Place 2 leaves red leaf lettuce in a wide rim pasta bowl or plate (per serving). Slice each cooked chicken breast into 4 slices (1 breast per serving) and place on lettuce. Brush with 1 ounce Honey Mustard Dressing (per serving).

Arrange oranges, cantaloupe, tomatoes, grapes, and apples around the outside of each bowl or plate. Top with walnuts. Drizzle remaining Dressing over salad. Yields 4 servings.

The Simply Great Cookbook II (Michigan)

Northwoods Chicken Salad

1 cup uncooked wild rice
5½ cups chicken broth
Juice of ½ lemon
1 chicken breast (2 halves) cooked, cooled and cut into bite-size pieces

3 green onions, sliced
½ red pepper, diced
2 ounces sugar pea pods, cut into 1-inch pieces
1 cup cashews

DRESSING:
2 large cloves garlic, minced
1 tablespoon Dijon mustard
½ teaspoon salt
¼ teaspoon sugar

¼ teaspoon freshly ground pepper
¼ cup herb vinegar
⅓ cup olive oil

Rinse wild rice. Combine with chicken broth in 3-quart sauce pan. Cover and bring to boil. Reduce heat and simmer for 45 minutes, drain. Cool in bowl. Add lemon juice, chicken, onion, and red pepper. Blend all dressing ingredients and toss with rice mixture. Refrigerate at least 2 hours before serving. Stir in pea pods and cashews. Serves 5–6.

The Clovia Recipe Collection (Minnesota)

Fruited Chicken Salad

3 tablespoons lemon juice
4 cups cubed, cooked chicken
1 cup sliced celery
1 cup cantaloupe balls
1 cup green grapes, halved

⅓ cup finely chopped onion
1 teaspoon salt
½ teaspoon pepper
½ cup mayonnaise or salad dressing or vanilla yogurt
¼ cup chopped almonds

Mix lemon juice with chicken. Add remaining ingredients. Toss until mixed.

What's on the Agenda? (Wisconsin)

Chilled Chicken Salad with Fruit and Rice

2½ cups cooked, cubed
   chicken
1½ cups cooked brown or
   white rice
1 cup halved green grapes
¾ cup thinly sliced celery
1 (8-ounce) can pineapple
   tidbits, drained
1 (11-ounce) can Mandarin
   oranges, drained

½ cup slivered almonds,
   toasted in a teaspoon of butter
½ cup mayonnaise
1 cup ranch dressing
Salt and freshly ground pepper
   to taste
Lettuce leaves

In a large bowl combine all ingredients except lettuce. Toss gently. Serve on lettuce-lined plates. Serves 4.

What's Cookin' (Michigan)

Sharon's Seafood Salad

2 cups crabmeat, chopped
2 cups chopped lobster
1 pound small shrimp, cooked,
   peeled, deveined
4 stalks celery, finely chopped

1 (16-ounce) jar prepared sour
   cream dill salad dressing
2 tablespoons chopped fresh dill
Sliced almonds

In large mixing bowl, combine crabmeat, lobster, shrimp, and celery. In small bowl, combine dressing and dill. Add to seafood mixture and toss gently. Refrigerate several hours or overnight. Stir before serving on lettuce leaves; sprinkle top with sliced almonds. Yields 6 servings.

Something Special (Michigan)

Steak and Mushroom Salad

DRESSING:

½ cup good olive oil
½ cup wine vinegar
2 tablespoons Dijon mustard
Freshly ground black pepper

1 garlic clove, crushed
1 teaspoon salt
½ teaspoon sugar

Combine ingredients in jar and shake well. Set aside.

SALAD:

12 small fresh mushrooms
1–1½ pounds roast or steak,
  cooked and thinly sliced
12 cherry tomatoes, halved
1 (14-ounce) can artichoke
  hearts, drained

1 head lettuce
2 tablespoons chopped parsley
3 tablespoons blue cheese,
  crumbled

Wash and rinse mushrooms and pat dry. Slice and combine in a bowl with beef and tomatoes. Cut artichokes in half or quarters and add to beef. Marinate several hours or overnight in Dressing.

Line salad bowl with chilled lettuce and arrange beef slices on it. Add marinated tomatoes, mushrooms, and artichokes. Sprinkle with parsley and cheese.

Renaissance Cuisine (Michigan)

In 1939, the Packard Motor Car Company unveiled the first air-conditioned car at the 40th National Automobile Show in Chicago, Illinois. The innovation received widespread acclaim at the auto show, but the expensive accessory would not be within the reach of the average American for several decades. The Packard Motor Car Company, which for many years built Detroit's most prestigious luxury cars, built 1.5 million vehicles on the site from 1903 to 1954. The factory complex, designed by Albert Kahn, included the city's first use of reinforced concrete for industrial construction. At its opening, it was considered the most modern automobile manufacturing facility in the world.

Warm Pork and Spinach Salad

1 pound boneless pork loin, into thin strips
1 pound fresh spinach leaves, coarsely shredded
3 cup watercress sprigs or other lettuce
1 cup thinly sliced celery
1 cup seedless green grapes
½ cup thinly sliced green onion
1 (8-ounce) can sliced water chestnuts, drained
1 large Golden Delicious cut apple, cored and chopped
1 cup low-calorie Italian salad dressing
2 tablespoons white wine
2 tablespoons Dijon-style mustard
1 tablespoon packed light brown sugar
2 teaspoons sesame seeds

Spray nonstick skillet with Pam and stir-fry pork until cooked, about 4 minutes. Set aside and keep warm. In large serving bowl combine spinach, watercress, celery, grapes, green onion, water chestnuts, and apple. Toss to mix.

In small pan combine salad dressing, wine, mustard, and brown sugar. Heat until sugar dissolves, stirring constantly. Stir cooked pork into hot dressing to coat well. Remove pork, pour half of dressing over greens in bowl and mix. Place pork strips on top of salad. Sprinkle with sesame seed. Pass remaining dressing (or pour on salad). Serves 6.

Thank Heaven for Home Made Cooks (Wisconsin)

Citrus Tuna Salad

1 (6-ounce) box lemon Jell-O
¼ teaspoon onion salt
¼ teaspoon salt
⅛ teaspoon white pepper
2 cups boiling water
½ cup orange juice
2 cups chopped celery

1 cup sliced stuffed olives
2 cans white water pack tuna, drained
2 cups green grapes, halved
½ cup slivered almonds
⅔ cup cream
3 tablespoons salad dressing

Combine Jell-O, onion salt, salt, and white pepper. Add boiling water and stir well. Cool to room temperature, then add orange juice. Refrigerate. When it starts to congeal, add celery, olives, tuna, grapes, and almonds. Whip cream and fold it into the salad dressing. Fold into salad mixture. Put into 12 individual salad molds and refrigerate overnight.

Dorthy Rickers Cookbook: Mixing & Musing (Minnesota)

Herring Salad

1 (16-ounce) jar herring in wine sauce
2 pared medium potatoes, cooked and finely cubed
1 (16-ounce) can beets, cut up
1 medium apple, pared and finely cubed
1 tablespoon finely chopped onion

2 medium-sized sweet pickles, finely cubed
1 tablespoon sugar
2 tablespoons white vinegar
¼ teaspoon pepper
½ cup whipped cream (optional)

Mix all ingredients together lightly. If using whipped cream, fold in right before serving. Garnish with sieved, hard-cooked egg yolk and finely chopped egg whites.

Favorite Recipes of Pommern Cooks (Wisconsin)

Gatehouse Chicken Pasta Salad

DRESSING:

⅔ cup olive oil
5 tablespoons red wine
   vinegar
¼ cup chopped fresh basil
   leaves (or 2 tablespoons dried)
3 tablespoons grated Parmesan
   cheese

1 tablespoon fresh oregano
   (or ½ tablespoon dried)
1 teaspoon salt
½ teaspoon ground black
   pepper

Prepare dressing first. In a large blender, mix together all ingredients; set aside.

SALAD:

4 cups cooked, cubed chicken
8 ounces rotelle pasta,
   cooked, rinsed, drained
1½ cups broccoli florets,
   cooked 2 minutes, rinsed,
   chilled

1 red bell pepper, sliced thin
1 green bell pepper, sliced thin
½ cup sliced, pitted black olives
1 cup cherry tomatoes, halved
½ cup mayonnaise

In a large bowl, combine chicken, pasta, and vegetables; toss Salad with oil and vinegar Dressing. Refrigerate 8 hours or overnight. At serving time toss Salad with mayonnaise. Serves 6–8.

Cranbrook Reflections (Michigan)

©XRAY10, WWW.GARDENVISIT.COM

The Cranbrook Educational Community in Bloomfield Hills, Michigan, is a National Historic Landmark founded by newspaper mogul George Gough Booth. Cranbrook campus consists of Cranbrook Schools, Cranbrook Academy of Art, Cranbrook Art Museum, Cranbrook Institute of Science, and Cranbrook House and Gardens. Taking its name from Cranbrook, England, the birthplace of the founder's father, Cranbrook House, built in 1908, is the oldest manor home in metropolitan Detroit.

Bacon, Lettuce and Tomato Salad

1 (7-ounce) box Creamettes
  shells, cooked and drained
1½ pounds bacon, diced,
  fried and drained
½ head lettuce, shredded
2 or 3 tomatoes, seeded
  and diced
1 tablespoon finely diced
  onion
Pepper to taste
Mayonnaise or Miracle Whip
  to coat

In large bowl, mix the first 6 ingredients together. Mix with mayonnaise or Miracle Whip to coat. Refrigerate until ready to serve. Yields 12 servings.

Hint: The shells, bacon and tomatoes may be prepared the day before and refrigerated.

St. Mary's Family Cookbook (Wisconsin)

Basil Tortellini Salad

2 (9-ounce) packages cheese
  tortellini
1 red bell pepper, cut into
  strips
3 cups chopped broccoli
  flowerets
4 carrots, sliced
½ cup chopped walnuts,
  toasted

Cook pasta according to package directions. Drain, rinse with cold water, and drain again. Combine pasta, red pepper, broccoli, and carrots.

DRESSING:
2 cups Miracle Whip Salad
  Dressing
4 tablespoons chopped fresh
  basil, or 2 teaspoons dried
½ cup grated Parmesan cheese
4 tablespoons milk
½ teaspoon pepper
1 clove garlic, minced

Mix salad dressing, basil, Parmesan cheese, milk, pepper, and garlic. Toss with pasta mixture. Chill 24 hours. Before serving, mix and top with nuts.

Cooking with Friends (Michigan)

Marco Polo Salad

1 pound spaghetti
¾ cup olive oil, divided
2 cloves garlic, crushed
1 tablespoon basil
1 tablespoon oregano
1 teaspoon salt
1 teaspoon coarsely-ground
 pepper
½ cup half-and-half

1 green pepper, cut julienne
1 red pepper, cut julienne
½ cup chopped parsley
⅔ pound Jarlsberg cheese, cut
 julienne
½ cup toasted and chopped
 pecans
¾ cup or ¼ pound freshly
 grated Parmesan cheese

Cook spaghetti until al dente. Drain and toss with 2 tablespoons of the olive oil. Set aside. Mix together garlic, the rest of the olive oil, basil, oregano, salt and pepper. Pour half-and-half into mixture, whisking at the same time. Toss into pasta. Add green and red pepper, parsley, Jarlsberg cheese, and pecans; toss together. Sprinkle Parmesan cheese on top. Serve at room temperature. Makes 8–10 servings.

Our Favorite Recipes (Minnesota)

Veggie Lovers' Salad

Delicious! Special flavor is given to this salad by the nutmeg.

½ package rainbow rotini
1 cup carrots, chopped
1 cup cucumber, chopped
1 cup frozen peas

1 stem fresh broccoli, chopped
½ cup onions, chopped
½ cup celery, cut
¾ cup ripe olives, sliced

DRESSING:
1 cup salad dressing
½ cup sugar
¼ cup cider vinegar

¼–½ teaspoon nutmeg
Salt and pepper

Cook noodles according to package directions. Rinse with cold water and drain. Add noodles to chopped vegetables. Pour dressing over and refrigerate. Makes a large salad.

Old Westbrook Evangelical Lutheran Church Cookbook (Minnesota)

Grape Salad

4 pounds red and green seedless grapes
1 (8-ounce) package cream cheese, softened
1 (8-ounce) carton sour cream
½ teaspoon vanilla
½ cup granulated sugar
½ cup brown sugar
Crushed nuts

Wash and dry grapes. Put in a large bowl. Beat together cream cheese, sour cream, vanilla, and granulated sugar. Fold into grapes. Sprinkle brown sugar and nuts on top. Refrigerate. Serves 8–10.

Come and Discover Special Appetites (Michigan)

It Ain't The Waldorf But It'll Do Salad

2 cups unpeeled chopped apples (2 medium)
2 teaspoons fresh lemon juice
¼ cup raisins (or snipped pitted dates)
¼ cup seedless grapes
¼ cup chopped celery
¼ cup fat-free whipped dressing
¼ cup plain nonfat yogurt
3 tablespoons chopped walnuts

In a medium bowl toss apples in lemon juice. If grapes are large, cut in half. Stir in raisins (or dates), grapes and celery. In a small bowl combine mayonnaise and yogurt. Fold dressing into apple mixture. Cover and chill for 2–24 hours. To serve arrange on lettuce leaves on four individual plates and sprinkle with walnuts. Makes four ³/₄-cup servings.

Spice of Life Cookbook (Wisconsin)

Fresh Apple Salad

8 cups chopped tart red
   apples, unpeeled
1 (20-ounce) can pineapple
   chunks, drained and juice
   reserved

2 cups seedless green grapes
1–2 teaspoons poppy seed
1 1/2 cups toasted pecans

DRESSING:
Reserved pineapple juice
1/4 cup butter
1/4 cup sugar
1 tablespoon lemon juice

2 tablespoons cornstarch
2 tablespoons water
1 cup mayonnaise

Combine pineapple juice, butter, sugar, and lemon juice in a small saucepan. Heat to boiling. Combine cornstarch and water to make a thick paste. Add to the hot mixture. Cook until thick and smooth. Cool COMPLETELY before adding mayonnaise. Combine salad ingredients (except pecans) and add dressing. Refrigerate until ready to serve. Add pecans right before serving.

Feeding the Flock (Minnesota)

Mandarin Orange and Almond Salad

1/2 head of lettuce, shredded
1 cup celery, chopped
1 tablespoon parsley, minced
2 green onions and tops,
   sliced
1 can mandarin oranges,
   drained

1/2 teaspoon salt
2 tablespoons sugar
2 tablespoons vinegar
1/4 cup salad oil
Few dashes of Tabasco
Pepper
1/4 cup caramelized almonds

Place lettuce, celery, parsley, green onions, and oranges in salad bowl. Shake together salt, sugar, vinegar, salad oil, Tabasco, and pepper. To caramelize almonds, put 2 tablespoons sugar in skillet; cut 1/4 cup almonds crosswise. Add almonds to sugar. Stir constantly over low heat until sugar melts, turns brown and collects on almonds. Remove from heat and break apart. Toss all ingredients together. Makes 6 servings.

A Thyme for All Seasons (Minnesota)

Cherry-Cran Salad

1 (20-ounce) package frozen,
   pitted, tart red cherries,
   thawed
1 (3-ounce) package cherry
   Jell-O
1 (8-ounce) can jellied
   cranberry sauce
1 (3-ounce) package lemon
   Jell-O

1 cup boiling water
1 (3-ounce) package cream
   cheese, softened
⅓ cup mayonnaise
1 (8¼-ounce) can crushed
   pineapple
½ cup whipping cream
1 cup tiny marshmallows
2 tablespoons chopped walnuts

Drain cherries; reserve syrup. If needed, add water to syrup to make 1 cup liquid; bring liquid to boiling. Remove from heat. Add cherry flavored Jell-O; stir to dissolve. With fork, break up cranberry sauce; stir into cherry Jell-O until smooth. Stir in drained cherries. Turn into 9x9x2-inch dish; chill until mixture is almost firm.

Dissolve lemon Jell-O in boiling water. Beat cream cheese with mayonnaise; gradually add lemon Jell-O. Stir in undrained pineapple; chill separately until partially set.

Whip cream; fold into lemon mixture with marshmallows. Spread atop almost-set cherry layer; sprinkle with nuts. Cover; chill until firm. Great with turkey or ham. Makes 12 servings.

Cooking with Friends (Michigan)

Cranberry Wine Salad

2 (3-ounce) packages
   raspberry Jell-O
2 cups boiling water
1 (16-ounce) can whole
   cranberry sauce

1 (8-ounce) can crushed
   pineapple, undrained
¾ cup port wine (or sweet
   vermouth)
¼ cup chopped walnuts

Dissolve Jell-O in boiling water; stir in whole cranberry sauce, crushed pineapple and wine. Chill until partially set. Fold in chopped walnuts. Pour mixture into 6½-cup mold. Chill until firm.

Look What's Cooking at C.A.M.D.E.N (Wisconsin)

Salad-In-A-Sandwich

A loaf of crusty French bread soaks up all the fresh and exciting flavors in this salad-in-a-sandwich. Serve it with lasagna or Italian spaghetti, as picnic fare, or for a summer lunch.

2 teaspoons minced garlic
½ teaspoon cracked black
  pepper
1 (2-ounce) can anchovy
  fillets, well drained
1 tablespoon balsamic
  or red wine vinegar
2 tablespoons olive oil
⅔ cup coarsely chopped
  stuffed green or Greek
  olives, or a combination

1 long loaf French bread
1 small red onion, thinly sliced
1 medium green bell pepper,
  thinly sliced
1 medium red bell pepper,
  thinly sliced
2 medium tomatoes, sliced
Additional vinegar, olive oil,
  and cracked black pepper
2 tablespoons chopped fresh
  basil or pesto (optional)

In a medium bowl, mash garlic and ½ teaspoon cracked black pepper with a fork until a paste is formed. Coarsely chop anchovies and mash them into the garlic paste. Stir in vinegar, olive oil and chopped olives. Slice bread loaf in half horizontally and pull out some of the inside bread from each half. (Bread scraps can be used to make croutons, dried for bread crumbs or donated to the birds.) Place bottom half of loaf on a large sheet of aluminum foil and spread olive mixture evenly over bread surface. Layer onions, peppers, and tomatoes over this. Sprinkle additional vinegar, olive oil and black pepper on the cut surface on the top bread half. Sprinkle with chopped basil or spread with pesto, if available. Place it on the stacked sandwich; press down firmly.

Wrap the loaf securely in the aluminum foil and weight it with whatever heavy articles are available: books, cans, etc. Keep it weighted one hour or longer. Refrigeration isn't necessary unless it won't be served for several hours. To serve, remove foil, insert toothpicks along the length of the loaf, and slice. The sandwich tastes best at room temperature. Makes 3–4 lunch-size servings, twice that as side dish.

Fresh Market Wisconsin (Wisconsin)

Blue Cheese Dressing

1 cup mayonnaise
4 ounces crumbled Blue
  cheese
3 tablespoons milk
2 tablespoons lemon juice

2 teaspoons sugar
1 tablespoon chopped onion
¼ teaspoon Worcestershire
¼ teaspoon dry mustard
¼ teaspoon salt

Combine all ingredients.

Mt. Carmel's "Cooking with the Oldies" (Wisconsin)

Pepper-Onion Mayonnaise

2 tablespoons finely chopped
  parsley
3 tablespoons finely chopped
  green pepper
1 tablespoon finely chopped
  red pepper
1 tablespoon finely chopped
  onion

2 tablespoons finely chopped
  pimento
1 cup mayonnaise
⅛ teaspoon paprika
2 teaspoons lemon juice
¼ teaspoon salt
⅛ teaspoon pepper

Combine parsley, green pepper, red pepper, onion, and pimento. Add mayonnaise, paprika, lemon juice, salt and pepper. Mix well. Add to your favorite green salad. Toss. Extra dressing will keep well in refrigerator for several days. Makes 1½ cups.

Apples, Brie & Chocolate (Wisconsin)

Saltless Seasoning

Use to season meats, vegetables, and salad dressings. Pop a bowl of popcorn, and sprinkle on just a bit while still hot. It's great to season Chex mix-type mixtures.

½ teaspoon garlic powder
¼ teaspoon ground thyme
½ teaspoon onion powder
½ teaspoon paprika

½ teaspoon ground celery seed
½ teaspoon pepper
½ teaspoon dry mustard

Mix together and store in closed container in a dry place.

Michigan Magazine Family and Friends Cookbook II (Michigan)

Vegetables

© NATIONAL PARK SERVICE

U.S. FISH AND WILDLIFE SERVICE

DWARF LAKE IRIS

Sleeping Bear Dunes National Lakeshore covers a 35-mile area of Lake Michigan's eastern coastline, as well as Michigan's North and South Manitou Islands. The dunes rise an impressive 460 feet above Lake Michigan. Living among the dunes is the dwarf lake iris— Michigan's official wildflower.

Kraut for Bratwurst & Kraut

Large head of cabbage,
  shredded
Large red onion, sliced
2 tablespoons olive oil
2 refrigerator packages (not
  canned) sauerkraut, drained,
  squeezed
3 tablespoons sugar, brown
  or white

3 tablespoons vinegar, any kind
2 tablespoons dried dill weed
  (4–5 tablespoons, if using
  fresh)
2 tablespoons celery seeds
Salt and pepper to taste
  (optional)

In heavy saucepan, sauté cabbage and onion in olive oil until soft. Add drained sauerkraut, sugar, and vinegar. Mix and let cook about 5 minutes on high. Reduce heat; add dill weed, celery seeds, salt and pepper, if desired, and let simmer, covered, for about an hour. This concoction can cook for up to 2 hours. I usually grill brats over charcoal and, when they're done, I put them in a pan over cooked kraut to keep warm. Serve in buns. Serves 6–8.

Historically Delicious (Michigan)

Brewed Sauerkraut

3 strips bacon, diced
1 cup chopped onion
2 pounds sauerkraut, rinsed
  and drained
1 (12-ounce) can beer

2 tablespoons brown sugar,
  packed
½ teaspoon caraway seeds
Pepper to taste
1 cup coarsely shredded carrot

Fry bacon in 2-quart saucepan until crisp. Remove, drain, and set aside. Add onions to pan and sauté; stir in sauerkraut, beer, sugar, caraway seeds, and pepper. Bring to a boil, cover, and simmer for one hour. Add carrots and simmer uncovered for an additional 20 minutes, until carrots are tender. Spoon into serving bowl and garnish with bacon pieces. Serves 6.

Drink Your Beer & Eat It Too (Wisconsin)

Purple Passion Cabbage

½ cup chopped onion
2 tablespoons butter or
  margarine
2 pounds red cabbage,
  shredded

⅓ cup sugar
1 tablespoon lemon juice
⅓ cup cider vinegar
2 teaspoons salt
Pepper

Sauté onion in butter until soft. Add remaining ingredients and cook for 20–30 minutes or until cabbage is tender. Best if made the day before serving and reheated. Makes 6–8 servings.

Fat 3 grams per serving/Vit C/Fiber/Cruciferous.

Minnesota Heritage Cookbook II (Minnesota)

Sweet-Sour Red Cabbage

½ medium head red
  cabbage, shredded
¼ cup butter
½ medium onion, diced
1 tablespoon soy sauce

¼ cup vinegar
¼ cup sugar
1 raw sliced apple
¼ cup water
1 tablespoon flour

Place all ingredients, except flour, in a covered kettle and let simmer for at least an hour. Then stir and sift in the flour to thicken.

Family Fare (Wisconsin)

Emigrants from Glarus, Switzerland, settled in the Little Sugar River Valley in the heart of Green County, Wisconsin, in 1845. New Glarus is now truly "Little Switzerland" with the architecture in the Swiss Emmenthal style. Each year there is a Heidi Festival that features a play, alphorn playing, yodeling, folk dancing, and flag throwing.

Scandinavian Salmon-Cheese-Potato

4 large potatoes
1 (7-ounce) can salmon,
　drained
¼ cup chopped green onion
1 egg
1 teaspoon dried dill weed

Little salt and pepper
6 tablespoons milk
2 cups Jarlsberg cheese,
　shredded (any favorite
　cheese will do)
1 tablespoon melted butter

Bake potatoes. Slice off top and carefully scoop out pulp. In bowl, mix potato, salmon, onion, eggs, dill, salt and pepper and milk. Stir in ³/₄ of cheese. Spoon mixture back into shells. Sprinkle with rest of cheese and brush with melted butter. Bake at 400° for 20 minutes.

Celebration of Grace (Wisconsin)

Refrigerator Mashed Potatoes

We used this at Potato Day several times, using 250 pounds red and white mashing, potatoes—served about 350 people!

5 pounds red potatoes
2 (3-ounce) packages cream
　cheese
1 cup sour cream

1 teaspoon salt
¼ teaspoon pepper
2 tablespoons butter

Peel and cook potatoes. Drain and mash. Add cream cheese, sour cream, salt, pepper, and butter. Beat all together at low-speed with electric mixer. Place in covered container and store in fridge.

　　To serve, place desired amount in baking dish; dot with butter. Cover and heat in microwave or oven until hot. Can make patties if desired. Roll in crushed bread crumbs and fry on both sides.

The Ultimate Potato Cookbook (Minnesota)

Spunky Twice-Baked Potatoes

7 large baking potatoes
½–¾ cup milk
1 (3-ounce) package cream cheese, softened
6 tablespoons butter
⅛ teaspoon garlic powder
⅛–¼ teaspoon white pepper
Salt
6 ounces Cheddar cheese, shredded

Scrub, dry, pierce and bake potatoes at 425° for one hour. About 10 minutes before potatoes are done, blend milk, cream cheese, butter, garlic powder, and pepper until smooth. Add more milk or butter if necessary to get the right consistency. Heat in a saucepan; do not boil. When potatoes are done, remove and immediately slice lengthwise, leaving shell intact. Spoon out cooked potato into large bowl; salt to taste. With electric mixer, beat potatoes slightly, and gradually add cream cheese mixture. Spoon mixture into shells of 6 potatoes; top with cheese. Heat in oven for about 20 minutes or microwave on high power until cheese is melted. Makes 6 servings.

From Minnesota: More Than a Cookbook (Minnesota)

Michigan Spuds Bake

Excellent for family or guests.

10–12 medium potatoes
½ cup margarine, cut up
½ cup chopped onions
2 cups shredded Cheddar cheese
2 cups sour cream
1 teaspoon salt
¼ teaspoon pepper

Boil potatoes till done, but still firm. Drain well; refrigerate. Peel and grate potatoes coarsely. Gently mix with all remaining ingredients. Bake in greased 9x13-inch casserole dish at 350° for 30–40 minutes or till bubbly. Cool for 5 minutes before cutting into squares for serving. Serves 12.

Some Enchanted Eating (Michigan)

Zesty Pizza Potatoes

4 large potatoes
8 ounces shredded mozzarella,
  Monterey Jack or Cheddar
  cheese (3½ cups)
4 green onions, sliced
½ teaspoon oregano
½ teaspoon basil
2 medium tomatoes, sliced or
  one pint stewed tomatoes
½ pound cooked Italian
  sausage or ground beef
Parmesan cheese

Bake potatoes at 400° until fork tender. In small bowl toss cheese, onions, oregano, and basil. Slice cooked potatoes lengthwise. Place cut sides up in baking dish. Sprinkle with half the cheese mixture. Top with tomatoes and meat, then remaining cheese mixture. Bake at 400° for 20 minutes or until golden brown and heated through. Sprinkle with Parmesan cheese if desired.

Wisconsin's Best (Wisconsin)

Herb-Roasted Potatoes

5 tablespoons Grey Poupon
  mustard
2 tablespoons olive oil
1 clove garlic, chopped
½ teaspoon Italian seasoning
6 medium red-skinned potatoes
  (about 2 pounds), cut into
  chunks

Mix all ingredients except potatoes in small bowl. In plastic bag, toss potatoes with mixture. Place in a greased 9x13-inch baking pan. Bake at 425° for 35–40 minutes or until potatoes are fork-tender, stirring occasionally.

McManus Family Recipes Volume 3 (Michigan)

Potato Wedges

Use your own favorite seasoning in this recipe. Instead of Italian seasoning, you may want to try substituting grated Parmesan cheese, garlic salt, basil, paprika, or something to compliment the main course for the meal.

4 medium Michigan potatoes
¼ cup butter
1 teaspoon Italian (or other)
  seasoning

Salt and pepper to taste
Parsley for garnish (optional)

Preheat oven to 450°. Cut each potato into 4 lengthwise wedges. Place on ungreased cookie sheet with skin side down. Melt butter; stir in seasoning. Brush potatoes with seasoned butter. Season with salt and pepper, as desired. Bake for 30–35 minutes, or till potatoes are tender. Arrange on serving platter. Garnish with parsley, if desired.

Good Food from Michigan (Michigan)

Colcannon

Who would believe that potatoes and cabbage combined with a few other well-chosen ingredients could seem so heavenly? This is Irish country food at its very simple best, from Executive Chef Tim Gurtner, 52 Stafford, Plymouth.

4 large potatoes, peeled
  and diced, about 4 cups
1 cup heavy whipping cream
½ teaspoon chopped garlic
1 teaspoon dried parsley
  flakes

1 teaspoon salt
½ teaspoon white pepper
1 cup chopped green cabbage
1 leek, white part only, diced

In an ovenproof medium saucepan over medium heat, place potatoes, cream, garlic, parsley, salt and pepper. Cook, stirring occasionally until mixture comes to a boil, about 5 minutes. Cover and bake in preheated 400° for 20 minutes.

While mixture bakes, blanch cabbage and leeks in boiling, salted water in a small saucepan just until tender, about one minute. Drain well, discarding liquid. Fold cabbage and leeks into potato mixture. Makes 6–8 servings.

Encore Wisconsin (Wisconsin)

Baked Sweet Potatoes and Apples

3 large apples
5–6 tablespoons butter,
   divided
3 large sweet potatoes, boiled,
   skinned

1 teaspoon salt
½ cup maple syrup
½–1 cup crushed cornflakes
   (optional)

Pare, core, and slice apples; fry in 3 tablespoons butter until light brown. Slice potatoes. Arrange apples and potatoes in layers in a buttered baking dish. Sprinkle with salt. Pour syrup over dish; sprinkle with cornflakes, if desired. Dot with remaining butter. Bake 350° about 35 minutes.

Great Lakes Cookery (Michigan)

Sweet Potato Mash

4 sweet potatoes, peeled,
   cubed large
2 tart apples, cored, diced
   large
½ yellow onion, diced large

½ cup maple syrup
Salt and pepper to taste
4 tablespoons butter, cut in
   small pieces

Preheat oven to 350°. Combine all ingredients, except butter, in greased baking dish. Dot top with butter. Cover and bake 30 minutes. Stir thoroughly. Cover again and bake until everything is soft, about 20 minutes. Turn into mixing bowl and mash, leaving some lumps. Taste and adjust seasoning.

McManus Family Recipes Volume 3 (Michigan)

Twice-Baked Yams

2 pounds yams (about
   6 medium)
Vegetable oil
¼ cup sour cream
¼ cup milk
2 tablespoons packed brown
   sugar

2 tablespoons butter or
   margarine
⅛ teaspoon salt
2 tablespoons pecans, coarsely
   chopped

Rub yams with oil; prick with fork to allow steam to escape. Bake at 375° until tender, 35–45 minutes. Cut lengthwise; scoop out inside, leaving a thin shell. Mash yams until no lumps remain. Beat in sour cream and milk, then brown sugar, margarine, and salt until light and fluffy. Stir in pecans. Increase oven to 400°. Place shells in ungreased baking dish. Fill shells with mixture. Top each with pecan half. Bake, uncovered, until filling is golden, about 20 minutes.

Sunflowers & Samovars (Wisconsin)

Tangy Carrot Dish

1½ pounds carrots, peeled
¼ cup water reserved from
   cooking carrots
1 teaspoon onion and juice,
   grated

½ teaspoon yellow mustard
½ cup mayonnaise
¼ cup cheese, grated
½ teaspoon salt
¼ teaspoon pepper

Slice carrots ½-inch thick. Cook in a small amount of water until crisp-done; drain. Reserve ¼-cup water for sauce. Combine water, onion and juice, mustard, mayonnaise, cheese, salt and pepper. Add carrots and spoon into buttered 2-quart casserole.

TOPPING:
1 cup fresh bread crumbs
¼ cup butter, melted

½ teaspoon paprika

Combine topping and sprinkle over carrot mixture. Bake at 350° for 20 minutes. Yields 8 servings.

St. John Evangelical Lutheran Church (Wisconsin)

Broccoli Casserole

¼ cup margarine
¼ cup chopped onion
¼ cup chopped celery
½ (10¾-ounce) can cream
  of mushroom soup

⅔ cup uncooked rice
½ (8-ounce) jar Cheez Whiz
1 (10-ounce) package frozen
  chopped broccoli, thawed,
  drained, partially cooked

Preheat oven to 350°. In medium skillet, melt margarine. Add onions and celery and sauté until transparent. Remove from heat and set aside. In medium bowl mix soup, rice, and Cheez Whiz. Add onions and celery and gently add broccoli. Pour into well-greased 2-quart casserole and bake 35–40 minutes. Easy to double this recipe.

A Taste of Home (Wisconsin)

WWW.WIKIPEDIA.ORG

Paul Bunyan is a character of legend and lore, who is usually believed to be a giant as well as a lumberjack of unusual skill. A myth about the formation of Great Lakes was created centered around his sidekick, Babe the Blue Ox: Paul Bunyan needed to create watering holes large enough for Babe to drink from.

Onions Onions Onions

3 tablespoons butter
2 large sweet (Vidalia) onions,
  thinly sliced
2 red onions, thinly sliced
2 Bermuda or Spanish onions,
  thinly sliced
2 leeks, washed, thinly sliced

1½ cups grated Havarti cheese
1 (6-ounce) package herbed
  Boursin or Allouette cheese,
  crumbled
1½ cups grated Gruyère cheese
¾ cup white wine

Preheat oven to 350°. Butter a large baking dish. Layer onions in dish–1/3 of each type. Sprinkle with salt and pepper. Top with Havarti. Make another layer and top with herbed cheese. Make another layer and top with Gruyère. Dot top with butter; pour wine over all. Bake 1 hour. Cover with foil if getting too dark. Serves 6–8.

Tasteful Art (Michigan)

Vegetables in Wisconsin Beer Batter

1⅓ cups flour
2 tablespoons Parmesan
  cheese
1 tablespoon parsley
1 teaspoon salt
Dash of garlic
1 (12-ounce) can Wisconsin
  beer, at room temperature
  and flat

2 eggs, separated
Green peppers, cauliflower,
  onion, artichoke hearts,
  zucchini or broccoli,
  cut into bite-sized pieces
Oil for deep frying

In a large bowl, combine flour, cheese, parsley, salt, and garlic. Stir in beer and egg yolks. Beat egg whites until stiff and fold into beer mixture. Dip vegetable pieces into batter. Heat oil to 375° and fry a few pieces of batter-dipped vegetables at a time in oil until golden. Drain on paper toweling. Serve immediately.

License to Cook Wisconsin Style (Wisconsin)

Zucchini Casserole

3 tablespoons butter
3 tablespoons all-purpose flour
1 (14½-ounce) can stewed
   Italian tomatoes
1 small onion, chopped
1 small green bell pepper,
   chopped

1 tablespoon brown sugar
1 teaspoon salt
3 zucchini, peeled, sliced
Grated cheese
Bread crumbs

Melt butter, add flour and blend. Add tomatoes, onion, green pepper, brown sugar, and salt. Pour over zucchini in a 2-quart casserole dish or larger depending on size of zucchini. Cover with grated cheese and bread crumbs. Bake at 350° for 1 hour.

Blissfield Preschool Cookbook (Michigan)

Oven-Fried Zucchini Spears

3 tablespoons seasoned
   dried bread crumbs
1 tablespoon grated Parmesan
   cheese
⅛ teaspoon garlic powder
⅛ teaspoon paprika

⅛ teaspoon freshly ground
   black pepper
2 medium zucchini
2 teaspoons olive oil
2 teaspoons water

Preheat oven to 475°. On a shallow plate, combine all ingredients, except zucchini, oil, and water; set aside. Slice off ends of zucchini. Cut each zucchini lengthwise into quarters; cut each quarter in half.

In large plastic bag, combine oil, zucchini, and water; close bag and shake well to moisten zucchini. Dredge zucchini in bread crumb mixture. Arrange zucchini in single layer on nonstick baking sheet. Bake until golden, 10–12 minutes. Makes 2 servings.

The Fruit of Her Hands (Michigan)

Zucchini Surprise

½ cup chopped onion
1 cup Bisquick baking mix
½ cup Parmesan cheese
2 tablespoons parsley flakes
½ teaspoon salt
½ teaspoon oregano

½ teaspoon seasoned salt
½ cup vegetable oil
4 eggs, slightly beaten
Dash of pepper and garlic
3 cups thinly sliced, unpeeled
 zucchini (2 medium-sized)

Mix together all ingredients except zucchini. Stir in zucchini. Place in greased 9x13-inch baking dish. Bake uncovered at 350° for 20–25 minutes or until golden brown. Makes 8–10 servings.

50 Years of Regal Recipes (Wisconsin)

Vegetable Tostadas

2 cups thinly sliced zucchini
 (1 medium)
4 ounces fresh mushrooms,
 sliced
2 tablespoons chopped
 green pepper
1 cup thinly sliced onion
 (1 medium large)
¼ cup chopped celery

Nonstick pan spray
4 flour tortillas
½ cup low-fat, low-sodium
 shredded Cheddar cheese
4 tablespoons fat-free sour cream
1 tomato, chopped
2 teaspoons hot pepper sauce
 or to taste

Combine vegetables, except tomatoes, in saucepan and simmer 10–12 minutes or microwave on HIGH for 6–8 minutes.

Spray small sauté pan with nonstick spray. Set on medium-high heat. Brown tortillas quickly on both sides and place on cookie sheet. Spoon vegetable mixture on each tortilla and top with cheese. Bake tortillas in 350° oven until cheese melts, about 3–5 minutes. To serve, top with sour cream, chopped tomatoes, and a few dashes of hot pepper sauce. Makes 4 servings.

Hint: You may substitute 4 ounces canned no-salt mushrooms, undrained, for fresh mushrooms.

Spice of Life Cookbook (Wisconsin)

Eggplant Hater's Ratatouille

I concocted this when inundated with lots of fresh garden produce. Since I despise eggplant, this is my own version of ratatouille. It's filthy cheap to make in summer when vegetables are plentiful. It's so good for you, you'd hardly believe it tastes so delicious.

5 tablespoons butter
1 medium zucchini, peeled
  and cut into ½-inch strips
1 medium green pepper,
  diced
1 medium onion, cut into
  chunks
2–3 large fresh tomatoes,
  cut in chunks

8 ounces fresh mushrooms,
  sliced
1 (8-ounce) can tomato paste
½ teaspoon garlic powder
1 teaspoon sugar
Pepper to taste
½–¾ pound grated
  mozzarella cheese

Melt butter in medium saucepan. Add zucchini, green pepper, onion, tomatoes, and mushrooms. Cover and sauté until soft. Drain off excess liquid. Add ¾ can of tomato paste, garlic powder, sugar, and pepper. (If you like a little kick to it, add crushed hot peppers or Tabasco, to taste). Heat through and serve, covered with grated cheese.

Note: This can be served in one large or several small casseroles as a side dish to meat or fish. Can also be served over spaghetti or cooked spaghetti squash. Ground beef may be added to make a main dish.

Foxy Ladies (Wisconsin)

Garden Ratatouille

Ratatouille is a vegetable stew topped with cheese and baked. Great way to use a lot of veggies from the garden. Freezes well.

3 tablespoons extra virgin olive oil
1 onion, diced
3 cloves garlic, minced
1 bell pepper, diced
Crushed red pepper flakes to taste
1 large eggplant, peeled, 1-inch cubes*
2 zucchini, sliced half-moon
2 summer squash, sliced
Kosher salt and black pepper to taste
1 tablespoon dried Italian seasoning
¼ pound fresh green beans, cleaned, cut in half
1 quart whole Roma tomatoes, crushed, with juice
1 tablespoon chopped fresh flat leaf parsley
½ pound grated mozzarella
¼ pound grated Parmesan

Place large Dutch oven on stovetop on medium heat. Pour in olive oil and warm. Sauté onion, garlic, bell pepper, and red pepper flakes until wilted. Add eggplant, zucchini, and squash, and sauté an additional 10 minutes. Add salt, pepper, Italian seasoning, green beans, and crushed tomatoes. Cook, uncovered, over low heat an additional 45 minutes, stirring occasionally. Stir in parsley and spoon into large oven-proof casserole dish. Top with grated cheeses and brown under broiler until cheese is melted and beginning to brown. Serves 8–10.

*When you peel eggplant, it discolors fairly quickly, so wait until the last minute.

Tasteful Garden Treasures (Michigan)

Eggplant Italienne

1 pound hamburger
1 cup chopped onion
1 (21-ounce) jar Ragu
  Italian Sauce
1 large eggplant
Mild olive oil

1–2 cups small-curd cottage
  cheese
½ pound mozzarella cheese,
  cubed
Parmesan cheese

Brown meat and onion slightly. Add Ragu Sauce and simmer 10 minutes. Peel and slice eggplant. Put on an oiled cookie sheet and pour oil over so all pieces are well oiled. Brown under broiler, turning each piece. Place in 9x13-inch pan. Add cottage cheese, mozzarella cheese, and sauce in layers with sauce on top. Bake 30–40 minutes, until bubbly. Serve with Parmesan cheese.

Cherry Berries on a Cloud and More (Wisconsin)

Summer Squash Casserole

6 cups sliced yellow or green
  summer squash
¼ cup chopped onion
1 cup condensed cream of
  chicken soup
1 cup sour cream

1 cup shredded carrot
1 (8-ounce) package herb
  seasoned stuffing mix
½ cup melted butter or
  margarine

Cook squash and onion in boiling salted water for 5 minutes; drain. Combine cream soup and sour cream. Fold in squash and onion. Stir in carrots. Combine stuffing mix and butter. Spread ½ of stuffing mix in bottom of 12x7½x2-inch baking dish. Spoon vegetable mix atop. Sprinkle remaining stuffing over veggies. Bake at 350° for 25–30 minutes. Yields 6 servings.

Feeding the Flock (Minnesota)

Indian Squash

1 large winter squash
½ teaspoons salt
2 teaspoons sugar
3 tablespoons soft butter

1½ teaspoons water
3 tablespoons light or dark
   molasses

Cook halved and seeded squash in salt water about 20 minutes. Place halves in baking dish. Make mixture of other ingredients, fill squash and bake in a 350° oven until tender. Makes 2 servings.

Minnesota Heritage Cookbook I (Minnesota)

Fried Green Tomatoes in Cream

We try never to let a tomato get away from us. When the days shorten, so that our bounty of tomatoes can no longer catch enough sun to turn them a rich red, we bring them in to store in our fruit cellar or paper bags. The window sill is not the answer. They'll look awful pretty there but they'll taste awful poorly. In the total dark, they will ripen nicely after 2–3 weeks. If we can't wait that long, we make good things like India Relish or Green Tomato Apple Pie for dinner, Fried Tomatoes in Cream . . . a favorite taste treat.

4 green tomatoes, unpeeled
All-purpose flour
Salt and freshly ground pepper

2–3 tablespoons butter
2 teaspoons brown sugar
½ cup heavy cream

Slice tomatoes ½-inch thick. Dredge in flour mixed with salt and freshly ground pepper to taste. In a large, heavy skillet, melt butter over medium heat. When it begins to sizzle, add tomato slices, sprinkling each with a pinch or so of brown sugar. When slices have browned and are just beginning to soften, turn off heat and immediately pour in cream. Gently turn tomatoes in the thickening cream; serve immediately. Serves 4.

Hollyhocks & Radishes (Michigan)

Country Tomato Pie

This is very good served with sausages for a brunch or as a simple supper dish with a pretty green salad.

2–3 large tomatoes
1 (9-inch) pie shell, baked
3 green onions, thinly sliced
1 tablespoon chopped fresh
   basil, or 1 teaspoon dried

Salt and freshly ground pepper
   to taste
¾–1 cup mayonnaise
1 cup grated sharp Cheddar
   cheese

Preheat oven to 350°. Peel tomatoes by dipping in boiling water for 10 seconds or so, to split skins. Thickly slice tomatoes, then layer in baked and cooled pie shell, sprinkling each layer with green onions, basil and salt and pepper to taste. Combine mayonnaise and cheese, and spread over tomatoes. Bake 30 minutes. Serves 4–6.

Hollyhocks & Radishes (Michigan)

Tomato Cheese Pie

1 (7.5-ounce) tube
   buttermilk biscuits
2–3 large tomatoes, sliced
Sweet basil
Salt and pepper
1 small green pepper, sliced

1 large onion, sliced
1 cup mushrooms, sliced
¼ cup olive oil
1½ cups mayonnaise
1 cup grated Monterey Jack or
   mozzarella cheese

Line a deep 10-inch pie dish with biscuits, pressing edges together to form a crust. Place half of tomatoes on biscuits. Season with salt, pepper, and basil. Sauté green pepper, onion, and mushrooms in oil. Drain. Place on top of tomatoes. Add remaining tomatoes. Season again. Combine mayonnaise and cheese and spread over top. Bake at 350° for 40–45 minutes.

All in Good Taste I (Wisconsin)

Creamed Spinach

Minnesota's vast iron ranges supply 70% of the iron mined in the United States. The known deposits of the state's richest ore have been exhausted. But the Minnesota earth still contains approximately 15 billion tons of valuable low-grade ore. Here is a recipe rich in iron.

2 packages frozen chopped
  spinach
1 medium onion, chopped
8 tablespoons butter, divided
6 tablespoons cream

6–8 tablespoons Parmesan
  cheese
Salt and pepper
½ cup seasoned bread crumbs

Cook spinach according to package directions and drain well. Sauté onion in 6 tablespoons butter until tender. Mix onion and butter with spinach, cream and cheese. Salt and pepper to taste. Put in 1-quart casserole. Mix bread crumbs with 2 tablespoons melted butter. Sprinkle over spinach mixture. Bake at 350° for 30 minutes. Serves 4–6.

Winning Recipes from Minnesota with Love (Minnesota)

Greek Spinach

A great combination of flavors!

2 pounds fresh spinach
1 tablespoon olive oil
½ cup pine nuts (or walnuts)
3 tablespoons chopped basil
2 tablespoons Italian parsley

1 clove garlic, minced
1 small onion, finely chopped
2 tablespoons cider vinegar
Dash of salt

Wash and tear the spinach, removing heavy stems. Heat a large skillet. Add the oil and nuts and saute until golden. Add remaining ingredients. Stir, cover, and cook 2 minutes, until the spinach is barely tender.

Herbs in a Minnesota Kitchen (Minnesota)

CHISHOLM CHAMBER
OF COMMERCE

Northeastern Minnesota's Iron Range includes four major iron ore deposits: Mesabi Range (one of the largest bodies of iron ore in the world), Vermilion Range, Gunflint Range, and Cuyuna Range. Chisholm's 81-foot Iron Man Statue was built as a tribute to the iron ore miners of the region. It is the third largest structural memorial in the United States, dwarfed only by the Statue of Liberty and the St. Louis Gateway Arch.

Spinach Pie

This pie freezes well. It can be made ahead and reheated in the oven or in a microwave oven.

2 (10-ounce) packages frozen, chopped spinach
2 tablespoons butter
½ cup chopped onion
1 clove garlic, chopped fine
8 ounces (2 cups) grated mozzarella cheese
3 tablespoons butter

3 tablespoons flour
1½ cups milk
1¼ teaspoons salt
¼ teaspoon pepper
Dash of nutmeg
Dash of dill weed
6 eggs, well beaten
1 (10-inch) or 2 (8-inch) pie crusts

TOPPING:
Grated Cheddar cheese (about ⅓ cup)

Slices of onion and tomato

Cook spinach as directed on package and press out water. Melt 2 tablespoons butter and sauté onion and garlic. Stir this into the drained spinach. Mix in the mozzarella cheese.

Melt 3 tablespoons butter and stir in 3 tablespoons flour. Add milk and cook, stirring constantly until thick. Add the salt and pepper, nutmeg, and dill weed. Stir this into the spinach mixture. Then fold in the beaten eggs. Pour into unbaked pie shells. Bake at 350° for 45–60 minutes (depending on the size of pie shells). During the last 10 minutes of baking, sprinkle grated cheese on top and place slices of onion and tomato decoratively on top of pie.

From Timm's Hill Bed and Breakfast.
Have Breakfast with Us II (Wisconsin)

Layered Spinach Supreme

1 cup Bisquick Baking Mix
¼ cup milk
2 eggs
¼ cup finely chopped onion
1 (10-ounce) package frozen
   chopped spinach, thawed,
   drained, (or 10 ounces
   fresh chopped spinach,
   wilted with hot water)

½ cup grated Parmesan cheese
4 ounces Monterey Jack cheese,
   cut into ½-inch cubes
1 (12-ounce) carton creamed
   cottage cheese
½ teaspoon salt
2 cloves garlic, crushed
2 eggs

Heat oven to 375°. Grease baking dish (12x7½x2-inch). Mix baking mix, milk, 2 eggs, onion; beat vigorously for 20 strokes; spread into dish. Mix remaining ingredients; spoon evenly over batter in dish. Bake until set (about 30 minutes); let stand 5 minutes before cutting.

Marketplace Recipes Volume II (Wisconsin)

Minnesota Logginberries

Better known as baked beans.

2 cups dried navy beans
Pinch of baking soda
½ pound diced bacon or
   salt pork
4 tablespoons brown sugar
3 tablespoons molasses

½ teaspoon dry mustard
1 medium onion, chopped
2 tablespoons ketchup
½ teaspoon salt
Water

Soak beans overnight in water to cover. Then, add pinch of soda to beans and boil for 10 minutes. Drain and add the rest of the ingredients with enough water to cover. Pressure-cook at 15 pounds for 30 minutes, or bake, covered, at 350° for 6–8 hours or until tender. Serves 6–8.

Winning Recipes from Minnesota with Love (Minnesota)

Cowboy Beans

4 bacon strips, chopped
1 large onion, chopped
3 tablespoons ketchup
1 teaspoon garlic salt
1 teaspoon chili powder
½ teaspoon ground cumin
¼ teaspoon dried red
   pepper flakes, optional

1 bay leaf
1 (16-ounce) can whole tomatoes
   with liquid (puréed in blender)
3 (15-ounce) cans pinto beans,
   drained
2 tablespoons brown sugar
1 tablespoon yellow mustard

Lightly brown bacon in a heavy 3-quart saucepan or Dutch oven. Add onion and cook until transparent. Stir in remaining ingredients. Cook over medium-low heat for one hour, covered, stirring often so they do not stick to pan or burn. Add water if too thick.

Fifth Avenue Food Fare (Wisconsin)

Beer Baked Beans

1 (32-ounce) can baked
   beans
1 cup beer
½ cup brewed coffee
½ cup chopped tomato
¾ cup chopped onion

3 frankfurters, cut in 1-inch
   diagonal pieces
1 tablespoon horseradish
½ cup ketchup
½ cup molasses

Place all ingredients in oven-proof dish and mix well. Bake at 325° until hot, approximately one hour, stirring occasionally. If beans appear to be drying out, add small amount of additional beer. Serves 6–8.

Drink Your Beer & Eat It Too (Wisconsin)

Since the mid-1800s, Milwaukee has been synonymous with beer and breweries. In fact, Milwaukee was touted as the "beer capital of the world." And, indeed, the city has been home to some of America's largest brewers—Pabst, Schlitz, Miller, and Blatz. Even Milwaukee's baseball team, the aptly named Brewers, play in the corporate-sponsored Miller Park. Pabst even brewed a beer named after the town, Old Milwaukee beer. Today, Miller is the only company still brewing in the city.

Gumbo Beans

Very nice for picnics.

1 (15-ounce) can green beans, drained

1 (15-ounce) can wax beans, drained

1 (15-ounce) can navy beans, drained

1 (15-ounce) can lima beans, drained

1 (16-ounce) can pork and beans, use juice

1 (15-ounce) can kidney beans, use juice

1 (6-ounce) can tomato paste

1 (10¾-ounce) can tomato soup

1 pound pork sausage, fried with 1 cup chopped onion

1 tablespoon BBQ sauce

1 tablespoon chili powder

Mix all ingredients and pour into an oven-proof baking dish. Bake at 350° for 1 hour. May be cooked in crockpot also.

Celebrating 300 Years of Detroit Cooking (Michigan)

Bean Casserole

Great for picnics or pot lucks.

1 pound spicy ground sausage

1 medium onion, chopped

1 medium green bell pepper, chopped

½ stick butter

1 cup ketchup

1 cup brown sugar

1 (14½-ounce) can stewed tomatoes

1 (15-ounce) can pork & beans

1 (15-ounce) can kidney beans, drained

1 (15-ounce) can butter beans, drained

1 (15-ounce) can lima beans, drained

Brown sausage; set aside. Brown onion and green pepper with butter. Combine drained sausage, onion mixture, and all remaining ingredients. Place in oven-proof dish and bake at 350° for 1 hour or more. Serves 8–10.

Seasoned Cooks II (Michigan)

Crisp Pickle Slices

4 quarts of sliced cucumbers
6 medium onions, sliced
3 cloves of garlic
1 green pepper, sliced
1 sweet red pepper, sliced
⅓ cup salt

3 cups white vinegar
5 cups sugar
1½ teaspoons turmeric
1½ teaspoons celery seed
2 tablespoons mustard seed

Slice cucumbers thin; add sliced onions, garlic, and peppers, cut in narrow strips. Add salt, cover with ice, let stand 3 hours. Drain. Combine remaining ingredients. Pour over cucumber mixture. Heat to boiling. Seal in hot sterilized jars.

Four Seasons at Hawks Inn (Wisconsin)

Michigan Farm Apple Relish

This is a recipe Chef Robert Nelson learned from his mother more than 50 years ago. His Farm Relish will liven up grilled meats, or provide a tangy topping for an omelette.

2 quarts chopped tomato
2 cups sliced Michigan Empire
   apples
1 cup diced celery
1 cup chopped onions
2 chopped green bell peppers
2 chopped red bell peppers

1½ cups Michigan apple cider
   vinegar
1 whole cinnamon stick
2 tablespoons yellow mustard
   seeds
½ tablespoon whole cloves
2¾ cups Michigan beet sugar

Combine all ingredients in large kettle. Simmer slowly 1 hour, ot till mixture is thick and clear. Fish out cinnamon stick. Cool and store. Serves 64.

Michigan Gourmet Cookbook (Michigan)

Pasta, Rice, Etc.

The Mall of America in Bloomington, Minnesota, is the largest mall in America in total enclosed floor space. It is the most visited shopping mall in the world with more than 40 million visitors annually (or roughly eight times the population of the state of Minnesota). The mall employs over 12,000 workers, and even has an indoor amusement park.

Bow Tie Pasta & Chicken

1 (8-ounce) package bow-tie
  pasta
¾ cup sun-dried tomatoes
Small amount of water
2 cloves garlic, finely chopped
2 tablespoons olive oil
½ pound chicken breast,
  julienned into ½-inch strips
1½ cups broccoli florets,
  very small

1 teaspoon basil
Pinch of red pepper flakes,
  crushed
Salt and ground pepper to taste
¼ cup white wine
¾ cup chicken broth
1 tablespoon grated Parmesan
  cheese

Cook and drain pasta. Simmer tomatoes in water till softened; drain and slice. Saute* garlic in olive oil in large skillet, stirring constantly. Add chicken and broccoli; saute* till tender. Add sun-dried tomatoes, basil, seasonings, wine, and broth. Cook 3–5 minutes, stirring occasionally. Toss in bow-tie pasta. Add Parmesan cheese. Serves 4.

Bringing Grand Tastes to Grand Traverse (Michigan)

Herb Garden Pasta

What a treat—pasta and produce fresh from the garden!

1 pound uncooked pasta
⅓ cup olive oil
2 medium zucchini, sliced
2 bell peppers (yellow and red)
1 cup chopped red onion
2 medium tomatoes, cut into
  wedges

¼ cup chopped fresh basil
¼ cup chopped fresh chives
¼ cup chopped fresh parsley
Salt and pepper
½ cup freshly shredded
Parmesan cheese

Cook pasta according to package directions; drain. While pasta is cooking, heat oil in skillet. Cook zucchini, peppers, and onion until slightly crisp, stirring occasionally. Add pasta and remaining ingredients. Serves 8.

Herbs in a Minnesota Kitchen (Minnesota)

Lazy Lasagne

SAUCE:

1–1½ pounds Italian sausage
2 (8-ounce) cans tomato sauce
2 (6-ounce) cans tomato paste
1–2 cloves garlic, minced
1 cup water

1 tablespoon dried basil
1 tablespoon dried oregano
1 tablespoon sugar
1 teaspoon salt

Brown sausage in Dutch oven; drain well. Add remaining sauce ingredients and simmer to blend flavors.

CHEESE MIXTURE:

1 pound ricotta cheese
12 ounces cottage cheese
½ cup freshly grated
   Parmesan cheese
¼–½ teaspoon pepper

2 tablespoons chopped fresh
   parsley
2 eggs, beaten
1 teaspoon salt

Combine cheese mixture ingredients and set aside.

1 (8-ounce) package uncooked
   lasagne noodles or 8-ounce
   sheet fresh pasta

1–1½ pounds mozzarella
   cheese

To assemble, cover bottom of 9x13-inch pan with ¼ of the sauce. Arrange ½ of pasta over sauce. Top with ¼ of sauce, then ½ of cheese mixture, then ½ of mozzarella. Spread with ¼ more sauce. Repeat layers (pasta, remaining cheese mixture, remaining mozzarella) and end with sauce. Cover with foil and bake at 375° for 30–35 minutes longer. Let stand 10–15 minutes. Cut into squares to serve. Makes 10–12 servings.

Minnesota Heritage Cookbook II (Minnesota)

Penne Roberto

Penne Roberto is Chef Fedorko's favorite recipe because it is simple, light, fresh and easy to prepare at home.

1 large yellow onion, finely diced

4 large tablespoons chopped garlic

6 tablespoons extra virgin olive oil, divided

12 Roma tomatoes, peeled and roughly chopped

½ cup chopped, fresh basil or 4 tablespoons dry basil, divided

Salt and freshly ground pepper to taste

6 ounces pancetta (Italian bacon) or any good-quality bacon

10 ounces dry Penne pasta

4 ounces Wisconsin Parmesan cheese, grated

Sweat onions and garlic in 4 tablespoons oil to flavor oil. When onions are translucent, add tomatoes and a little over ½ of the basil. Cook approximately 20 minutes and season with salt and freshly ground pepper.

Cook bacon until crisp and all fat is rendered; drain. Cook pasta in large amount of boiling, salted water until al dente; chill under cold, running water to stop cooking process.

When you're ready to serve, run pasta under hot water to heat; allow to drain. In large serving bowl, mix remaining oil and basil, toss with pasta, and season with salt and pepper. Top with tomato sauce, bacon, and freshly grated Parmesan cheese. Yields 4 servings.

Recipe from Ristoranté Brissago, Lake Geneva.
Our Best Cookbook 2 (Wisconsin)

For 41 years, Wisconsin has celebrated the traditional Wisconsin Fish Fry at Port Fish Day in Port Washington. Known as The World's Largest Outdoor Fish Fry, it lures about 50,000 people each year. If your stomach is feeling especially ready to reel in some fish, try your best at the "Smoked Fish Eating Contest." In a 12-hour day, the event serves about 10,000 pounds of fish and 13,000 pounds of cottage fries.

Stuffed Shells

1 (12-ounce) package
  jumbo shells
1½–2 pounds hamburger
1 (20-ounce) jar Prego
  Spaghetti Sauce with
  Mushrooms

2 eggs, beaten
1 (16-ounce) carton small-curd
  cottage cheese
2 cups shredded mozzarella
  cheese

Cook shells according to package directions; drain. In a large skillet, cook hamburger; drain. Pour ½ jar sauce into 13x9-inch baking dish. In a large bowl, mix together hamburger, eggs, cottage cheese, and mozzarella cheese. Fill shells with above mixture and place in baking dish. Pour remaining sauce over shells. Sprinkle with mozzarella cheese. Bake in a 350° oven for about 30 minutes. Refrigerate leftovers.

Look What's Cookin' at Wal-Mart (Wisconsin)

Fat-Free Pasta Primavera

1 cup sliced zucchini
½ cup sliced mushrooms
¼ cup sliced onion
½ cup sliced red/green pepper
½ cup green beans, cut in
  ½-inch diagonal pieces
1 rounded tablespoon flour
1 (13-ounce) can evaporated
  skimmed milk

½ teaspoon salt
¼ teaspoon pepper
1 tablespoon sliced fresh basil
½ cup chicken broth
½ cup white wine
Your favorite pasta
Parmesan cheese

Spary frying pan with Pam. Sauté first 5 ingredients 4–5 minutes and remove from heat. Meanwhile, spread flour in another large skillet. Add can of evaporated skim milk and stir. Do not boil as milk will separate. Add salt, pepper, and fresh basil. When liquid reaches a nice sauce consistency, add chicken broth, wine, and sautéed vegetables, and serve over hot cooked pasta. Sprinkle lightly with Parmesan cheese. Serves 4.

Seasoned with Love (Wisconsin)

Mushroom-Spinach Pasta

This tasty recipe is low in both fat and sodium because of the fresh, low-fat and salt-reduced ingredients.

2 cups low-fat (1 percent)
  cottage cheese
6 ounces low-fat cream cheese,
  softened
Vegetable oil cooking spray
½ cup finely chopped onion
½ pound fresh mushrooms,
  cleaned, sliced
⅓ cup dry white wine
¼ teaspoon crushed dried
  thyme

Dash of pepper
1 (6½-ounce) can evaporated
  skim milk
1 (10-ounce) package frozen
  chopped spinach, defrosted,
  well drained
16 ounces spaghetti, cooked
  according to package
  directions, omit salt and fat
⅓ cup freshly grated Parmesan
  cheese

In a food processor fitted with a metal blade, combine cottage cheese and cream cheese until smooth. Spray medium-size saucepan with cooking spray. Add onion and mushrooms and cook until tender. Add white wine, thyme, and pepper. Stir in cheese mixture, evaporated skim milk, and spinach; heat thoroughly, stirring occasionally. Place hot spaghetti on a large platter; top with sauce and toss gently. Sprinkle with Parmesan cheese. Serves 8.

Variation: For a zestier version, increase the thyme to ½ teaspoon and add ½ teaspoon garlic powder and a dash of nutmeg. Add these to the recipe with the white wine.

Heart Smart Cookbook II (Michigan)

Spaghetti Pie

You might want to make two pies and freeze one.

**6 ounces spaghetti (can use
  fettucini)**
2 tablespoons butter
⅓ cup grated Parmesan cheese
2 eggs, well beaten
**1 pound ground beef or
  bulk Italian sausage**
½ cup chopped onion
¼ cup chopped green pepper
1 (8-ounce) can tomatoes, cut up

1 (6-ounce) can tomato paste
1 teaspoon sugar
**1 tablespoon dried oregano,
  crushed**
¼ teaspoon salt
**1 (8-ounce) carton cottage
  cheese, drained**
**½ cup shredded mozzarella
  cheese**

Cook spaghetti (you should have 3¼ cups). Stir butter into hot spaghetti. Stir in cheese and eggs. Form mixture into a crust in a buttered 10-inch pie dish.

In skillet cook meat, onion, and green pepper until meat is brown and vegetables are tender. Drain off excess fat. Stir in undrained tomatoes, tomato paste, sugar, oregano, and salt.

Spread cottage cheese over bottom of crust. Fill with tomato mixture. Cover with foil and chill 2–24 hours. Bake at 350° covered for 60 minutes. Uncover; sprinkle with mozzarella cheese. Bake 5 minutes more, until cheese melts.

Thank Heaven for Home Made Cooks (Wisconsin)

Horicon Marsh in south central Wisconsin was formed from an extinct glacial lake. The marsh encompasses 32,000 acres, most of it open water and the largest freshwater cattail marsh in the United States. Attracting thousands of nesting waterfowl and migratory birds, it is Wisconsin's most popular place to bird-watch.

Chicken Spaghetti

3 pounds chicken breasts,
  cooked
2 cups chopped celery
2 cups chopped green bell
  pepper
2 cups chopped onions
1 (12-ounce) can mushroom
  stems and pieces
1 pound grated Cheddar cheese

2 (14-ounce) cans chicken broth
1 (10¾-ounce) can cream of
  chicken soup
4 (10¾-ounce) cans cream of
  mushroom soup
1 (12-ounce) jar chopped
  pimento
1 (8-ounce) can sliced ripe olives
1 (20-ounce) box spaghetti

Cut chicken into bite-size pieces. Sauté celery, peppers, and onions in olive oil. Add mushrooms, cheese, broth, soups, pimentos, olives, and chicken. Cook spaghetti and mix with other ingredients. Heat as a casserole at 350° for 20 minutes. Can be frozen and reheated. Serves 16.

Our Best Home Cooking (Michigan)

Excellent Pesto

1½ cups packed fresh sweet
  basil leaves
⅓ cup fresh grated
  combination Parmesan
  and Romano cheese
½ cup extra virgin olive oil

¼ teaspoon salt
⅛ teaspoon fresh ground
  black pepper
1½ large cloves garlic
¼–½ cups chopped pine nuts
  or walnuts (optional)

Place all ingredients except nuts into food processor bowl. Blend with blade attachment till smooth. Stir in nuts. Serve with pasta, as a spread, etc.

Variations: Lemon Basil Pesto—substitute lemon basil leaves. Cinnamon Basil Pesto—substitute cinnamon basil leaves.

The Madison Herb Society Cookbook (Wisconsin)

Alpler Macaroni

**6 medium potatoes, peeled
and cut into bite-sized
pieces**
2 cups macaroni
Chopped onions

1 cup grated Swiss cheese
¼ cup butter
Paprika
½ pint cream

Cook potato pieces in salted water with more water than usual for 8–10 minutes, then add 2 cups of macaroni and cook together until macaroni is done. Pour into colander to drain.

Spray a 13x9-inch baking dish with nonstick spray (or butter it). Add half of potato-macaroni mixture, then ½ cup grated cheese (or as much as you like), then the rest of the potato mixture and another ½ cup cheese. Top with onion (as much as you like) sautéed in butter. Sprinkle with paprika. Pour cream over the top. Cover and bake in 350° oven for 20–30 minutes or until heated through.

Old World Swiss Family Recipes (Wisconsin)

Deluxe Macaroni and Cheese

**2 cups small-curd cottage
cheese**
1 cup sour cream
1 egg, lightly beaten
¼ teaspoon salt

Garlic salt and pepper to taste
**2 cups shredded sharp
Cheddar cheese**
**½ (7-ounce) package elbow
macaroni, cooked, drained**

In large bowl, combine cottage cheese, sour cream, egg, salt, garlic salt, and pepper. Add Cheddar cheese; mix well. Add macaroni and stir until coated. Transfer to a greased, 2½-quart baking dish. Bake, uncovered, at 350° for 25–30 minutes, or until heated through. Serves 6–8.

Red Flannel Town Recipes (Michigan)

Polish Noodles and Cabbage

¼ cup butter
½ cup peeled and chopped
   yellow onions
4 cups chopped or thinly
   sliced cabbage

1 teaspoon caraway seeds
½ teaspoon salt
½ teaspoon ground pepper
1 (8-ounce) package noodles
½ cup sour cream (optional)

Melt butter in large skillet. Add onion; sauté until transparent. Add cabbage and sauté 5 minutes, or until tender, but still crisp. Stir in caraway seeds, salt and pepper. Meanwhile, cook noodles in salted water as directed on package. Do not overcook. Drain well. Stir noodles into cabbage, and add sour cream. Cook 5 minutes longer, stirring frequently. Serves 4–6.

St. Frederick Parish Centennial Recipe Collection (Wisconsin)

Pork-Sauerkraut Casserole

2 pounds pork steak, cubed
1 package dry onion soup mix
1 can cream of mushroom soup
3 cups water
1 large can sauerkraut,
   well-drained

1 (4-ounce) can mushrooms
1 (8-ounce) package wide
   noodles, cooked
1 can French-fried onion rings
   (optional)

Brown meat. Add onion soup mix, mushroom soup, and water. Simmer 2 hours. Add to meat mixture the sauerkraut, mushrooms, and noodles. Let stand for 3 hours or overnight. Bake one hour at 350°. Top with onion rings during last 10 minutes of baking time. Makes 8 good servings.

Centennial Cookbook (Wisconsin)

Tuna Noodle Delight

"Using your noodle" in more ways than one, this tuna dish is enjoyed by everyone who tries it. It makes a large amount.

1 cup sour cream
1 can celery soup
1 (8-ounce) package fine
  noodles, cooked
1 large can chunk tuna

1 (4-ounce) can mushrooms
1 (4-ounce) jar pimientos
2 teaspoons dry onion soup mix
2 tablespoons soy sauce
1 cup grated Cheddar cheese

Mix sour cream with soup. Add rest of ingredients and mix. Put in buttered casserole dish. Bake at 325° for 45 minutes.

Sparks from the Kitchen (Wisconsin)

Spartichokes

Nice party or buffet dish.

2 cups cooked brown rice
4 eggs, beaten
⅔ cup milk
2 tablespoons margarine,
  melted
2 tablespoons chopped onion
2 tablespoons chopped parsley

1 teaspoon seasoned salt
½ teaspoon salt
1 cup cooked, drained, chopped
  spinach
1 cup chopped artichoke hearts
2 cups shredded Cheddar cheese

Mix together rice, eggs, milk, margarine, onion, parsley, and salts. Add spinach, artichokes, and Cheddar cheese; stir till blended. Pour into casserole dish and bake at 325° for 45 minutes. Serves 6–8.

Some Enchanted Eating (Michigan)

Mushroom-Wild Rice Casserole

1 (6-ounce) box Uncle Ben's
  wild rice with seasonings
½ green bell pepper, diced
½ pound fresh mushrooms,
  sliced
¼ cup margarine, melted

2 tablespoons flour
½ teaspoon salt
⅛ teaspoon pepper
½ cup chicken bouillon
½ cup dry white wine

Preheat oven to 325°. Grease a 1½-quart casserole. Prepare rice according to package directions. In skillet, sauté green pepper and mushrooms in margarine until mushrooms are lightly browned. Add flour, salt, and pepper. Gradually stir in bouillon and wine. Cook over low heat, stirring constantly until slightly thickened. Add cooked rice. Place in casserole and bake uncovered 30 minutes. Makes 6 servings.

Eet Smakelijk (Michigan)

Wild Rice

1 cup wild rice
½ cup chopped onion
¼ cup butter
1 cup chopped celery
¼ teaspoon sage
¼ teaspoon basil
1 tablespoon parsley flakes

½ cup slivered almonds,
  browned (optional)
2 (4-ounce) cans mushrooms
  and juice
1 can consommé or chicken
  stock

Wash rice and soak 3 hours or overnight; drain. Put all together in a 2-quart dish and bake at 350° for 1½ hours. Can't be beat! Warm up; add a little water (don't want it too dry).

Potluck Volume II (Minnesota)

Northern wild rice (*Zizania palustris*) is an annual plant native to the Great Lakes region of North America and Canada. Harvesting wild rice by canoe is still practiced in these regions (as the seed heads are tapped, most of the rice falls into the canoe, but some falls in the water to seed the bed for future years). Wild rice is the state grain of Minnesota.

Varenyky
(Filled Dumplings)

This is a favorite dish of the Ukrainian people.

POTATO-CHEESE FILLING:

1 tablespoon grated onion	1 cup cottage cheese or grated
1 tablespoon butter	Cheddar cheese
2 cups cold mashed potatoes	Salt and pepper to taste

Combine all ingredients. Mixture should be thick.

DOUGH:

2 cups all-purpose flour	½ cup cold water
1 egg	Potato-Cheese Filling

Place flour in a deep bowl. Add egg and water to make a medium-soft dough; knead till smooth. Cover and let rest for 10 minutes. Prepare Filling. It should be thick enough to hold its shape. Roll the dough quite thin. Cut rounds with a 3-inch cutter. Put round on the palm of the hand; place a spoonful of Filling on it, fold over to form a half circle and press edges together with fingers. Place Varenyky on a floured tea towel and cover. At this time, they can be frozen. To cook, drop a few Varenyky at a time into a large quantity of rapidly boiling water. Stir very gently to separate. Cooking time will depend on size and thickness. They are ready when well puffed (approximately 5 minutes). Remove and drain.

Historically Delicious (Michigan)

Kluski Dumplings

1 cup flour	¼ teaspoon salt
¼ cup milk	2 eggs

Mix all ingredients together, like a heavy pancake batter. Drop off tip of teaspoon in boiling salted water. (Use a Spatzle maker for smaller dumplings.) Dumplings come to the top when done. Remove with slotted spoon. Delicious in chicken soup.

Sharing Our Best (Wisconsin)

Broccoli Quiche

1 (10-ounce) box frozen
   chopped broccoli
¼ cup bacon bits
1 deep-dish frozen pie crust or
   Parmesan pie crust
¾ cup shredded Jarlsberg
   cheese

4 eggs
1 cup half-and-half
½ teaspoon salt
Dash of pepper

Cook broccoli as directed; drain well, squeezing to remove as much moisture as possible. Sprinkle bacon bits on crust, then add drained broccoli, and top with cheese. Mix eggs, half-and-half, salt, and pepper together. Pour into pie shell. Bake 50 minutes at 425°. Reduce heat to 325° and continue to bake until quiche is set (about 25 minutes more). Serves 6–8.

Soul Food (Michigan)

Chicken and Asparagus Quiche

There is nothing finer than the very first spring crop of Michigan asparagus.

1 unbaked 8- or 9-inch pie
   shell
¾ cup finely diced cooked,
   chicken
¼ cup finely diced ham
2 cups cut cooked asparagus,
   ½-inch pieces

1 cup shredded Swiss cheese
3 eggs
Milk or light cream
Pinch of nutmeg
Pinch of pepper
6 whole cooked asparagus
   spears for garnish

Preheat oven to 425°. Into unbaked pie shell, place chicken, ham, asparagus, and Swiss cheese. Break 3 eggs into a large measuring cup; add enough milk or cream to make 1¼ cups. Add pinch each of nutmeg and pepper. Beat well with fork. Pour over mixture in pie shell. Decorate with cooked asparagus spears. Bake 15 minutes at 425°; reduce heat to 300° and bake 30–40 minutes, or till cold knife inserted into center comes out clean. Serves 6–8.

Cranbrook Reflections (Michigan)

Cheddar Chicken Harvest Pie

This is a great success served with fresh salad.

1 cup finely shredded Cheddar
cheese
2 pie crusts
¼ cup butter
2 cups broccoli florets (or ½
cauliflower and ½ broccoli)
1 large carrot, sliced
½ cup chopped onion

3 cloves garlic, minced
2 cubes chicken bouillon,
dissolved in 2 cups boiling
water
1 tablespoon lemon juice
1 teaspoon poultry seasoning
¼ cup flour

Press cheese into top and bottom crusts. In large skillet, melt butter; add broccoli, carrot, onion, and garlic, and cook till veggies are crisp-tender. To dissolved bouillon, add lemon juice and poultry seasoning; gradually add flour to thicken. Fold into vegetables. Place mixture into prepared crust in 9-inch pie pan. Cover with top crust and cut slits in top. Place on baking sheet and bake at 375° for 35 minutes; cool slightly before serving. Serves 6–8.

Soul Food (Michigan)

A joint venture between the United States and Canada, the St. Lawrence Seaway is a system of locks, canals, and channels that permits ocean-going vessels to travel from the Atlantic Ocean to the North American Great Lakes, as far as Lake Superior. It extends from Montreal to Lake Erie, including the Welland Canal. The seaway is named after the St. Lawrence River, which it follows from Lake Ontario to the Atlantic Ocean. This section of the seaway comprises stretches of navigable channels within the river, a number of locks, as well as canals made to bypass rapids and dams in the waterway. The seaway (sometimes referred to as Highway H_2O) opened in 1959. The Great Lakes are today used as a major mode of transport for bulk goods. In 2002, 162 million net tons of dry bulk cargo were moved on the Lakes. This was, in order of volume: iron ore, grain, and potash. The iron ore and much of the stone and coal are used in the steel industry.

The Wisconsin Herb Blend

1 teaspoon dried rosemary, crushed

2 teaspoons dried basil, crushed

4 teaspoons dried onion flakes

2 teaspoons dried lemon balm, crushed

2 teaspoons dried parsley, crushed

1 teaspoon dried tarragon, crushed

2 teaspoons dried oregano, crushed

2 teaspoons dried garlic flakes

Mix thoroughly, put in airtight container and allow time to "mellow."

Note: Other variations are possible simply by adding combinations of favorite herbs and spices to this basic blend.

The Madison Herb Society Cookbook (Wisconsin)

Spice-It-Up Seasoning Mix

1 tablespoon paprika

1 tablespoon garlic powder

1 tablespoon onion powder

1 tablespoon black pepper

1 tablespoon salt

1 tablespoon cayenne pepper

1 tablespoon crushed parsley flakes

1 teaspoon coriander

1 teaspoon granulated Splenda sweetener

½ teaspoon leaf thyme

½ teaspoon leaf tarragon

½ teaspoon dried lemon peel

Combine all ingredients and mix well. Place in a sealed shaker jar. Makes about ¹⁄₂ cup. Use as a general seasoning.

Recipes from Joan's Kitchen (Michigan)

Meats

An international leader in dairy and cheese technology for more than 150 years, Wisconsin is home to more dairy farms than any other state—nearly 15,000 dairy operations (about 20 percent of the nation's total) with over 1.25 million dairy cows. Most of the state's dairy farms are family owned and operated.

Beef Burgundy

Crockpot works very well for this recipe.

2 pounds chuck or round
  steak
1 tablespoon Kitchen
  Bouquet
1/4 cup cream of rice cereal
4 medium carrots
2 cups sliced onions
1 clove garlic (optional)

2 teaspoons salt
1/8 teaspoon pepper
1/8 teaspoon marjoram
1/8 teaspoon thyme
1 cup Burgundy, or a dry red
  wine
1 (6-ounce) can mushrooms
  and broth

Trim excess fat from meat. Cut into 1¹/₂-inch cubes. Place in 2-quart casserole and toss with Kitchen Bouquet. Stir in cream of rice cereal. Wash and scrape carrots. Cut into quarters length-wise, and half cross-wise. Add to meat. Add sliced onions. Mix seasonings together and add to meat. Add Burgundy and mush-rooms with broth. Cover tightly. Bake at 350° for about 2¹/₂ hours, or until meat is tender. Stir every 30 minutes. Add more Burgundy and/or beef broth if more liquid is desired. Serve with noodles, rice or mashed potatoes. Serves 6–8.

Our Favorite Recipes (Minnesota)

Pepper Steak

2 pounds round steak, cubed
2 tablespoons fat
1 can stewed tomatoes
3 tablespoons soy sauce
2 tablespoons flour
1/8 teaspoon pepper
2 teaspoons beef bouillon
  (instant)

1 cup hot water
1 large onion, chopped
1 cup celery, cut in 1-inch size
  pieces
3 green peppers, chopped
1 can sliced mushrooms

Brown cubed meat in fat. Remove meat. Stir tomatoes, soy sauce, flour, pepper, beef bouillon, and water into drippings. Heat to boiling. Turn heat to low and add beef strips, onion, and celery. Cover and simmer about 45 minutes to one hour or until tender. Add green pepper and mushrooms and simmer until pepper is tender. Serve over cooked rice or noodles. If too thick add a little water or white wine.

Sharing Our Best/Home of the Good Shepherd (Minnesota)

Crockpot Swiss Steak

1–1½ pounds round steak
Flour
2 teaspoons dry mustard
Salt and pepper, to taste
1 onion, finely chopped
2 carrots, grated
1 stalk celery, finely chopped
1 (16-ounce) can tomatoes
2 tablespoons Worcestershire
2 teaspoons brown sugar

Mix flour, mustard, salt and pepper. Brown the Swiss steak that has been coated with seasoned flour. Put the browned meat into a crock-pot. Sauté the onion, carrots, and celery. Add the tomatoes, Worcestershire and brown sugar; stir and heat. Pour the heated mixture over the meat in crockpot. Cover. Cook on LOW 6–8 hours.

Note: If desired, peeled and halved potatoes can be added to the crockpot also. Delicious!

Recipes from St. Michael's (Minnesota)

French Dip Sandwich au Jus

3–5 pounds boneless rump
  roast
1 large sweet onion, cut in
  ¼-inch slices
¼ cup margarine
½ cup soy sauce
1 clove garlic
1½ teaspoons Kitchen Bouquet
  sauce
1 package dry onion soup mix
4–5 cups water
French rolls
1 cup shredded Swiss cheese

Place roast in a crockpot or slow cooker. Brown the onions in the margarine and place on top of roast. Combine the next 5 ingredients and pour over the roast and onions. Cook on LOW for 8–10 hours. Remove meat and slice. Make sandwiches with bread, meat, and cheese. Put au jus in small bowls and dip sandwiches.

Treasured Recipes from Treasured Friends (Minnesota)

Italian Beef

1 (6-pound) round roast	½ teaspoon oregano
3 large onions	¼ teaspoon basil
1 tablespoon salt	½ teaspoon Italian seasoning
½ teaspoon onion salt	½ teaspoon salt
½ teaspoon garlic salt	1 teaspoon Accent

Place meat in roaster half filled with water, salt, and onions. Roast until tender. Let stand overnight in cold place. Slice very thin. Strain liquid and add remaining ingredients. Bring to boiling point. Place sliced beef and seasoned liquid in layers in large saucepan. Serve on French or Italian bread.

The Palmyra Heritage Cookbook (Wisconsin)

Italian Beef Hoagies

1 (4-pound) boneless sirloin tip roast, halved	2 cups water
	1 (16-ounce) jar mild pepper rings, undrained
2 envelopes Italian salad dressing mix	18 hoagie buns, split

Place roast in a slow cooker. Combine salad dressing mix and water; pour over roast. Cover and cook on low for 8 hours or until meat is tender. Remove meat; shred with a fork and return to slow cooker. Add pepper rings with juice and heat through. Spoon ¹/₂ cup meat mixture onto each bun. Makes 18 hoagies.

Come and Discover Special Appetites (Michigan)

Braised Sirloin Tips

2 pounds beef, 1-inch cubes
1 (10½-ounce) can beef
  consommé
⅓ cup red Burgundy or
  red cranberry cocktail
2 tablespoons soy sauce

1 clove garlic, minced
¼ teaspoon onion powder
2 tablespoons cornstarch
¼ cup water
4 cups hot cooked rice

Brown meat all sides. Add consommé, wine, soy sauce, garlic, and onion powder. Heat to boiling. Reduce heat and simmer one hour. Blend cornstarch and water. Pour into meat. Cook one minute more. Serve over rice. Makes 8 servings.

St. Mark's Lutheran Church Cookbook (Wisconsin)

Main Street Main Dish

1 (3½- to 4-pound) beef
  blade pot roast
Flour
Vegetable oil
Salt and pepper
2 cups sliced onion
¼ cup water
¼ cup ketchup
⅓ cup dry sherry
1 clove garlic, minced

¼ teaspoon dry mustard
¼ teaspoon dried marjoram
¼ teaspoon dried rosemary
¼ teaspoon dried thyme
1 medium bay leaf
1 (8-ounce) can sliced
  mushrooms, drained
2 tablespoons flour
2–3 cups water

Trim excess fat from meat. Dredge meat in a little flour. In large skillet, brown meat on both sides in a little oil. Sprinkle generously with salt and pepper; add onion. Stir ¼ cup water, ketchup, sherry, garlic, and seasonings together; add to skillet. Add mushrooms. Cook, covered, over low heat or bake at 325° for 2 hours.

Remove meat to serving platter. Discard bay leaf. Sprinkle 2 tablespoons flour into drippings in skillet; cook and stir until mixture thickens. Boil and stir one minute. Gradually add water until gravy is desired consistency. Serves 6–8.

From Minnesota: More Than a Cookbook (Minnesota)

Sauerbraten

4 pounds chuck roast
1 cup water
1 cup cider vinegar
2 medium onions, sliced
2 bay leaves

2 teaspoons salt
½ teaspoon pepper
12 peppercorns
6 whole cloves
¼ cup brown sugar

GRAVY:
¼ cup brown sugar
¼ cup raisins

6 gingersnaps

Place meat in earthenware or glass bowl. Combine the other ingredients and heat to boiling. Pour over the meat and allow to cool. Marinate 3–4 days in the refrigerator; turning meat twice daily. Do not pierce meat with a fork.

Drain meat and set marinade aside. Brown meat on all sides in hot fat in a heavy skillet. Add the marinade, cover pan and simmer slowly 3–4 hours or until tender. Remove meat from skillet and slice across the grain into scant ¹/₂-inch slices. Strain the liquid. Melt ¹/₄ cup brown sugar in skillet; add liquid gradually and stir until sugar dissolves. Add ¹/₄ cup of raisins and 6 crushed gingersnaps. Cook until smooth and thickened. If gravy is too thin, thicken with a flour and water paste. Return meat to gravy and heat. Makes 6 servings.

Create Share Enjoy! (Wisconsin)

Sauerbraten (see recipe above) is one of the best known German dishes. It is traditionally served with red cabbage, potato dumplings (Kartoffelklöße), spätzle, boiled potatoes, or noodles. While many German-style restaurants in America pair potato pancakes with sauerbraten, this is common only in a small part of Germany.

Beef-Broccoli Strudel

1 pound ground beef
¼ cup dried bread crumbs
1 medium onion diced
½ cup sour cream
1 (10-ounce) package
   broccoli, thawed (leaves)
   and squeezed dry

4 ounces shredded mozzarella
   cheese (more if desired)
1¼ teaspoons salt
¼ teaspoon pepper
½ pound phyllo dough
½–1 cup melted butter or
   margarine

Brown ground beef; add onions and cook until transparent. Add all remaining ingredients except phyllo and butter. Brush each sheet of phyllo with melted butter, layering sheets as you go. Starting at short end of phyllo, evenly spoon beef mixture to cover about half of the rectangle. From beef mixture side, roll phyllo jellyroll fashion. Place roll seam-side-down on cookie sheet. Brush with remaining butter. Bake 45 minutes at 350°. Cool 15 minutes for easier slicing. Serves 6.

Create Share Enjoy! (Wisconsin)

Corned Beef and Cabbage

3–4 pounds lean corned beef
2 garlic buds, cut in half
1 onion, chopped
2 bay leaves
10 peppercorns

2 tablespoons pickling spices
3 potatoes, quartered
6 small carrots, halved
4 sticks celery, cut in pieces
1 head cabbage, quartered

Put the corned beef in a big soup kettle and cover it with cold water. Add all of the other ingredients except the vegetables and bring water to a boil. Reduce the heat to a slow boil or simmer. Simmer for 3 hours per pound of corned beef. At this point, stop! Refrigerate overnight and remove all fat from the top.

When cooking the next day, bring to a slow boil and add potatoes, carrots, and celery. Cook for $1/2$ hour or until vegetables are tender. During the last 15 minutes of cooking time, add the cabbage. Do not overcook the cabbage. Serve with buttered rye bread.

Blessed Be the Cook (Wisconsin)

Cranberry Sauerkraut Meatballs

2 pounds ground beef
2 eggs
1 envelope regular onion
  soup mix
½ cup water
1 cup finely crushed cracker
  crumbs

Mix together and shape into meatballs. Brown in a skillet.

SAUCE:

1 (16-ounce) can sauerkraut,
  drained and snipped
1 (8-ounce) can cranberry
  sauce (whole or strained)
¾ cup chili sauce or ketchup
2 cups water
⅓ cup brown sugar

Mix together and pour half of the sauce in a 9x13-inch baking dish. Arrange meatballs on sauce. Pour remaining sauce over meatballs. Cover with foil and bake for one hour at 325°. Remove foil. Bake another 30–40 minutes. Serve hot over noodles or rice.

The Best Cranberry Recipes (Wisconsin)

Smothered Swiss Steak

1 medium onion, sliced
2 tablespoons flour
¼ teaspoon paprika
Salt and pepper to taste
1 pound round, Swiss or cubed
  steak, cut into 3–4 pieces
1 teaspoon Kitchen Bouquet
  (optional)
½ cup water or beef broth

Place layer of onion slices in bottom of crockpot or baking dish. Mix flour, paprika, salt and pepper together and dredge steak pieces till lightly coated with flour mixture. Place $^1/_2$ meat pieces on onion; add another layer of onions, and remaining meat. Mix water or broth and Kitchen Bouquet; pour over entire meat mixture. In crockpot, cook 6–8 hours. In oven, cook 2–2$^1/_2$ hours. If gravy is desired, add more water and thicken with white sauce for the last $^1/_2$ hour of cooking.

Centennial Cookbook Welcome Corners (Michigan)

Barbecued Beef on Buns

1 (3-pound) boneless beef
  chuck roast
1 medium onion, chopped
½ cup chopped celery
Water
1½ cups ketchup
¼ cup packed brown sugar
¼ cup vinegar

2 tablespoons dry mustard
2 teaspoons salt
2 teaspoons Worcestershire
1 teaspoon chili powder
½ teaspoon paprika
½ teaspoon garlic salt
Few drops hot pepper sauce
Hamburger buns

Place beef, onion, and celery in a Dutch oven; add water to almost cover meat. Bring to a boil; reduce heat. Cover and simmer for $2^1/_2$–3 hours or until meat is tender.

Remove meat; strain and reserve cooking liquid. Trim and shred meat; return to Dutch oven. Add 2 cup of strained cooking liquid (save remaining cooking liquid) and chill. Skim and discard fat. Add ketchup, brown sugar, vinegar, and seasonings. Cover and simmer for one hour, stirring occasionally. If mixture becomes too thick, add additional reserved cooking liquid. Serve on hamburger buns. Yields 15–20 servings.

Favorite Recipes of Lester Park & Rockridge Schools (Minnesota)

Today, northeastern Minnesota is the only area in the lower 48 states where wolves still thrive. The International Wolf Center in Ely enlightens visitors about the myths and realities of these curious creatures. The center opened in June 1993, and features Gray wolves viewable through large windows that allow visitors to watch them communicate, play, hunt, and eat.

Hamburger Kraut Hot Dish

1½ pounds hamburger
1 small onion, chopped
1 (15-ounce) can sauerkraut
1 can cream of mushroom
   soup
1 can cream of celery soup
¾ cup water
5 ounces uncooked egg noodles
Slices American or Velveeta
   cheese

Brown hamburger and onion. Place in 9x13-inch pan. Cover with sauerkraut. Heat soups and water. Pat dry noodles over kraut. Cover with soup mixture. Bake covered in 350° oven for 45 minutes. Top with cheese slices and return to oven until melted.

One Hundred Years of Sharing (Minnesota)

Layered Tostada Bake

1 pound ground beef
½ cup chopped onion
1 (1¼-ounce) envelope taco
   seasoning mix
1 (8-ounce) can tomato sauce
1 (16-ounce) can refried beans
   (can use hot chili beans)
1 (4-ounce) can whole green
   chiles, drained, seeded and
   chopped
2 eggs
1 egg beaten
1 cup Bisquick baking mix
½ cup cornmeal
¼ cup milk
2 tablespoons oil
1 cup dairy sour cream
2 cups shredded Cheddar cheese

Heat oven to 375°. Grease oblong baking dish (12 x 7½ x 2). Cook and stir ground beef and onion in skillet until beef is brown; drain. Stir in seasoning mix, tomato sauce, beans, chiles. Mix 1 egg, baking mix, cornmeal, milk, and oil until moist, beat vigorously 30 seconds. Spread dough in dish. Spoon beef mixture over dough. Mix sour cream, 1 beaten egg and cheese. Spoon over beef mixture. Bake 30 minutes. Let stand 10 minutes before cutting. Garnish with green pepper rings, if desired. Makes 6–8 servings.

People Pleasers (Minnesota)

Beef-Potato Nacho Casserole

2 pounds ground beef
¾ cup chopped onion, divided
1 (1¼-ounce) package taco seasoning mix
¾ cup water
1 (8-ounce) can tomato sauce
1 (4-ounce) can chopped green chiles, drained
1 (16-ounce) can red kidney beans, rinse, drained
1 (24-ounce) package frozen potatoes, thawed
1 (11-ounce) can nacho cheese soup, undiluted
½ cup milk
¼ cup chopped green bell pepper
¼ teaspoon sugar
1 teaspoon Worcestershire
Paprika

Brown beef. Sauté ½ cup onion in skillet; drain. Stir in taco mix, water, and tomato sauce. Bring to a boil and simmer 1 minute. Spread meat mixture into greased 9x13-inch baking pan. Top with green chiles, beans, and potatoes.

In bowl, combine soup, milk, ¼ cup onion, green pepper, sugar, and Worcestershire; pour over potatoes. Sprinkle with paprika. Cover with foil and bake at 350° for 1 hour. Remove foil and bake 15 minutes more till light golden brown. Let stand 10 minutes before cutting. Makes 8 servings.

Heavenly Helpings (Michigan)

Located between Detroit, Michigan, and Windsor, Ontario, the first auto traffic tunnel built between two nations was the mile-long Detroit-Windsor Tunnel under the Detroit River. The Detroit-Windsor Tunnel is the only international vehicular underwater border crossing in the world. It has been recognized as one of the great engineering wonders of the world and remains one of the busiest crossings between the United States and Canada. Construction took 26 months and cost $23,000,000. It first opened to traffic on November 3, 1930. The maximum depth of the roadway beneath the river surface is 75 feet.

Potato Pizza

1 package frozen hash brown squares
1 pound browned ground beef
1 (15-ounce) jar Prego
1 can Cheddar cheese soup (undiluted)
1 (8-ounce) package mozzarella cheese

Spray a 9x13-inch pan lightly with Pam. Line with frozen hash browns. Mix ground beef, Prego, and Cheddar cheese soup. Heat through. Pour over hash browns. Cover with foil and bake at 375° for 45 minutes. Take foil off and cover with mozzarella. Bake 15 minutes more. Let stand 10 minutes before serving.

If desired, you can add a pizza topping of your choice to the hamburger mixture.

The Ultimate Potato Cookbook (Minnesota)

Beef 'n' Potato Bake

4 cups frozen hash brown potatoes (thawed)
3 tablespoons oil
¼ teaspoon pepper
1 pound ground beef
¾-ounce package brown gravy mix
1 cup water
½ teaspoon garlic salt
1 (10-ounce) package frozen mixed vegetables
1 cup shredded Cheddar cheese
Canned French fried onion rings

In shallow 1½-quart baking dish, combine potatoes, oil, and pepper. Press firmly to bottom and sides of dish. Bake shell uncovered at 400° for 15 minutes. Brown beef and drain. Add gravy mix, water, and garlic salt. Bring to slow boil. Add vegetables and cook on medium for 5 minutes. Add ½ cup cheese; place into potato shell. Bake uncovered at 350° for 15 minutes. Sprinkle with remaining cheese and onion rings; return to oven for 5 minutes.

The Oke Family Cookbook (Minnesota)

Potato Hamburgers

1 pound lean ground beef
1 cup grated raw potato
3 tablespoons minced onions
1 tablespoon minced parsley
1 egg
1 teaspoon salt
¼ teaspoon pepper

Mix well. Shape into ¹/₂-inch thick patties. Place on broiler rack. Brush with your favorite barbecue sauce. Broil three inches from heat until well browned. Turn and broil other side. Baste occasionally with barbecue sauce (or tomato sauce or ketchup).

To pan fry, brown on one side, turn and brown on other side. Reduce heat and fry until done.

People Pleasers (Minnesota)

Best Ever Sloppy Joes

1 (14-ounce) can petite-diced tomatoes
¹/₃ cup red wine vinegar
1¹/₃ cup ketchup
2–3 tablespoons brown sugar
1½ pounds ground sirloin
1 cup chopped celery
½ cup chopped bell pepper
3 garlic cloves, diced
1–2 tablespoons chili powder
1 teaspoon diced leaf oregano
1 cup chopped yellow onion

Mix together tomatoes, vinegar, ketchup, and brown sugar until sugar is dissolved; set aside. Brown meat together with remaining ingredients. Drain and add to tomato mixture in a Dutch oven. Cook over medium heat 10–15 minutes. Serve on buns. Makes about 5¹/₂ cups.

Taste of Clarkston: Tried & True Recipes (Michigan)

Greek Style Meatloaf

2½ pounds ground chuck
½ pound finely diced feta
   cheese
10 pitted black olives, chopped
1 small onion, peeled, diced
1 tablespoon oregano
1 tablespoon ground cumin

1 tablespoon paprika
1 teaspoon black pepper
1½ teaspoons salt
1 tablespoon garlic powder
1 egg
½ cup bread crumbs

In large bowl, mix all ingredients thoroughly. In a jellyroll pan, shape meat into a loaf, making sure there are no bubbles. For easier and firmer shaping, wet hands before shaping.

Bake in preheated 350° oven 1 hour, or till temperature registers 165° on meat thermometer. If meat seems to be browning too quickly, cover with foil. Remove from oven; let meatloaf stand 15 minutes to firm up. Slice and serve with mashed potatoes and gravy. Makes 8 servings.

Opaa! Greek Cooking Detroit Style (Michigan)

PHOTO © NATIONAL PARK SERVICE

Bridalveil Falls empties into Lake Superior at Pictured Rocks National Lakeshore in Michigan's Upper Peninsula. Pictured Rocks became the first designated National Lakeshore in the United States in 1966. The park offers spectacular scenery of the hilly shoreline between Munising and Grand Marais, with natural archways, waterfalls, and sand dunes.

Stuffed Cabbage Rolls

1 large head cabbage
1 pound hamburger
2 eggs
½ cup rice, uncooked

1 teaspoon salt
¼ teaspoon pepper
1 small onion, cut fine

Simmer cabbage leaves to soften. Combine remaining ingredients and mix well. Place mixture into cabbage leaves and roll up. Place layer of cabbage leaves in bottom of casserole dish. Place rolls on top.

SAUCE:

1 large onion, chopped
2 (8-ounce) cans tomato sauce
2 (29-ounce) cans tomatoes
2 tablespoons lemon juice

¼ teaspoon pepper
1 teaspoon salt
1 teaspoon Worcestershire
½–1 cup brown sugar

Combine all ingredients in saucepan; bring to a boil. Pour Sauce over rolls; place in 375° oven covered for 1 hour. Bake uncovered at 250° for 2 more hours.

Country Cookbook (Michigan)

Crazy Meatballs

2 pounds ground beef
1 cup bread crumbs

1 package dry French onion
    soup mix

Mix ground beef, crumbs and soup mix; shape into balls.

SAUCE:

1 bottle chili sauce
1 cup cranberry sauce
½ cup brown sugar

1 cup water
1 (15-ounce) can sauerkraut,
    drained

Simmer chili sauce, cranberry sauce, sauerkraut, brown sugar, and water till mixed. Pour over meatballs in 9x13-inch baking pan. Bake at 325° for 2 hours.

Home Cookin': First Congregational United Church of Christ (Michigan)

Norwegian Meatballs

A good reason to use the chafing dish tucked away in your cupboard . . .

1¼ pounds lean ground beef
¾ pound ground pork and
  veal combined
2 slices soft white bread
  without crusts
⅔ cup light cream
2 eggs, lightly beaten
1 small onion, grated
2 small or 1 large clove garlic,
  minced
1 tablespoon chopped parsley

1 teaspoon salt
¼ teaspoon pepper
¼ teaspoon nutmeg
¼ teaspoon allspice
2 tablespoons margarine
1 tablespoon oil
1½ quarts beef bouillon
¼ cup flour
1 cup water
Salt and pepper to taste

Mix together beef, pork, and veal in a large bowl. In separate bowl, soak bread in cream for a few minutes, then add to meat. Next add eggs, onion, garlic, parsley, salt, pepper, nutmeg, and allspice. Mix thoroughly, using hands, and shape into 1-inch balls; refrigerate for 30 minutes. Heat margarine and oil in skillet and fry meatballs until lightly browned.

In a large kettle or Dutch oven, heat the beef bouillon. Drop browned meatballs into bouillon and simmer covered for 20 minutes. Mix flour and water together, add to broth and simmer 10 minutes longer. Season to taste with salt and pepper. Makes 8 servings.

Minnesota Heritage Cookbook I (Minnesota)

Upper Peninsula Pasties

DOUGH:

1½ cups shortening

4 cups all-purpose flour

1½ teaspoons salt

10–12 tablespoons water

Cut shortening into flour to which salt has been added and mix as you would for a pie crust. Add enough water to make a soft dough. Chill in refrigerator while making the Filling.

FILLING:

1 pound tender beef stew meat, diced into ½-inch pieces

½ pound pork, cut into ½-inch pieces

2–3 medium potatoes, quartered, sliced

1 small onion, diced

1½ teaspoons salt

¼ teaspoon pepper

Small amounts of parsnips, carrots, or rutabagas

Butter or margarine

Mix all ingredients in a bowl, except butter. Divide Dough into 6 equal parts. Roll each section into an 8- or 9-inch circle. Put $^1/_6$ of the Filling on each circle and dot top of each with a pat of butter. Finish by folding Dough over to make a half-circle; crimp edges with a fork and prick top 3–4 times. Bake one hour in 350° oven. Makes 6 pasties.

Red Flannel Town Recipes (Michigan)

Michigan is the only state to consist entirely of two peninsulas. The Upper Peninsula is the northern of the state's two major land masses. It is commonly referred to simply as the Upper Peninsula, the U.P., or Upper Michigan, and more casually as the "Land Above the Bridge." The Upper Peninsula contains almost one-third of the land area of the state of Michigan but just three percent of the total population. Residents are frequently called Yoopers (derived from "U.P.-ers") and have a strong regional identity. The land and climate are not very suitable for agriculture, although the economy has occasionally thrived from logging and mining. Yoopers call people in the "mitten" trolls since they live "below the bridge."

The Lower Peninsula of Michigan is sometimes dubbed "the mitten," owing to its shape. The Upper Peninsula is separated from the Lower Peninsula by the Straits of Mackinac, a five-mile-wide channel that joins Lake Huron to Lake Michigan.

Like the entire Lower Peninsula of Michigan, most of the Upper Peninsula observes eastern time. However, the four counties bordering Wisconsin are in the central time zone.

Pasties

(Meat and Potato Turnovers)

6 cups sifted flour
3 teaspoons salt
1½ teaspoons baking powder
2 cups shortening or lard
1–1½ cups ice water
3 cups thinly sliced potatoes
1½ cups sliced carrots
  (optional)
1½ cup chopped rutabaga
  (optional)

3 cups chopped onion
Salt and pepper
2 pounds beef sirloin, round or
  flank steak, cut in ½-inch
  pieces
¾ pound pork butt, ground
  or chopped (optional)
½ cup butter melted with
  ½ cup water

Mix flour, 3 teaspoons salt and baking powder in a large bowl. Add shortening and cut in with a pastry blender. Add ice water, a little at a time, until dough can be easily handled. Divide dough into 6 pieces, wrap in waxed paper and refrigerate for 30 minutes.

For each pasty: Roll out dough into a 9-inch circle. Layer potatoes, carrots, rutabaga and onion; sprinkle with salt and pepper. Add beef, pork, more salt and pepper, ending with a second layer of potatoes. Fold in half, moistening edge with cold water, and seal edges. Crimp edge with a fork. Place on greased cookie sheet. In the top of each pasty, cut a small hole with a sharp knife.

Bake pasties in 425° preheated oven for 15 minutes. Turn oven to 350° and bake 35–45 minutes or until they are nicely browned. After ½ hour of baking, remove from oven and spoon the butter-water mixture into the hole, return to oven and complete baking. Serve hot or cold. Pasties freeze and reheat well. Yields 6 large pasties.

Minnesota Heritage Cookbook I (Minnesota)

My Mother's Potato Pasty

3 cups flour
1 cup shortening

½ teaspoon salt
⅓ cup cold water

Mix as for pie crust. Roll thin and put on cookie sheet.

FILLING:

Sliced raw potatoes
Leftover roast beef
Gravy
1 medium onion, chopped

Salt and pepper
1 egg
¼ cup milk

Layer potatoes, beef, gravy, onion, salt and pepper over half of crust. Fold over crust and pinch together. Bake at 350° for 40 minutes. Beat egg and milk together. Cut a "U" on top of the crust and pour mixture over. Replace crust and bake 10 minutes more. Cut in squares and serve.

The Palmyra Heritage Cookbook (Wisconsin)

Barbecued Pork Ribs

I think it's the combination of honey, chicken broth, and wine-based soy sauce which makes for such a pleasing sauce. We wouldn't think of using the bottled stuff after finding this recipe—and the ribs won't taste any better on the grill!

4 pounds ribs (spareribs or
** country style)**
1 cup hot chicken broth or
** bouillon**
3 tablespoons sugar

5 tablespoons honey
3 tablespoons Kikkoman Soy
** Sauce**
2 Tablespoons ketchup
1 teaspoon salt

If the ribs are fatty, cover with water and boil for 10 minutes. Remove from water and place in baking dish. Mix remaining ingredients and pour over ribs. Marinate ribs for 2 hours, turning occasionally. Bake at 300° for 2–2½ hours, again turning ribs occasionally. Makes 5–6 servings.

A Thyme for All Seasons (Minnesota)

Weekend Spareribs

3 pounds country-style spareribs
1½ cups ketchup
¼ cup Worcestershire
⅓ cup red wine vinegar
¼ cup packed brown sugar
2 teaspoons salt
½ teaspoon garlic salt
¼ teaspoon pepper

Combine spareribs with enough water to cover in a large saucepan. Boil 1½–2 hours or until tender. Place ribs in a 9x13-inch baking pan. Pour a mixture of ketchup, Worcestershire, vinegar, brown sugar, salt, garlic salt, and pepper over the ribs. Marinate, covered, in refrigerator for several hours. Bake at 350° for 45 minutes.

Dawn to Dusk (Michigan)

Oven Roasted Honey and Beer Ribs

2–3 pounds baby back ribs
½ cup chopped onion
2 cloves garlic, minced
1 tablespoon cooking oil
¾ cup chili sauce
½ cup beer
¼ cup honey
2 tablespoons Worcestershire
¼ teaspoon dry mustard

Place ribs, bone side up, in a shallow roasting pan. Bake at 350° for 1 hour. Drain fat. Turn ribs, meat side up.

While meat is cooking, make sauce. In shallow saucepan, cook onion and garlic in hot oil until tender. Stir in chili sauce, beer, honey, Worcestershire, and dry mustard. Simmer, uncovered, for 20 minutes. Makes 1½ cups sauce.

Spoon some sauce over ribs. Bake, covered, for 45–60 minutes or until tender, adding sauce often. Pass remaining sauce. Serves 4.

Soul Food (Michigan)

Lemon Grilled Ribs

Make this sauce ahead of time to have it handy.

½ cup water
1 chicken bouillon cube
3 tablespoons brown sugar
1 cup pineapple juice
2 cloves garlic, minced
¼ cup minced onion

¼ cup ketchup
¼ cup lemon juice
2 tablespoons cornstarch
Salt and pepper to taste
3 pounds spare ribs or
   country-style ribs

Combine all ingredients except ribs in saucepan. Bring to a boil, stirring well. Lower heat and simmer 5 minutes; set aside.

Cut ribs into serving-size pieces (3 or 4 ribs per person). Place ribs bone side down on grill over slow coals. Grill about 20 minutes; turn meaty side up again and grill about 20 minutes longer; brush meaty side with sauce mixture. Continue to grill without turning 20–30 minutes; baste occasionally. Brush sauce on both sides of ribs; let cook 2–3 minutes on each side. Makes 4–6 servings.

Great Lakes Cookery (Michigan)

Oriental Pork Almandine

1 pound boneless pork chops,
  or cutlets
⅓ cup all-purpose flour
2 cups chicken broth
3 tablespoons soy sauce
½ cup sliced almonds
2 tablespoons butter

¼ pound mushrooms, sliced
1 medium onion, sliced
  lengthwise
2 cups celery, diagonally sliced
Green onions, sliced (optional)
Hot cooked rice, chow mein
  noodles or egg noodles

Trim excess fat from pork chops. Cut meat in ³/₄-inch cubes. Roll in flour. Put in 3-quart saucepan and sauté over high heat, stirring frequently, till lightly browned. Stir in broth and soy sauce. In small skillet, toast almonds lightly in 1 tablespoon butter. Remove from skillet; set aside. Melt remaining butter in skillet. Add mushrooms and onion. Sauté till onion is tender. Add mushrooms, onion, and celery to pork. Bring to a boil and simmer, covered, 30 minutes, or till pork is tender. Stir in almonds. Turn into serving dish. Garnish with green onions, if desired. Serve over rice or noodles.

Pleasures from the Good Earth (Michigan)

Orange-Cranberry Pork Chops

This is cranberry country, so here's one of our favorite ways to enjoy them. Try this same recipe for cut-up chicken; just reduce the baking time to 30–35 minutes.

6 (½- to ¾-inch-thick)
  pork chops
Salt and freshly ground
  pepper to taste

2 cups whole cranberry sauce
Juice and grated rind of 1
  orange

Preheat oven to 325°. Slightly warm, then grease, a large skillet with the fatty edges of the chops, then arrange chops in pan. Brown quickly on both sides over medium-high heat, seasoning with salt and freshly ground pepper to taste.

Remove chops to a shallow baking dish, large enough to accommodate them in 1–2 layers. Pour off any fat from skillet, but do not scrape. Combine cranberry sauce, orange juice and rind, saving a little rind for garnish, if you wish. Pour into still-hot skillet, and immediately stir with a flat whisk to loosen browned bits. Pour over chops. Bake, covered, for 45 minutes or until tender. Serves 4–6.

Hollyhocks & Radishes (Michigan)

Trainwreck Pork Chops

1 (8-ounce) can stewed
  tomatoes
¼ cup instant minced onion
1 teaspoon garlic salt
1 teaspoon crushed oregano
1 teaspoon sugar

½ teaspoon pepper
1 (8-ounce) can tomato sauce
1 tablespoon hickory smoke
  barbecue sauce
4 loin pork chops (¾-inch
  thick)

Break up tomatoes with spoon and add onion, garlic salt, oregano, sugar, pepper, tomato sauce, and barbecue sauce. Pour $1/2$ of mixture into shallow 2-quart casserole. Trim fat from chops and arrange in sauce, then pour remaining sauce over top. Bake covered at 350° for one hour. Serve over hot cooked noodles.

Duluth Woman's Club 70th Anniversary Cookbook (Minnesota)

Pork Chops and Wild Rice

1 small package Uncle
  Ben's Wild Rice
6–8 pork chops, depending
  on size
1 medium onion, minced
1 cup finely chopped celery
1 cup chopped green pepper
1 (8-ounce) package fresh
  mushrooms, chopped
  (optional)

1 teaspoon salt
¼ teaspoon garlic salt
⅛ teaspoon pepper
2 tablespoons drippings from
  meat
1 cup milk
1 can mushroom soup

Make rice as directed on package. Fry pork chops on both sides until brown, season with salt and pepper as you fry. Mix vegetables, seasonings, rice, and meat drippings from pan (add a little water to frypan to get enough drippings). Put vegetable mixture in a buttered 9x13-inch cake pan. Arrange chops over vegetables. Pour milk and soup, mixed together over chops. Cover and bake in 350° oven for 1¼ hours.

Sacred Heart Centennial Cookbook (Wisconsin)

French Meat Pie

2 cups potatoes, put thru
  food grinder (can use
  frozen hash browns)
1 large onion, ground
4 pounds ground lean pork
  (shoulder pork)
½ teaspoon ground savory

½ teaspoon allspice
½ teaspoon sage
½ teaspoon cinnamon
Salt and pepper to taste
4 (9-inch) deep-dish pie crusts,
  with top crusts (use purchased
  frozen or homemade)

In enough water to cover, cook potato and onion until tender. Add meat and spices and simmer 30 minutes. Drain, put into pie crusts, and cover with top crusts. Bake at 400° for 20 minutes. If desired, freeze for later use; take right from freezer and bake again at 400° for 25–30 minutes or until hot and ready to serve. Makes about 4 pies.

Marketplace Recipes Volume I (Wisconsin)

Ham Logs with Raisin Sauce

1 pound ground ham
½ pound ground pork
¾ cup milk
½ cup oatmeal (raw)

1 egg
½ teaspoon salt
Dash of pepper

Combine ingredients; form into 6 logs. Put in baking dish. Cover with the following sauce.

SAUCE:

½ cup brown sugar
1 tablespoon cornstarch
¾ cup cold water

2 tablespoons vinegar
2 tablespoons lemon juice
¼ cup seedless raisins

Combine brown sugar and cornstarch; gradually add water, vinegar, lemon juice, and raisins. Heat to boiling, stirring. Bake at 350° for 40–45 minutes, basting with the raisin sauce.

People Pleasers (Minnesota)

Ham and Asparagus Casserole

3–4 tablespoons butter
1 teaspoon grated onion
Dash of garlic salt
1 teaspoon paprika
½ teaspoon salt
⅛ teaspoon pepper
2 tablespoons flour

3 cups milk
2 cups grated sharp Cheddar
cheese
2 (10-ounce) packages frozen
asparagus
1 cup poultry stuffing crumbs
2 cups sliced cooked ham

Melt 2 tablespoons butter and blend in grated onion and seasonings along with flour. Slowly add milk and heat, stirring constantly till thickened. Add cheese and stir till melted. Cook asparagus according to directions and cut into 1-inch lengths. Preheat oven to 375°. In bottom of 2-quart buttered casserole, sprinkle a layer of stuffing crumbs. Add layer of ham and one of asparagus. Now pour part of cheese sauce over and repeat layer of ham, asparagus, and sauce till ingredients are used. Top with remaining crumbs and butter. Bake 45 minutes, or till bubbly and browned. Serves 6–8.

Recipes & Remembrances II (Michigan)

Corn Dogs

1 cup all-purpose flour
⅔ cup yellow cornmeal
1½ teaspoons sugar
1 teaspoon onion salt
½ teaspoon baking powder
Dash of pepper

2 tablespoons shortening
1 egg, slightly beaten
Spicy mustard
⅔ cup milk
Oil
1 pound frankfurters

You will need wooden skewers. Combine flour, cornmeal, sugar, onion salt, baking powder, and pepper in a large bowl. Cut in shortening until particles are the size of coarse crumbs. Combine egg, 1 tablespoon mustard, and milk. Add to dry ingredients. Stir until blended. Heat 3 inches of oil in deep saucepan to 365° on deep-fat frying thermometer. Dry off frankfurters. Insert skewer; spread or dip in batter. Put into hot oil and fry 2–3 minutes until golden brown. May serve on skewers with more mustard for dipping. Makes 8–10.

Dell & Barry's Holiday Delights for All Seasons (Michigan)

Herbed Lamb Stew

1 tablespoon oil
1 pound lean lamb leg or
   shoulder, cut into ½-inch
   cubes
2 tablespoons flour
2 cups water
1 (8-ounce) can tomato sauce
1 cup chopped onion
1 clove garlic, minced
⅛ teaspoon salt/pepper

1 cup peeled, diced potatoes
1 cup frozen peas
1 cup sliced carrots
1 cup sliced mushrooms
1 cup sliced zucchini or squash
2 tablespoons parsley
1 tablespoon fresh chopped
   oregano leaves or ¾
   teaspoon dried

In Dutch oven, heat oil to medium heat. Add lamb; sauté until slightly brown. Reduce heat, add flour and stir constantly until thick. Slowly add water, tomato sauce, onion, garlic, salt, pepper, and blend well. Cover and cook over low heat for 30 minutes; stir occasionally. Add vegetables, parsley, and oregano. Cook 30 more minutes. Yields 6 servings.

Anoka County 4H Cook Book (Minnesota)

Elk, Venison, or Moose Oven Burgundy

2 tablespoons flour
2 tablespoons soy sauce
2 pounds venison, elk, or
   moose
4 carrots, cut in chunks
2 large onions, sliced thin

1 cup thinly sliced celery
¼ teaspoon pepper
¼ teaspoon marjoram
¼ teaspoon thyme
1 cup Burgundy wine

Blend flour with soy sauce in Dutch oven. Cut meat into 1½-inch cubes. Add meat to soy sauce mixture and toss to coat. Add carrots, onions, celery, pepper, marjoram, thyme, and wine to meat; mix gently. Cover tightly and cook in 325° oven for 3 hours. Serve with rice, noodles, or mashed potatoes.

Wild Game Recipes from the Heart of the U.P. (Michigan)

Batter Fried Venison

1 cup finely crushed crackers
1 large onion

1 venison round steak, boned,
   sliced, (¼- to ⅜-inch thick)

Run crackers through blender until finely crushed. Dice onion very fine and mix with the crackers. Using a large coated paper to work on and a meat tenderizing hammer, pound onion, and cracker mix into venison on both sides. Each piece of meat will expand almost double in size. Fry in hot oil or bacon drippings, turning once, for about 1½ minutes on each side. Serve hot as a main dish or cool for sandwiches.

What's Cook'n? (Wisconsin)

Known for its wolf and moose populations, Isle Royale National Park is a U.S. National Park in the state of Michigan off the coast of the Upper Peninsula (even though it is closer to Canada and Minnesota). Isle Royale, the largest island in Lake Superior, is over forty-five miles long and nine miles wide at its widest point. As of the 2000 census there was no permanent human population.

Beef or Venison Barbecue

1 chuck roast or venison
(about 3 pounds)
½ cup chopped onion
1 tablespoon sugar
2 teaspoons dry mustard
2 teaspoons salt
½ teaspoon pepper
2 teaspoon paprika
⅓ cup vinegar
1 tablespoon Worcestershire
1 cup ketchup
1 cup water

Trim excess fat from roast. Place roast in crockpot or Dutch oven. Combine remaining ingredients in a small bowl and mix well. Pour over meat and cover. In Dutch oven simmer for 2½ hours or until very tender. In crockpot simmer for 5–6 hours or until very tender. Remove meat and using 2 small cooking forks, shred it. Return to sauce and check periodically to see that it doesn't burn. If sauce thickens too much, add a little more liquid. Recipe is best if made at least 24 hours before serving. Freezes well. If you prefer a sweeter sauce, add sugar. Yields 12–15 servings on buns.

Cardinal Country Cooking (Wisconsin)

Down-Home Stir-Fry

½ pound venison
Milk for soaking
2 tablespoons shortening
½ cup chopped green bell
pepper
½ cup chopped onion
½ cup mushrooms
1 cup chopped broccoli
½ teaspoon salt, or to taste
½ teaspoon garlic salt
½ teaspoon seasoning salt
3 tablespoons soy sauce
1 cup chopped tomatoes

Cut venison into strips and soak in milk for 1 hour. Melt shortening in large frying pan. Heat to medium-high. Remove meat strips from milk, drain, and place in frying pan. Stir, then add peppers, onions, mushrooms, and broccoli. Stir; season with salt, garlic salt, seasoning salt, and soy sauce. Stir; add tomatoes and cook 6 more minutes, stirring often. Serve over rice.

Mrs. Boone's Wild Game Cookbook (Michigan)

Venison Mushroom Simmer

2 pounds venison steak, cut
   into thin strips
2 tablespoons shortening
1 medium onion, chopped
1 clove garlic, minced
1 (4-ounce) can mushroom
   pieces, undrained

¼ cup soy sauce
2 beef bouillon cubes
½ teaspoon salt
Dash of pepper
2½ cups water
¼ cup cornstarch

In large skillet or wok, brown meat in shortening. Add onion and garlic; cook until tender. Add mushrooms, soy sauce, bouillon, salt and pepper, and 2 cups of water. Cover and simmer until tender, 30–40 minutes. Combine cornstarch with ½ cup water and stir into meat mixture. Cook and stir until thickened. Serve over rice or noodles. Makes 6 servings.

Maple Hill Cookbook (Minnesota)

Marinade for Almost Anything

1½ cups salad oil
¾ cup soy sauce
¼ cup Worcestershire
2 tablespoons dry mustard
2½ teaspoons salt

1 tablespoon pepper
½ cup red wine vinegar
1½ teaspoons parsley
2 cloves garlic, crushed
⅓ cup lemon juice

Combine ingredients. This is good for any grilled entrée, chicken, beef, pork, even fish. May marinate overnight, refrigerate. Makes 3¼ cups.

All in Good Taste II (Wisconsin)

Poultry

© TRAVEL MICHIGAN

Dog sled racing has become a major attraction in the Great Lakes area with several major races each year, including the U.P. 200 in Marquette, Michigan, one of the top mid-distance races in the lower 48 states. Minnesota's John Beargrease Sled Dog Marathon spans 400 miles from Duluth to Grand Portage and back, the longest in the lower 48.

Chicken with Bing Cherry Sauce

2 eggs	Plain bread crumbs
2 tablespoons water	1 (5-ounce) can Durkee French
2 tablespoons oil	Fried Onions, crushed
4 whole chicken breasts	1 cup chicken broth

Mix together eggs, water, and oil. Dip chicken in bread crumbs, then in egg mixture, then in crushed onion rings. Put in glass baking dish. Add chicken broth. Bake at 350° for 1 hour.

BING CHERRY SAUCE:

1 (8-ounce) jar currant jelly
½ (16-ounce) bottle chili sauce
1 (16-ounce) can pitted black
   cherries with juice

1½ tablespoons cornstarch,
   mixed with water to dissolve

Heat all ingredients in saucepan. Serve with chicken.

The Fruit of Her Hands (Michigan)

Baked Chicken Breasts Supreme

1½ cups plain yogurt or sour
   cream
¼ cup lemon juice
½ teaspoon Worcestershire
½ teaspoon celery seed
½ teaspoon sweet paprika
1 clove garlic, minced

½ teaspoon salt (optional)
¼ teaspoon pepper
8 boneless, skinless chicken
   breast halves
2 cups finely crushed dry bread
   crumbs

In a large bowl, combine yogurt or sour cream, lemon juice, Worcestershire, celery seed, paprika, garlic, salt, and pepper. Place chicken in mixture and turn to coat. Cover and marinate overnight in refrigerator.

Remove chicken from marinade; coat each piece in crumbs. Arrange on shallow baking pan. Bake uncovered at 350° for 45 minutes or until juices run clear. Serves 6–8.

Favorite Recipes from Our Kitchens to Yours (Michigan)

Grilled Chicken Breast with Lemon Sauce and Angel Hair Pasta

I enjoyed Chef Tom D'Olivo's (Maria's Italian Cuisine, Oconomowoc) light and lovely entreé on my birthday this May on Maria's sunny outdoor patio. The flavors are perfect in this pretty dish—and it is simple to assemble and serve.

SAUCE:

4 tablespoons butter
4 tablespoons flour
3 cups chicken stock

½ cup Chablis wine
1 lemon, washed

Make sauce by melting butter in medium saucepan. Whisk in flour until blended. Let cook for 2 minutes, stirring constantly. Gradually whisk in chicken stock and wine. Grate zest from lemon; set aside. Squeeze juice from lemon (you will need about 4 tablespoons juice) and whisk into sauce. Cook over medium-high heat, stirring constantly until thickened, about 3 minutes. Whisk in zest at end of cooking; set aside.

CHICKEN BREAST:

4 chicken breast halves (4 ounces each), skinned, ¼-inch thick, boned and pounded

Grill chicken breasts over hot coals or on high setting of gas grill, about 3 minutes per side or until juices run clear. Remove to warm serving plate.

PASTA:

4 tablespoons minced
shallots (about 2 large)
2 tablespoons butter

8 ounces angel hair pasta,
cooked and drained

Sauté shallots and butter together in small skillet until shallots are transparent, about 2 minutes. Mix into cooked pasta. Divide pasta and chicken breasts among four serving plates. Pour ¼ of sauce over each chicken breast and drizzle over pasta. Makes 4 servings.

Encore Wisconsin (Wisconsin)

Forgotten Chicken

1 cup white rice (not instant)
1 (10¾-ounce) can cream of
  mushroom soup
1 (10¾-ounce) can cream of
  celery soup
1 cup hot water
4–6 pieces boneless, skinless
  chicken breasts
1 envelope dried onion soup

In a greased (bottom and sides) 9x13-inch pan place raw rice. Combine soups with water. Cover rice with mixture. Place chicken on top of soup. Sprinkle chicken with dried onion soup. Cover with foil (no peeking). Bake at 325° for 2 hours. Serves 4.

The Manor Cookbook (Michigan)

Stir-Fried Chicken

4 boneless, skinless chicken
  breasts
3 carrots, chopped
2 potatoes, peeled, chopped
1 tablespoon olive oil
2 teaspoons crushed garlic
½ small red onion, sliced, or
  1 bunch green onions,
  chopped
1 cup sliced button mushrooms
½ cup marsala
2 teaspoons honey
1 tablespoon jalapeño mustard
  or stone-ground mustard
½ teaspoon salt
½ teaspoon pepper

Rinse chicken and pat dry. Cut into ½-inch-wide strips. Boil carrots and potatoes in water to cover in a saucepan for 4–5 minutes. Drain; set aside. Heat olive oil and garlic in a sauté pan. Add chicken. Stir-fry over medium to medium-high heat until chicken begins to brown. Add onion, mushrooms, carrots, and potatoes, and mix well. Add wine. Reduce heat to medium-low. Simmer 3–5 minutes. Stir in a mixture of honey and mustard. Sprinkle with salt and pepper. Serve with pita bread or a salad. Yields 4–6 servings.

The Flavors of Mackinac (Michigan)

Spicy Tandoori

1 pound skinless, boneless
  chicken breasts
1 pound skinless, boneless
  chicken thighs
½ cup plain low-fat yogurt
Juice and grated peel of 1
  lemon
2 teaspoons each: paprika,
  ground cumin, and coriander

1 teaspoon freshly ground
  pepper
½ teaspoon pumpkin pie spice
½ teaspoon allspice
 Pinch of cayenne pepper, or to
  taste

With sharp knife, make several cuts into meat. Combine remaining ingredients, and pour over chicken in glass or plastic bowl and refrigerate all day, or overnight, turning occasionally.

Remove chicken, and discard marinade. Grill chicken about 6 inches from charcoal, turning each piece frequently, 30–40 minutes, until golden brown. Serves 6.

The Spice of Life Cookbook (Michigan)

Chicken Breasts in Wine

This is delicious served with wild rice. The sauce may be placed in a dish and served with the meal.

6 chicken breasts
1 cup rosé wine
¼ cup soy sauce
¼ cup vegetable oil
1 teaspoon garlic salt

3 tablespoons water
¼ teaspoon oregano
¼ teaspoon marjoram
1 teaspoon ginger
2 tablespoons brown sugar

Brown chicken breasts slightly. Place in baking dish. Mix rest of ingredients and pour over chicken breasts. Cover with foil and bake for 1½ hours at 375°. Remove foil the last half hour. Turn breasts once during baking.

If you like to do things well in advance of company, skip the pre-browning and pour sauce over chicken and chill for several hours in the refrigerator. Serves 6.

A Thyme for All Seasons (Minnesota)

Cheesy Tomato Basil Chicken Breasts

SAUCE:

3 tablespoons butter
2 cups cubed tomatoes
⅓ cup chopped onion
1 (6-ounce) can tomato paste
1 tablespoon basil leaves

½ teaspoon salt
¼ teaspoon pepper
2 teaspoons minced fresh garlic
3 whole chicken breasts,
　skinned, halved

Heat oven to 350°. In 9x13-inch baking pan, melt butter in oven. Meanwhile, stir together remaining Sauce ingredients; set aside. Place chicken in baking pan, turning to coat with butter. Spoon Sauce mixture over chicken. Bake for 30–40 minutes or till chicken is no longer pink.

TOPPING:

1 cup fresh bread crumbs
¼ cup chopped fresh parsley
2 tablespoons butter, melted

6 ounces mozzarella cheese,
　cut into strips

Combine all ingredients except cheese. Place cheese strips over chicken; sprinkle with Topping mixture. Continue baking 5–10 minutes, or till chicken is fork tender and bread crumbs are browned.

Blissfield Preschool Cookbook (Michigan)

Chicken Minnetonka

Elegant and easy.

2 whole chicken breasts, halved, skinned and boned
¼ cup butter
1 teaspoon dried rosemary, crushed

2 teaspoons chopped chives
¼ teaspoon pepper
1 (8-ounce) can refrigerated crescent rolls

SAUCE:

1 tablespoon flour
1 (4-ounce) can sliced mushrooms

¼–⅓ cup dry white wine
½ cup dairy sour cream

Heat oven to 375°. In skillet, sauté chicken breasts in butter with seasonings until almost done. Separate dough into 8 triangles. Place 4 triangles on large cookie sheet. Put one piece of chicken on each triangle. Put other triangles on top of chicken and seal edges. Bake about 25 minutes until golden brown.

To make sauce, add flour to drippings in skillet; bring to a boil over medium heat. Add mushroom liquid, wine and sour cream, stirring constantly. Stir in mushrooms; heat through. Serve sauce with baked chicken triangles. Serves 4.

From Minnesota: More Than a Cookbook (Minnesota)

Henry Wadsworth Longfellow wrote the epic poem "The Song of Hiawatha" in 1855, which referred to Minnesota and landmarks of the area such as Lake Minnetonka and Minnehaha Falls. This brought national interest to the area near Minneapolis. In the poem, Hiawatha "heard the Falls of Minnehaha calling to him through the silence."

Touch of Italy Chicken

4 chicken breasts, skinned
  and boned
Italian seasoning
Salt and pepper
½ (10-ounce) package fresh
  spinach, cooked and drained
Provolone cheese

4 teaspoons plus ½ cup (1 stick)
  butter, divided
2 eggs
2½ cups bread crumbs
1 teaspoon Italian seasoning
1 teaspoon paprika

Wash chicken breasts; place between wax paper and pound thin. Sprinkle breasts with Italian seasoning, salt and pepper. Place ¹/₄ of spinach down the center of each breast. Top with a finger of provolone cheese. Top with one teaspoon butter. Fold chicken like an envelope, encasing spinach, cheese and butter.

    Beat eggs. Combine bread crumbs, Italian seasoning and paprika and mix well. Dip chicken in egg, then in bread crumbs, holding so envelopes don't unfold. Let dry in refrigerator for 15 minutes then re-dip in egg and crumbs. (You can bake at this time or hold them in the refrigerator for several hours.) When ready to bake, melt the stick of butter and roll the chicken in the butter, turning to coat. Place in a shallow baking dish and pour any remaining butter over the chicken. Bake at 375° for 25–30 minutes, turning once. Make a small cut in the chicken to check for doneness (no pink!) Makes 4 servings.

Apples, Brie & Chocolate (Wisconsin)

WWW.THEHOUSEONTHEROCK.COM

The world-famous House on the Rock in Spring Green, Wisconsin, may well be Wisconsin's most well known attraction. Designed by Alex Jordan, the house features "The Infinity Room" that projects 218 feet out over the scenic Wyoming Valley. With 3264 windows, there is indeed no other room like it in the world.

Cherry-Orange Chicken

2 (3-pound) fryers or chicken
  breasts
4 tablespoons margarine,
  melted
1 cup brown sugar
½ teaspoon orange peel
¼ teaspoon ground ginger
½ cup orange juice
1 (16-ounce) can dark sweet
  cherries, drained

Cut up and place chicken in 9x13-inch baking pan. Pour margarine over chicken. Mix and pour next 4 ingredients over chicken. Bake at 350° for 45 minutes. Remove from oven. Top with cherries. Bake for 30 minutes longer till tender and golden. Serves 6.

Bringing Grand Tastes to Grand Traverse (Michigan)

French Garlic Chicken

The French love garlic! Although the number of cloves may appear overwhelming at first, the results are magnifique!

2 large heads garlic (20–25
  cloves)
1½ cups chicken stock
2 tablespoons butter
1 tablespoon oil
3½–4 pounds chicken parts
1 lemon, peeled, thinly sliced
2 tablespoons flour
½ cup dry white wine
Salt and pepper to taste

Preheat oven to 350°. Separate cloves of garlic, set in a saucepan, cover with water, simmer 5 minutes. Drain and cover with cold water. Discard water and peel cloves. Simmer poached, peeled garlic cloves, partially covered, in stock 30 minutes. In a heavy skillet, melt butter and oil. When hot, brown chicken till golden. Transfer to a 9x13-inch pan and cover with garlic cloves (save stock) and lemon slices. Prepare sauce in skillet with flour, garlic stock, and wine. Skim fat, if necessary, and pour sauce over chicken. Cover with foil and bake 45–55 minutes. Serve with French bread to spread with poached garlic. Make be made ahead and reheated. Serves 4–6.

Cranbrook Reflections (Michigan)

Chicken Enchiladas

SAUCE:

2 (10¾-ounce) cans cream of
   chicken soup
1 cup sour cream

¼ teaspoon garlic salt
2 (4-ounce) cans chopped green
   chiles

Mix soup, sour cream, garlic salt, and chiles.

FILLING:

3 cups grated Cheddar or
   longhorn cheese
3 cups chopped cooked chicken

½ cup chopped green onions
12 flour tortillas

Combine cheese, chicken, onions, and about ⅓ of Sauce mixture; mix until moist. Place ½ cup of Filling mixture in center of each tortilla. Spread mixture over tortilla and roll up. Place seam side down, in baking dish. Pour remaining Sauce over rolled enchiladas, covering well. Bake 30 minutes at 350° until melted thoroughly. Serves 8.

a-MAIZE-ing Tailgating (Michigan)

One-Pot Chicken Dinner

Michigan is gorgeous, and cooking on the shores of Lake Superior is out of this world. One-pot meals, such as the one below, make it very easy. And then there is dessert. Bake a frozen blueberry pie in a Coleman oven on the shores of Lake Superior in a violent rain and windstorm, with pants rolled up, no shoes, tents going down on all sides, a martini in one hand and a pot holder in the other. Now that's good eating!

1 (50-ounce) can cooked
   whole chicken
Canned vegetables as desired,
   such as carrots, potatoes,
   green beans, or onions

2 cups chicken broth
Salt and pepper to taste
1 (20-ounce) package baking
   mix

Remove chicken from bones. Place chicken and can liquids in a 4-quart kettle. Add canned vegetables, chicken broth, salt and pepper. Heat chicken mixture. Prepare dumplings using directions on package of baking mix. Add dumplings to chicken and simmer until dumplings are cooked through. Serves about 8.

Between the Lakes (Michigan)

Chicken Salad Pockets

2 cups cubed cooked chicken breasts
1 medium cucumber, seeded, chopped
1 medium tomato, seeded, chopped
3 green onions, thinly sliced
¼ cup lemon juice
3 tablespoons canola oil
2 cloves garlic, peeled, minced
1 teaspoon sugar
½–1 teaspoon dried basil
4 (6-inch) pita breads, halved
2 cups shredded red leaf lettuce or romaine lettuce

In bowl, combine cubed chicken with cuke, tomato, and green onions. In a small bowl, combine lemon juice with oil, garlic, sugar, and basil. Fill each pita half with ½ cup shredded lettuce, then fill with ½ cup chicken salad mixture. Makes 4.

Fifty Nifty ... Cool Summer Recipes (Michigan)

Broccoli and Chicken Hot Dish

1 large package broccoli
1 chicken, cooked, boned, and cut in pieces
1 can cream of mushroom soup
1 can cream of chicken soup
½ cup mayonnaise
1 teaspoon lemon juice
½ cup grated Cheddar cheese
1 small can shoestring potatoes

Layer broccoli and chicken in 9x13-inch pan. Mix soups, mayonnaise, and lemon juice and pour over. Sprinkle cheese on top. Bake at 350° for one hour. When nearly done, top with shoestring potatoes. Bake a few minutes more to heat.

Our Favorite Recipes/Aurdal Lutheran Church (Minnesota)

Creamed Chicken with Cranberry Rollups

½ cup diced carrots
¼ cup diced celery
¼ cup diced white onion
Chicken broth
1½ cups cooked, diced chicken
½ cup water chestnuts

3 cups cream of chicken
 soup (or 1 can soup plus
 1 soup can of milk)
½ cup fresh snow peas
½ cup sliced fresh mushrooms
⅛ teaspoon pepper

Sauté carrots, celery, and onion in small amount of chicken broth, water or white wine, until tender. Add chicken, and remaining ingredients. Pour into a 3-quart casserole dish.

TOPPING:

2 cups biscuit mix
½ cup milk

1 (8-ounce) can whole berry
 cranberry sauce (1 cup)

Mix baking mix and milk until soft dough forms; beat 30 seconds. Turn onto cloth-covered surface well floured with baking mix; knead 10 times. Roll dough into rectangle, 12x9-inches; spread with cranberry sauce. Roll up, beginning at 12-inch side. Cut into 1-inch slices. Arrange slices so swirls show onto hot chicken mixture. Bake at 425° for 20–25 minutes or until rollups are golden brown.

Four Seasons at Hawks Inn (Wisconsin)

Wisconsin produces nearly one-third of the nation's crop of cranberries, and leads the nation in the production of cranberry juice. Harvest in late September attracts tens of thousands to "Cranberry Country."

Savory Chicken Scallop

4 cups diced cooked chicken
  (turkey may be used)
3 cups fine, soft bread crumbs
1½ cups cooked rice
¾ cup chopped onion
¾ cup diced celery
1 small jar (⅓ cup) pimento,
  chopped

¾ teaspoon salt
¾ teaspoon poultry seasoning
1½ cups broth (chicken
  bouillon may be used)
1½ cups milk
4 eggs, slightly beaten

Combine all ingredients, except mushroom sauce in large bowl. Spoon into buttered 9x13-inch baking dish. Bake in 350° oven for 50–55 minutes or until knife inserted comes out clean. Cut into squares and serve with Creamy Mushroom Sauce. Makes 12 servings.

CREAMY MUSHROOM SAUCE:

1 can condensed cream of
  mushroom soup
¼ cup milk

1 cup diary sour cream
A bit of onion

Combine ingredients in saucepan and heat slowly stirring well. Do not boil.

Bethany Lutheran Church Celebrating 110 Years (Minnesota)

Chicken Curry Hot Dish

2 (8-ounce) packages chopped
  broccoli, cooked and drained
5 cups diced chicken
2 teaspoons lemon juice
2 cans cream of chicken soup
½ cup milk
¾ cup mayonnaise

½ teaspoon curry powder
  (optional)
Mild or sharp Cheddar cheese
8 ounces herb stuffing mix
½ cup melted butter or
  margarine

Put cooked broccoli in a greased baking dish. Top with chicken; sprinkle with lemon juice and dot with butter. Cover with chicken soup mixed with milk, mayonnaise and curry powder. Top with shredded mild or sharp Cheddar cheese. Cover with stuffing mix which has been mixed with the melted butter. Bake at 350° for 30–45 minutes.

Sharing our Best to Help the Rest (Minnesota)

Barbecue Chicken Wings

20–24 chicken wings

Disjoint wings; save the tips for soup. Push meat to one end of wing to form a small drumstick (or can just buy drummettes).

BATTER:
1 cup cornstarch
¼ cup milk
2 eggs

½ teaspoon salt
½ teaspoon Ac'cent or MSG
Dash of garlic salt

SAUCE:
¾ cup sugar
¾ cup water
½ cup vinegar

1 tablespoon soy sauce
1 tablespoon ketchup

Dip chicken wings in Batter mixture, and deep-fry until golden brown. Remove from oil; place on paper towels to drain. Then dip in Sauce; place on cookie sheet. Bake at 350° for 30 minutes, basting often with Sauce.

Dell & Barry's Holiday Delights for All Seasons (Michigan)

Picnic Drumsticks

1½ cups plain yogurt
⅓ cup lemon juice
6 cloves garlic, minced
1 teaspoon salt, divided
1 teaspoon cayenne pepper, divided
⅓ cup Mucky Duck mustard (sweet and tangy)

30 drumsticks, skinned (about 6 pounds)
3 cups finely crushed saltine crackers
2 tablespoons oregano
1 tablespoon paprika
6 tablespoons unsalted butter, melted

Combine yogurt, lemon juice, garlic, $1/2$ teaspoon salt, $1/2$ teaspoon cayenne, and mustard in medium bowl; mix well. Spoon unto 2 shallow dishes. Rinse drumsticks; pat dry. Arrange in prepared dishes, turning to coat well. Marinate, covered, in refrigerator 3 hours to overnight.

Combine cracker crumbs, oregano, paprika, remaining $1/2$ teaspoon salt, and cayenne pepper in paper or plastic bag. Add drumsticks several at a time, shaking to coat with crumb mixture. Arrange in foil-lined baking pans; drizzle with butter. Bake at 375° for about 45 minutes, or till golden brown. Serve hot or at room temperature.

Note: Chicken can be wrapped in foil and refrigerated after cooking for next-day picnic or tailgate party.

Mucky Duck Mustard Cookbook (Michigan)

 With more than 11,000 inland lakes and 36,000 miles of rivers and streams, you can stand anywhere in Michigan, and you are never more than six miles from a lake or stream. And you're always within 85 miles of a Great Lake.

Spring Luncheon Hot Dish

2 cans cream of mushroom
  soup
2 cans cream of chicken soup
2 (15-ounce) cans evaporated
  milk
2 small packages slivered
  almonds

2 small cans mushrooms
2 small jars pimento, cut up
2 cups celery, cut up
4 cups cooked and boned
  turkey
4 cups chow mein noodles
  (reserve 1 cup for top)

Mix all ingredients; cover with reserved one cup noodles. Spoon into greased casserole dish. Bake for one hour at 350°. Serves 10.

Great Cooks of Zion Church (Minnesota)

Turkey Hash

One of the best reasons to have some turkey left over! Good for brunch with poached eggs perched on top, or Sunday supper with honeyed carrots and a green salad.

2 cups diced or ground cooked
  turkey
1 raw or cooked potato, diced
¼ cup finely chopped onion
2–3 tablespoons finely
  chopped green bell pepper
1 good pinch poultry seasoning

Salt to taste
Generous grinding of black
  pepper
½ cup good, rich turkey or
  chicken broth
¼ cup heavy cream
2 tablespoons butter

Toss together first 7 ingredients*. Stir in broth and cream. Over medium-high heat, melt butter in a heavy, 10-inch skillet until sizzling. Add hash, spreading out evenly in pan. Continue to cook over medium-high heat, without stirring, 5–10 minutes or until liquid has evaporated and hash is browning nicely on bottom. Turn hash, scraping pan well, then spread out evenly. Reduce heat to medium, and cook another 5 minutes or until crusty on bottom.

To serve, be sure to include all of those tasty, browned bits from the bottom of the pan . . . the best part! Serves 2.

*Note: If you have any left-over stuffing, you can add it to the hash mixture.

Hollyhocks & Radishes (Michigan)

Minnesota Turkey Tender

**10 slices cooked or baked
turkey breast, warm
1 (6-ounce) box chicken
flavored stuffing mix
½ cup cooked wild rice
⅔ cup roasted sunflower
seeds**

**½ cup finely chopped celery
1 cup water
2 teaspoons fresh parsley
1 can cream of chicken soup
¼ cup milk
1 (2-ounce) jar chopped
pimento**

Cover the bottom of a greased 9x13-inch baking dish with turkey slices. In a medium bowl, combine the stuffing mix, rice, and sunflower seeds, mixing well. In a saucepan, combine the celery and water and simmer for 5 minutes. Add to the stuffing mixture and stir well with a fork. Spread over the turkey. Combine parsley, soup, milk, and pimento and blend. Pour over turkey and stuffing. Bake at 350° for 20 minutes. Makes 6 servings.

Recipes from Minnesota with Love (Minnesota)

Grilled Turkey Tenderloins

**¼ cup soy sauce
¼ cup oil
¼ cup sherry
2 tablespoons lemon juice
2 tablespoons dehydrated
onion**

**¼ teaspoon ginger
Dash of pepper
Dash of garlic salt
1 pound turkey tenderloins,
1-inch thick**

Mix first 8 ingredients; add turkey and coat. Marinate overnight. Grill 6–8 minutes per side. Serves 4.

Bringing Grand Taste to Grand Traverse (Michigan)

Morel-Stuffed Grouse

Chicken breasts may be used in place of grouse.

4 shallots, thinly sliced
2 tablespoons butter, divided
3 cups chopped fresh morel mushrooms
¾ cup white wine, divided
1–2 tablespoons chopped fresh thyme, divided
½ cup whipping cream, divided

3 tablespoons fresh bread crumbs
Salt and white pepper to taste
4 skinless, boneless grouse (or chicken) breasts
1 tablespoon vegetable oil
Worcestershire
Cornstarch slurry* (optional)

Using a medium-size sauté pan, sweat shallots in 1 tablespoon butter. Add mushrooms and sauté briefly. Add 2 tablespoons wine and reduce by half. Add 2 teaspoons thyme leaves and 2 tablespoons cream and simmer a few minutes. Add bread crumbs and combine thoroughly. Add salt and pepper to taste.

Prepare grouse (or chicken) breasts by placing between sheets of plastic wrap and flattening gradually and uniformly with smooth side of meat mallet, taking care not to create holes or overly thin areas.

Place a small mound of mushroom mixture on each breast and roll, gently but firmly, tucking seam under. Repeat with remaining breasts. (You may prefer to secure rolls with skewers or large toothpicks—just don't forget to remove them before serving.)

Heat remaining butter and 1 tablespoon oil in a large, heavy sauté pan. Brown rolled breasts, turning to reach all areas. Remove breasts from pan and set aside. Add remaining white wine to pan and simmer, reducing by half. Add remaining cream and simmer several minutes. Return breasts to pan along with any juices that have accumulated. Simmer gently until grouse is cooked through. Correct sauce seasonings with salt, pepper, and Worcestershire. Thicken sauce with cornstarch slurry (*cornstarch mixed with a little water), if necessary, but remove breasts to a warm serving plate first. Yields 4 servings.

The Rustic Gourmet (Michigan)

Sautéed Duck Breasts

Carve the breasts from 4 mallards at the time they are shot. This eliminates plucking the birds and also conserves freezer space. Defrost breasts in a plastic bag, saving any juice that accumulates.

¼ **pound butter**	**4 tablespoons chopped parsley**
2 cloves garlic, minced	**4 tablespoons currant jelly**
8 duck breasts	**1 tablespoon Worcestershire**
Rind of 1 orange, cut in julienne	**Salt and pepper to taste**
strips, poached 2 minutes	**7 ounces Marsala**

In a large skillet, melt butter. Add minced garlic. When butter is bubbling, add duck breasts, and sauté them for 1 minute on each side. Remove breasts to a warm platter. Add to the butter in skillet the juices from defrosted breasts, poached orange rind, chopped parsley, currant jelly, Worcestershire, salt and pepper to taste, and Marsala. Blend this mixture well, then return breasts to sauce and simmer gently 2 more minutes. The breasts should be pink inside. Serve breasts with wild rice and any remaining sauce.

Mrs. Boone's Wild Game Cookbook (Michigan)

Surveys indicate that about half of all fishing in the Great Lakes region is done using a boat. The Great Lakes states have about 3.7 million registered recreational boats, or about a third of the nation's total. Minnesota ranks first nationally in the sales of fishing licenses per capita. But you don't have to own a boat! You can cast off docks and piers, or you can charter boats and captains in many areas for several hours or several days to do "big lake" fishing in the open waters of the Great Lakes.

A Few Facts About the Great Lakes

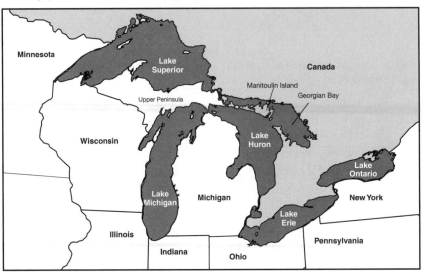

The Great Lakes are a collection of freshwater lakes located in eastern North America, on the Canada-United States border. The Great Lakes contain about one-fifth of all the freshwater on the planet and 95% of our nation's supply of fresh water. (School kids remember the names of the lakes by spelling "HOMES.")

Lake Superior is the largest of the Great Lakes in surface area and volume. Lake Superior could contain all the water in the other Great Lakes plus three more lakes the size of Lake Erie. It is particularly known for its clear, cold water with an average summer temperature of 40° F. Average depth is 483 feet, while the maximum depth is 1,332 feet.

Lake Huron is the second largest Great Lake by surface area (and third largest by volume). It has the longest shoreline of the Great Lakes, counting the shorelines of its 30,000 islands, and has the largest island in any lake in the world, Manitoulin Island (1,223 sq. miles). The average depth is 195 feet, and its deepest point is 750 feet. Lake Huron contains Georgian Bay, a bay so large that it is nicknamed "the Sixth Great Lake." Early explorers listed it as a separate lake because it is nearly separated from the rest of Lake Huron by Manitoulin Island and Bruce Peninsula.

Lake Michigan is the only Great Lake located entirely within the United States, making it the largest body of freshwater in the nation. The average depth is 279 feet, and its deepest point is 925 feet. It is the third largest Great Lake by surface area (and second largest by volume). The world's largest freshwater dunes line the lakeshore and are visited by millions of people annually who enjoy the numerous state and national parks as well as local beaches.

Lake Erie is the fourth largest of the Great Lakes in surface area and the smallest by volume. Lake Erie is also the southernmost, shallowest, and warmest of the Great Lakes. It has an average depth of 62 feet and a maximum depth of 210 feet. Because Lake Erie is the warmest, it is the most biologically productive of the Great Lakes, and its fisheries are widely considered the best in the world.

Lake Ontario is the smallest of the Great Lakes in surface area (fourth largest in volume). Its average depth, at 283 feet, is second only to Lake Superior, and its deepest point is 802 feet. Lake Ontario is the easternmost Great Lake, and the only one that does not border the state of Michigan. Lake Ontario lies 325 feet below Lake Erie, at the base of Niagara Falls.

Seafood

The Mississippi River begins its 2,300-mile journey to the Gulf of Mexico at the edge of a small glacial lake in northwestern Minnesota, Lake Itasca. This scenic area of Minnesota has remained relatively unchanged from its natural state. Most of the area has a heavy growth of timber that includes virgin red pine, Minnesota's state tree.

Lake Michigan Fish Boil

Share your catch with a crowd.

1–2 new potatoes per person
2 small onions per person
1 cup uniodized salt, divided

½ pound lake fish per person,
skinned, filleted, cut in 2-inch
chunks

Use a fish boil cooker or large pot with basket that allows room beneath the basket for potatoes and onions. Put potatoes and onions in water in bottom of cooker. Water should cover the bottom of the basket. Bring to a boil; add ½ cup salt. Bring again to a boil for 12 minutes. Add fish to basket; water should cover fish. Bring to a boil; add ½ cup more salt. Cook 15–18 minutes or till fish flakes; drain. Serve with drawn butter. Serves 10–12.

Variations: Steelhead, trout, Chinook or coho may be used.

Some Enchanted Eating (Michigan)

Beer Batter Fish

1 pound fish fillets
½ cup Mix
⅓ cup lemon juice

⅔ cup beer
1 cup vegetable oil

MIX:
1½ cups unsifted flour
**2¼ teaspoons baking
   powder**

¾ teaspoon baking soda
1½ teaspoons salt

Place fish on paper towels; pat dry. Coat fish with ½ cup Mix. In large bowl, combine remaining mixture, lemon juice, and beer (this will foam). Stir until consistency of pancake batter. In large skillet, heat oil over medium heat. Dip fish into batter; fry until golden brown on both sides. Drain on paper towels.

Dr. Martin Luther Church 100th Anniversary Cookbook (Wisconsin)

Baked Lutefisk

Soak 5 pounds of lutefisk in cold water for one hour; drain well. Preheat oven to 400°. Put lutefisk in an enamel roaster (others will stain) with rack in the bottom. Salt slightly. Do not add water; it will steam in its own juices. Cover roaster with heavy foil and then put the roaster cover on. Place in preheated oven for 20 minutes. If it is fork tender, it is done, and 20 minutes usually does it. Serves 4–5. Serve with melted butter or Creamy White Sauce.

CREAMY WHITE SAUCE:

5 tablespoons butter
5 tablespoons flour
2½ cups milk
2½ cups half-and-half
1 teaspoon salt

Melt butter and add flour. Stir until well blended. Add milk and half-and-half gradually. Cook in double boiler, about 10 minutes, or until thick, stirring constantly.

Red Oak Grove Lutheran Church Family Cookbook (Minnesota)

Oven-Fried Fish Sticks

1 pound cod
¼ cup cornmeal
¼ cup seasoned dry bread crumbs
½ cup skim milk
Vegetable oil cooking spray
⅓ cup low-fat mayonnaise
1 teaspoon lemon juice
2 tablespoons sweet pickle relish

Move oven rack to position slightly above middle of oven. Heat oven to 500°. Cut cod into 1x3-inch pieces. Mix cornmeal and bread crumbs together in small dish. Dip fish into milk, then coat with cornmeal-bread crumb mixture. Place in ungreased baking pan. Spray vegetable oil cooking spray over fish. Bake uncovered about 10 minutes or until fish flakes easily with a fork. In a small bowl, mix mayonnaise, lemon juice, and pickle relish. Refrigerate until ready to serve with fish. Makes 4 servings.

Heart Smart Kids Cookbook (Michigan)

Grilled Smoked Salmon with Fresh Dill Caper Mustard

Do try flavoring this grilled salmon with pre-soaked hardwood chips. Somehow the wood smoke adds heartiness to an otherwise delicate salmon. Chef/owner Jim Jensen (The Vintage, Wisconsin Rapids) suggests that this dish could be used as an entreé as well as an appetizer.

GRILLED SALMON:

4 salmon steaks or fillets (4 ounces each)
½ teaspoon salt or to taste
¼ teaspoon freshly ground black pepper

5 or 6 large hardwood chips, soaked in water for 10 minutes

Prepare grill to a medium temperature. Place pre-soaked wood chips on top of hot coals in the center of grill. Sprinkle surface of fillets lightly with salt and pepper, if desired and spray surfaces with vegetable oil spray. Place salmon on grill around edge of wood chips. Cover, close vents to avoid flame-ups, and grill without turning until cooked, about 8–9 minutes. Flesh should be opaque throughout.

DILL CAPER MUSTARD:

½ cup Dijon-style mustard
½ cup olive oil
1 tablespoon capers
2 tablespoons fresh dill, minced or 1 tablespoon dried dill weed

3 small cloves minced garlic
⅛ teaspoon freshly ground black pepper
Fresh lemon slices, for garnish
Fresh sprigs of dill, for garnish

While salmon cooks, make sauce by whisking mustard in small bowl. Slowly whisk in oil in a thin stream until oil is all absorbed in the emulsion. Mix in capers, dill weed, garlic, and pepper. Arrange salmon on plate, serve with a dollop (2 tablespoons) of Dill Caper Mustard and garnish with lemon slices or fresh sprigs of dill, if desired.

Encore Wisconsin (Wisconsin)

Grilled Salmon with Pineapple Salsa

PINEAPPLE SALSA:

2 cups coarsely chopped fresh pineapple
½ cup chopped red sweet pepper
¼ cup finely chopped red onion
2 tablespoons lime juice
1 small fresh jalapeño pepper, seeded, finely chopped
1 tablespoon snipped fresh chives
1 tablespoon honey

In medium bowl, combine chopped pineapple, red pepper, red onion, lime juice, jalapeño, snipped chives, and honey; set aside.

SALMON:

1 pound fresh skinless salmon fillets, 1 inch thick
1 tablespoon lime juice
¼ teaspoon ground cumin
Salt and pepper

Rinse salmon; pat dry. Brush both sides with lime juice; sprinkle with cumin, salt and pepper. Heat grill to medium heat; brush grill rack with oil. Grill salmon 8–12 minutes, turning once during grilling. Cut salmon into 4 pieces. Serve topped with Pineapple Salsa. Serves 4.

Fifty Nifty . . . Cool Summer Recipes (Michigan)

Zesty Grilled Tuna

This is perfect for those who don't like their fish too "fishy."

3 tablespoons soy sauce
3 tablespoons orange juice
1 tablespoon vegetable oil
2 tablespoons ketchup
¾ teaspoon chopped fresh parsley
½ shallot, chopped
1 clove garlic, minced
1 teaspoon lemon juice
½ teaspoon oregano
½ teaspoon pepper
1 pound tuna or swordfish fillets

Combine soy sauce, orange juice, oil, ketchup, parsley, shallot, garlic, lemon juice, oregano, and pepper in a large bowl; mix well. Add fish. Marinate at room temperature 1 hour. Grill until fish tests done. Yields 4 servings.

Dawn to Dusk (Michigan)

Open Fire Walleye Fish Fry

Here's one for walleye that's a bit different. It works best over an open fire. I call it "speed cooking." Four or five hungry campers standing around waiting to eat can have an adverse effect on camp morale.

**½ cup Jiffy, Bisquick, or
    pancake mix
1 teaspoon Italian seasoning
1 teaspoon poultry seasoning**

**1 egg
1½ cups club soda or beer
2 walleye fish fillets
Flour**

Combine all ingredients, except walleye and flour, for batter. This batter must be thin. Add milk or more club soda (or beer) until the consistency of a thin pancake batter. Roll fillets in flour; dip in batter, and fry in deep fat or oil until brown at the edges. Flip and cook until done. Serves 4.

Mrs. Boone's Wild Game Cookbook (Michigan)

Red Snapper à la Greektown

Both ancient and modern Greeks have been devoted to the sea. Some of the favorite fish of the Greeks are, unfortunately, not available in this country. However, we do have in America an abundance of fish to keep alive the recipes and traditions of Greek fish cookery.

**4 (1-pound) whole red snapper
Olive oil
3 teaspoons salt**

**2 teaspoons oregano
½ teaspoon black pepper
4 cloves finely chopped garlic**

Wash fish, drain, and pat dry. Brush olive oil on all parts of fish; set aside. In a bowl, mix all spices including garlic. Sprinkle spices all over fish and in cavity. Let stand 30 minutes before broiling. Broil (or charbroil) 20 minutes, or till brown and flaky.

LEMON OIL SAUCE:
**1 cup olive oil
½ cup lemon juice**

**¼ cup chopped parsley
½ teaspoon salt**

Mix all ingredients thoroughly in a saucepan and heat slowly. Spoon sauce over broiled fish. Serve with rice pilaf and a glass of dry white wine. Makes 4 servings.

Opaa! Greek Cooking Detroit Style (Michigan)

Stuffed Scrod

CRABMEAT STUFFING:

4 tablespoons finely chopped onion

2 sticks butter or margarine, melted

8 ounces crabmeat (Maryland lump or crab leg)

6 ounces white cream sauce

3 ounces plain bread crumbs

Sauté onion in butter or margarine until translucent in color. Let cool and mix with crabmeat, cream sauce, and bread crumbs; set aside.

8-ounces scrod fillets
Paprika and salt to taste
Oil

Lemon wedges
Parsley

Split fillets in half, starting at thickest end and leaving attached on one side. Place 2 ounces Crabmeat Stuffing on each scrod fillet. Roll lightly to shape and place on broiler pan. Dust with paprika, sprinkle with salt, and brush with oil. Place under broiler and cook 6–10 minutes or until fish flakes easily. Garnish with lemon wedges and parsley, and serve with tartar sauce.

Renaissance Cuisine (Michigan)

WWW.MICHIGAN.ORG

It is estimated that there have been well over 4,000 shipwrecks on the Great Lakes since 1679. Lake Superior's beautiful, yet unrelenting fury has earned her the reputation of being the most treacherous of the Great Lakes. Lake Superior was the location of the famous November 10, 1975 shipwreck of the *Edmund Fitzgerald*. This large cargo ship sank during an intense storm on a regular trip from Superior, Wisconsin, to Detroit, Michigan, carrying 26,000 tons of iron ore. The bell of the *Edmund Fitzgerald* is displayed in the Great Lakes Shipwreck Museum (shown above) as a memorial to her lost crew. The museum is the only one of its kind dedicated to the perils of maritime transport on the Great Lakes. It is fittingly located at Whitefish Point, Michigan, site of the oldest active lighthouse on Lake Superior. Artifacts and exhibits tell stories of sailors and ships who braved the waters of Superior and those who were lost to her menacing waves.

Swordfish Picata

**2 pounds fresh skinless
  swordfish**
½ cup peanut oil
Salt to season
2 cups flour for dusting
2 fresh lemons

½ cup dry sack sherry
**1½ cups thinly sliced fresh
  mushrooms**
**1½ tablespoons chopped
  parsley for garnish**

Slice swordfish into medallions 3 inches in diameter and approximately ¼-inch thick (12 pieces in all). Heat peanut oil in Teflon coated sauté pan; add salt to season. Dust swordfish medallions lightly with flour and place in hot oil. Allow to sauté until golden in color. Turn over medallions and cook until golden in color. Add juice of lemons and sherry.

Remove swordfish medallions from sauté pan and place 3 medallions on each plate. Add mushroom slices to sauté pan; mix with sherry and lemon sauce for 1 minute. Ladle mushroom sauce evenly over all 4 entrées using all the sauce. Sprinkle with chopped parsley. Serve immediately. Yields 4 servings.

The Simply Great Cookbook II (Michigan)

Tempura-Fried Soft-Shell Crab

2 cups Japanese rice flour
½ teaspoon salt
¾ teaspoon cayenne pepper
2 cups water

12 live soft-shell crabs (frozen crabs, if out of season)
Peanut oil
Chopped parsley

In a bowl, mix together rice flour, salt, and cayenne pepper. With a wire whisk, slowly stir water into mixture until batter is smooth and has the consistency of heavy cream. Add more flour or more water if necessary. Set aside.

Clean crabs; rinse them well. Then with a pair of scissors, snip the face off just behind the eyes. Lift up the back shell at this point and remove it with the gills. Reserve shells.*

With a spoon, clean out the mustard-colored bile sac and again rinse crab well. Place a damp cloth over crabs and refrigerate till ready to fry.

In a large pot, heat enough oil to cover crabs, about $1\frac{1}{2}$ inches deep, to 375°. Gently dip each crab in tempura batter and place in hot oil, top side down. Cook 2 minutes, flip over and cook another minute. Remove from oil and drain on paper towels. Garnish with chopped parsley and serve with tartar sauce. Yields 4 servings.

Note: Soft-shell crabs are blue crabs, a common species in the western Atlantic. As they grow, crustaceans such as crabs and lobsters must periodically "throw" their hard shell, leaving them with paper thin shells that harden after a few days.

*Dip the thin crab shells in batter and fry in oil. The fried shells are a unique snack, somewhat resembling potato chips.

The Simply Great Cookbook (Michigan)

Crabmeat Cobbler

½ cup Crisco
½ cup chopped green bell
 pepper
½ cup chopped onion
½ cup all-purpose flour, sifted
1 teaspoon dry mustard
½ teaspoon Ac'cent

1 cup milk
1 cup shredded American cheese
1 (6½-ounce) can crabmeat
2 tablespoons Worcestershire
1½ cups chopped tomatoes,
 drained
½ teaspoon salt

Melt Crisco in pan. Add green pepper and onion and cook till tender, about 10 minutes. Blend in sifted flour, dry mustard, Ac'cent, milk, and American cheese; cook, stirring constantly, till cheese is melted and mixture is very thick. Add crabmeat, Worcestershire, tomatoes, and salt.

CHEESE BISCUIT TOPPING:
1 cup all-purpose flour, sifted
2 teaspoons baking powder
½ teaspoon salt

¼ cup shredded American cheese
2 tablespoons Crisco
½ cup milk

Sift together flour, baking powder, and salt. Add cheese and Crisco. Cut in till mixture resembles coarse meal. Add milk. Mix only till all flour is dampened. Drop by rounded teaspoonsful on top of crabmeat mixture. Bake in 450° oven 15–20 minutes.

Allen Park Garden Club Recipe Book (Michigan)

©CHRIS LIGHT

The United States lightship *Huron* (LV-103) is the only surviving lightship type specifically built for service on the Great Lakes. Lightships were like floating lighthouses anchored in areas that were too impractical to construct a lighthouse. The *Huron* was launched in 1920 and spent 50 years guiding vessels through dangerous shoals. She was the last lightship on the Great Lakes and is now a museum in Port Huron, Michigan. Lightships have become obsolete, and there are none in operation today.

Charley's Bucket

1½ cups water
1 teaspoon salt
2 ears fresh corn (leave in husk, trim silk and outer leaves)
2 (1¼-pound) live Maine lobsters

½ Dungeness crab, or ½ pound King crab legs
4 redskin potatoes, pre-cooked
10 mussels, cleaned
10 steamer clams, cleaned
½ cup clarified butter

In a large kettle with a tight-fitting lid, put water and salt; bring to a boil. Place corn into water, followed by lobsters and crab. Set potatoes alongside the seafood. Cover tightly. Return water to a boil. Cook 7 minutes. The lobster is fully cooked when the shell is completely red. If dark areas are present, continue to cook.

Remove lid and add mussels and steamers. Cover and steam 5 additional minutes. Remove lid from kettle and if mussels and clam shells have opened, the Bucket is done. If shells have not opened, cover and continue steaming until they do. Serve with clarified butter for dipping shellfish and crustaceans. Yields 2 servings.

The Simply Great Cookbook (Michigan)

Shrimp Stroganoff

1 (12-ounce) package fettucini
2 tablespoons butter
2 tablespoons chopped onion
¾ pound fresh shrimp, peeled
1 can cream of shrimp soup

½ cup milk
½ cup sour cream
2 tablespoons chopped fresh parsley
½ teaspoon paprika
Salt and pepper to taste

Cook pasta according to package directions. Meanwhile, in a large skillet, melt butter; add onion and cook until tender. Add shrimp; cook 2–3 minutes, stirring constantly, until shrimp begin to turn pink. Blend in soup and milk; heat thoroughly. Stir in sour cream, parsley, and paprika. Season to taste with salt and pepper. Do not boil. Serve over hot pasta. Makes 2–4 servings.

Sharing Our Best (Wisconsin)

Jamboqumby

¼ cup butter
1 cup chopped onion
1 cup chopped green or
   red pepper or combination
2 cloves garlic
½ teaspoon thyme
½ teaspoon oregano
1 bay leaf

1 (28-ounce) can stewed
   tomatoes
⅛ teaspoon cayenne
½ teaspoon chili powder
1 (15-ounce) can tomato sauce
1 pound hot sausage (Italian
   or Andouille)
1½ pounds raw shrimp

Melt butter in saucepan and sauté onion and pepper until tender. Add garlic, thyme, oregano, bay leaf, tomatoes, cayenne, chili powder, and tomato sauce. Simmer covered for 15 minutes. Meanwhile sauté sausage until lightly browned and prick to extract the fat from the sausage. Cut into one-inch pieces and add to the pot. Continue to cook for another 15 minutes. Add cleaned raw shrimp and continue cooking for about 5 minutes. Remove bay leaf. Serve over cooked rice. Garnish with fresh-cut onion tops or chives. Makes 6 servings.

Apples, Brie & Chocolate (Wisconsin)

Impossible Seafood Pie

2 (10-ounce) packages broccoli
   or asparagus, thawed and
   drained
3 (6-ounce) packages frozen
   crabmeat and (or) shrimp,
   thawed and drained
½ cup sliced green onions
2 (2-ounce) jars chopped
   pimentos, drained

1 cup sour cream
1 (8-ounce) package cream
   cheese
1 cup Bisquick
4 eggs
1 teaspoon Nature's Seasoning
Dash of nutmeg
2 tomatoes

Preheat oven to 350°. Grease 9x13-inch pan. Spread vegetables, seafood, green onions, and pimentos in the pan. Beat sour cream, cream cheese, Bisquick, eggs, and seasonings, pour over ingredients in pan. Top with thin-sliced tomato and sprinkle with Parmesan cheese. Bake 35–40 minutes at 350°.

Winnehaha's Favorite Recipes (Minnesota)

Spicy Lime-Ginger Grilled Shrimp

Wonderful!

MARINADE:

¾ cup fresh lime juice
1 tablespoon minced fresh
  ginger
2 medium garlic cloves, minced
2 small shallots, finely chopped
2 tablespoons finely chopped
  fresh cilantro

½ teaspoon salt
⅛ teaspoon black pepper
⅛ teaspoon crushed red
  pepper flakes, or to taste
2½ tablespoons orange
  marmalade
⅓ cup olive oil

Combine all ingredients in small mixing bowl, whisking in oil last.

SHRIMP:

1½ pounds shrimp, shells on
4 large carrots, peeled
1 large European cucumber,
  halved, seeded, unpeeled

1 head red leaf lettuce
2 tablespoons finely chopped
  cilantro for garnish

Thread shrimp on skewers (4–6 per skewer) and ley them flat in a 13x19-inch non-aluminum dish. Pour ½ the Marinade over shrimp and marinate for ½ hour. Meanwhile, shred carrots and cucumber; put in medium mixing bowl. Add about 2 tablespoons remaining marinade; reserve rest for dipping.

When ready to serve, prepare grill for medium-high heat; place skewered shrimp flat on grill. Baste and grill till just pink. Arrange lettuce leaves on platter and mound cucumber-carrot mixture on top. Place skewered shrimp on top of vegetables and let guests help themselves. Garnish with chopped cilantro and pass remaining marinade for dipping. Have plenty of napkins.

Note: If using bamboo skewers, soak in water overnight before skewering shrimp to prevent them from catching fire on grill.

Recipes and Memories (Michigan)

Baked Seafood au Gratin

½ cup butter	3 tablespoons dry sherry
¾ cup flour	Dash of Tabasco
4–5 cups milk	1 tablespoon lemon juice
1 teaspoon salt	1½ cups cheese
Pepper, to taste	3 large or 6 small lobsters
1 teaspoon dry mustard	1 package frozen shrimp
1 teaspoon celery salt	1 package scallops
1 teaspoon onion juice	1 bag crab or 1 can crab
1 teaspoon Worcestershire	1 (8-ounce) can mushrooms

Make a cream sauce using flour, butter, milk, salt, pepper, mustard, onion juice, and celery salt; stir and cook until smooth. Add Worcestershire, sherry, Tabasco, and lemon juice. Add cheese; stir until cheese melts and is blended. Combine seafood (cut up into bite-size pieces) and mushrooms. Serve in individual seashells (keep sauce thick) and top with cheese and bread crumbs. Dust with paprika. If served on patty shells or toast, thin sauce.

Our Heritage Cookbook (Minnesota)

Cakes

Little House Wayside in Pepin County, Wisconsin, marks the birthplace of Laura Ingalls Wilder, author of the popular *Little House* series of children's books based on her pioneer family. The site contains a replica of the house that was described in the books as "Little House in the Big Woods." The site is now surrounded by farmland, although it was a dense hardwood forest when Laura was born in 1867.

Laura Ingalls Wilder's Gingerbread with Chocolate Frosting

1 cup brown sugar
½ cup shortening
½ cup molasses
2 teaspoons baking soda
1 cup boiling water
3 cups flour

1 teaspoon each: ginger, cinnamon, allspice, and nutmeg
¼ teaspoon cloves
½ teaspoon salt
2 eggs

Blend brown sugar and shortening; mix molasses well with this. Mix baking soda with boiling water (be sure cup is full of water after foam runs off into cake batter). Mix all well. Blend flour with spices and salt. Sift all into the mixture and mix well. Add lastly, 2 well-beaten eggs. The mixture should be quite thin. Pour into a greased 9x13-inch baking pan. Bake in a moderate oven (350°) for 30 minutes. Cool and frost with Boiled Chocolate Frosting.

BOILED CHOCOLATE FROSTING:

2 cups sugar
2 heaping tablespoons cocoa

⅔ cup milk
½ cup butter
2 teaspoons vanilla

Mix sugar and cocoa together; add milk, a little at a time, then the butter. Boil for 6 minutes. Remove from heat and add vanilla and let cool. Beat until creamy.

Note: May add one teaspoon table syrup when adding vanilla, to prevent sugaring.

Trinity Lutheran Church of Norden Anniversary Cookbook (Wisconsin)

Wisconsin Apple Cake

1¾ cups flour
1 teaspoon baking powder
2 tablespoons sugar
⅔ cup margarine
1 egg

6–8 apples
¼ cup margarine
1 cup sugar
3 tablespoons flour
½ teaspoon cinnamon

Sift first 3 ingredients into a bowl. Cut in ⅔ cup margarine until mixture resembles corn meal. Beat egg; add to flour mixture, mixing lightly. Press dough into a 9x13-inch pan with the fingers, bringing up the sides about 1-inch.

Core and peel apples. Cut into slices. Arrange close together in rows on the pastry dough. Cut the ¼ cup margarine into the remaining sugar, flour, and cinnamon until crumbly. Sprinkle the apples with sugar topping. Bake in 375° oven for about 45 minutes. Serve warm or cold, plain or with ice cream.

Celebration of Grace (Wisconsin)

Walnut Apple Cake
with Poured on Caramel Icing

1 cup oil
2 eggs
1½ cups sugar
1½ teaspoons vanilla
2 cups flour

¾ teaspoon baking soda
½ teaspoon salt
2 cups diced apples, peeled or
    unpeeled
1 cup chopped nuts

Mix oil, eggs, sugar, and vanilla. Add flour, soda, and salt. Add apples and nuts. Bake in sprayed 9x13-inch baking pan at 350° for 50–60 minutes. Ice while hot.

POURED ON CARAMEL ICING:
1 stick butter (½ cup)
3 tablespoons milk

¾ cup brown sugar

Boiled ingredients together for 2½ minutes. Ice while cake is hot.

Chickadee Cottage Cookbook (Minnesota)

Apple Cider Cupcakes
with Cider Cream Cheese Frosting

CUPCAKES:

3 cups unpasteurized apple
  cider
¾ cup vegetable shortening
1¾ cups sugar
2 large eggs

2 cups all-purpose flour, sifted
⅛ teaspoon ground cloves
1 teaspoon cinnamon
1 teaspoon baking soda
Pinch of salt

In large saucepan boil cider till it is reduced to about 1½ cups; let cool. In large bowl with mixer, beat shortening and sugar till mixture is fluffy; beat eggs in one at a time. Into bowl, sift together flour, cloves, cinnamon, baking soda, and salt. Stir in reduced cider and combine mixture well.

Divide batter among 18 paper-lined ½-cup muffin tins and bake in middle of preheated 375° oven 25 minutes, or till tester comes out clean. Transfer cupcakes to rack. Let cool and remove from tins.

FROSTING:

2 cups apple cider
2 (3-ounce) packages cream
  cheese, softened

½ cup powdered sugar
Pinch of salt

In saucepan boil cider until reduced to about ¼ cup; let cool. In a bowl with mixer, beat together cream cheese, powdered sugar, reduced cider and salt till smooth. Frost cupcakes.

Note: Can also reduce cider in glass measuring cup in microwave.

Heavenly Helpings (Michigan)

There are over 7.5 million apple trees in commercial production in Michigan, covering 37,000 acres, on 950 family-run farms throughout Michigan's Lower Peninsula. In 2006, Michigan harvested approximately 903 million pounds (21.5 million bushels) of apples. Michigan is the largest supplier of apple slices used in commercially prepared apple pies. Michigan apples are also a main source for applesauce, fresh-cut slices, and fresh and shelf-stable apple cider. The most prevalent variety remains the Red Delicious, followed closely by the Golden Delicious. The Gala is rapidly gaining, however.

Rhubarb Torte

GRAHAM CRACKER CRUST:

4 tablespoons melted butter or margarine, reserve 2 tablespoons

1 cup graham cracker crumbs
2 tablespoons sugar

Combine all ingredients, reserve 2 tablespoons crumb mixture. Pat remainder in 9x9-inch pan. Bake at 350° for 10 minutes. Cool.

3 tablespoons cornstarch
4 cups sliced rhubarb
½ cup water
Few drops red food coloring
1 recipe Graham Cracker Crust

1½ cups tiny marshmallows
1 (3½-ounce) package instant vanilla pudding mix

Combine sugar and cornstarch; stir in rhubarb and water. Cook and stir till thickened. Reduce heat; cook 2–3 minutes. Add food coloring. Spread on cooled Graham Cracker Crust. Cool.

Whip cream; fold in marshmallows. Spoon on rhubarb mixture. Prepare pudding according to package directions; spread over all. Sprinkle with reserved crumbs. Chill. Makes 9 servings.

The Octagon House Cookbook (Wisconsin)

Cheese Torte

1 envelope plain gelatine
¼ cup cold water
¾ cup hot water
Juice of ½ lemon or 1 teaspoon ReaLemon juice

12 ounces cream cheese
1 cup sugar
2 teaspoons vanilla
1 pint whipping cream, whipped
Graham cracker crust

Dissolve gelatine in cold water, then add hot water and lemon juice. Cream cheese and add sugar and vanilla. Add cooled gelatine. Fold in whipped cream. Pour in graham cracker crust. Makes enough for a 9x9-inch pan. For a 9x13-inch pan, make 1½ recipes.

Centennial Cookbook (Wisconsin)

Rhubarb Pudding Cake

4 cups cut-up rhubarb
1⅔ cups sugar, divided
¾ cup water
⅓ cup shortening
1 egg
1 cup all-purpose flour

1 teaspoon baking powder
¼ teaspoon salt
⅔ cup milk
½ teaspoon vanilla
Chopped nuts (optional)

Combine rhubarb, 1 cup sugar, and water in saucepan. Cook over medium heat, stirring occasionally for 10 minutes (keep hot). Cream shortening and remaining ⅔ cup sugar; add egg, beating until fluffy. Sift flour with baking powder and salt; add dry ingredients alternately with milk and vanilla. Turn into 2 greased and floured layer pans. Carefully spoon hot sauce over batter. Chopped nuts may be sprinkled on top, if desired. Bake at 350° for 35–40 minutes. Makes 9 servings.

Northcountry Kitchens Cookbook (Michigan)

WWW.BOATNERD.COM

Michigan is the only place in the world with a floating post office. For more than 100 years, the J.W. Westcott Company in Detroit has delivered mail to ships on the Great Lakes while they are still underway. It began in 1874 when Captain Westcott used a rowboat to deliver ship's orders to passing vessels. Mail delivery was added in 1895 and is delivered every day during the navigation season. It's a tricky exchange, as the pilot boat has to match the speed of the larger vessel, make the delivery, then pull away so as not to get caught in the bigger ship's wake.

Williamsburg Orange Cake

2¾ cups cake flour
1½ cups sugar
1½ teaspoons baking soda
¾ teaspoon salt
1½ cups buttermilk
½ cup margarine, softened

¼ cup shortening
3 eggs
1½ teaspoons vanilla
1 cup cut-up golden raisins
½ cup finely chopped nuts
1 tablespoon grated orange peel

Heat oven to 350°. Grease and flour 3 (8-inch) round layer pans. Beat all ingredients in large mixer bowl on low speed, scraping bowl constantly, 30 seconds. Beat on high speed, scraping bowl occasionally, 3 minutes. Pour into pans. Bake till wooden pick inserted in center comes out clean, 30–35 minutes; cool. Frost with Williamsburg Butter Frosting.

WILLIAMSBURG BUTTER FROSTING:

½ cup margarine, softened
4½ cups powdered sugar

4–5 tablespoons orange juice
1 tablespoon grated orange peel

Mix margarine and powdered sugar. Beat in orange juice and peel.

Allen Park Garden Club Recipe Book (Michigan)

Lemon Refrigerator Cake

1 tablespoon unflavored
   gelatin
¼ cup cold water
6 slightly beaten egg yolks
1½ cups sugar, divided
¾ cup lemon juice

1½ teaspoons lemon rind
6 egg whites
1 large angel food cake, torn into
   small pieces
1 cup heavy whipping cream,
   whipped

Soften gelatin in the cold water. Combine egg yolks, ³/₄ cup sugar, lemon juice, and lemon rind, and cook in a double boiler, stirring constantly until mixture coats a metal spoon. Remove from heat and add softened gelatin. Stir until dissolved. Beat egg whites until stiff and gradually add remaining ³/₄ cup sugar, beating constantly. Fold into custard. Layer some cake pieces in large oiled angel food pan. Pour part of the custard over cake. Alternate layers until all is used. Chill until firm. Unmold and frost with whipped cream. Serves 12–14.

Family Fare (Wisconsin)

Blueberry Cake

3 cups all-purpose flour
1½ cups sugar
1 tablespoon baking powder
⅓ teaspoon salt
½ cup shortening
1 cup plus 2 tablespoons milk
2 eggs
1½ cups blueberries

Sift flour, sugar, baking powder, and salt into a bowl and mix well. Beat shortening in a mixer bowl until creamy. Add flour mixture and milk. Beat 2 minutes, scraping bowl occasionally. Add eggs. Beat 1 minute. Stir in blueberries. Spoon into a greased 5x9-inch loaf pan. Bake at 350° for 50 minutes or until cake tests done. Cool slightly. Slice and serve with Hard Sauce for Blueberry Cake. Yields 12 servings.

HARD SAUCE FOR BLUEBERRY CAKE:

1 cup butter, softened
⅛ teaspoon salt
2 cups sifted powdered sugar
1 teaspoon vanilla or rum extract

Beat butter in a mixer bowl at high speed until creamy. Add salt and confectioners' sugar gradually, beating well after each addition. Beat until of sauce consistency, scraping bowl occasionally. Stir in vanilla. Chill, covered, 1 hour.

Note: May substitute 1 tablespoon cooking sherry for vanilla.

The Flavors of Mackinac (Michigan)

For centuries, Native Americans dwelling around the Great Lakes region of North America knew how to locate the best of the wild blueberry patches. Blueberries, both dried and fresh, were a staple in their diets and were also used as medicine. French explorer Samuel de Champlain noted this berry harvesting as early as 1615 during his travels through the Lake Huron area. The lowbush variety are considered the wild blueberries and are native to North America while the highbush blueberries have several cultivars. In Michigan's eastern Upper Peninsula, most of the land north of the Tahquamenon River is covered with blueberries—along the roads and out in open fields.

Classic Cranberry Cake with Sauce Topping

¾ cup butter, softened
1 cup sugar
2 eggs
1 cup sour cream
1¾ cups flour

¼ teaspoon baking soda
1½ teaspoons baking powder
2 cups fresh cranberries, halved
1 teaspoon vanilla

Cream butter and sugar; add eggs and sour cream. Reserve 2 tablespoons flour. Mix together the remaining flour, soda, and baking powder. Sprinkle the reserved flour over the halved cranberries and stir them into the batter with spoon. Add vanilla. Pour the batter into greased and floured 9x13-inch pan. Bake 30 minutes at 350°.

SAUCE TOPPING:
1½ cups granulated sugar
1 cup whipping cream

2 tablespoons butter
1 teaspoon vanilla

Mix sugar, cream, and butter in medium saucepan; boil 2 minutes, stirring constantly. Remove from heat. Add vanilla. Serve warm sauce over cake. Sauce may be reheated as used.

Blessed Be the Cook (Wisconsin)

Coconut Almond Carrot Ring

1½ cups flour
1½ teaspoons baking powder
½ teaspoon salt
1 teaspoon cinnamon
1 cup sugar
1 cup oil

2 eggs
1 cup grated carrots
1½ cups chopped almonds
½ cup raisins
⅔ cup coconut

Mix flour, baking powder, salt, and cinnamon. Beat sugar and oil at medium speed until well mixed. Stir in flour mixture. Add eggs and beat well. Stir in carrots, nuts, raisins, and coconut. Pour into greased and floured Bundt pan. Bake at 350° for 45 minutes. Frost with cream cheese frosting.

Celebrating 150 Years of Faith and Food (Wisconsin)

14-Carat Cake

2 cups sifted flour
2 teaspoons baking powder
1½ teaspoons baking soda
1½ teaspoons salt
2 teaspoons ground cinnamon
2 cups sugar
1½ cups salad oil
4 eggs

2 cups finely shredded, pared
   carrots
1 (8½-ounce) can crushed
   pineapple, drained
½ cup chopped walnuts
1 (3½-ounce) can flaked coconut
Cream Cheese Frosting

Sift together flour, baking powder, baking soda, salt, and cinnamon in mixing bowl. Add sugar, oil, and eggs. Beat at medium speed of electric mixer one minute. Stir in carrots, pineapple, walnuts, and coconut. Turn into 3 greased and floured 9-inch round cake pans. Bake in 350° oven for 40 minutes, or until cake tests done. Cool in pans on racks 10 minutes. Remove from pans; cool on racks.

CREAM CHEESE FROSTING:

½ cup butter or regular
   margarine
1 (8-ounce) package cream
   cheese, softened

1 teaspoon vanilla
1 (1-pound) box confectioners'
   sugar

Cream together butter, cream cheese, and vanilla in a bowl at medium speed of electric mixer. Gradually add confectioners' sugar, beating well until smooth and creamy. If mixture is too thick to spread, add a little milk. Fill layers and frost top and sides of cake.

Country Heart Cooking (Wisconsin)

Mom's Spice Cake

1¼ cups brown sugar
1 cup white sugar
¾ cup soft shortening
3 eggs, beaten thoroughly
2¾ cups flour
1½ teaspoons soda

1½ teaspoons cinnamon
¾ teaspoon nutmeg
¾ teaspoon cloves
1 teaspoon salt
1½ cups buttermilk

Cream together the sugars and shortening until fluffy. Beat in the eggs. Sift the dry ingredients together and stir in alternately with the buttermilk. Pour into a greased and floured 9x13-inch oblong pan. Bake at 350° for 35–40 minutes or until cake tests done. Cool.

BROWN SUGAR FROSTING:

1 cup brown sugar
12 tablespoons cream or
   half-and-half

4 tablespoons butter
1 teaspoon vanilla

Combine brown sugar and cream. Boil for exactly 3 minutes. Remove from heat and add butter and vanilla. Beat mixture until the gloss leaves. If mixture gets too stiff, add a little cream.

Treasured Recipes of Chippewa County (Minnesota)

WWW.WIKIPEDIA.ORG

The 45-foot Glockenspiel Tower in Ulm, Minnesota, is one of only a few free-standing carillon clock towers in the world. Beneath the bells and clock on the west side of the tower, three animated polka band figures perform 10 months out of the year. During the holiday season, from Thanksgiving until early January, the figures are replaced with a nativity scene. Directly below the main upper stage, a door slides up and a lower stage projects out to reveal three-foot-high animated figures that depict the history and development of the city.

Pecan Bourbon Cake

For those who don't like fruitcakes. This is a favorite at our house.

2 cups finely chopped pecans
1 cup bourbon, divided
3½ cups sifted all-purpose flour
1½ teaspoon baking powder
½ teaspoon nutmeg
½ teaspoon cinnamon

¼ teaspoon ground cloves
2 cups unsalted butter
2½ cups sugar
8 eggs, well beaten
1½ teaspoons amaretto liqueur

Preheat oven to 350°. Butter 2 (9-inch) loaf pans. Combine pecans and ½ cup bourbon; let stand. Sift together dry ingredients. Cream butter and gradually add sugar, then beaten eggs, and beat very well. Stir in flour mixture and mix just till combined. Stir in pecans and bourbon. Pour into pans and bake 1 hour. Cool in pans 15 minutes; turn out. Soak 2 pieces of cheesecloth in remaining bourbon. Wrap each cake in a piece of cheesecloth, then wrap in foil. Refrigerate for 1 week before serving.

Historically Delicious (Michigan)

Oatmeal Harvest Cake

1½ cups boiling water
1 cup oatmeal
½ cup shortening
1 cup brown sugar
1 cup white sugar

2 eggs, well beaten
1⅓ cups flour
1 tablespoon cinnamon
1 teaspoon baking soda
½ teaspoon salt

Pour boiling water over oatmeal. Let stand 20 minutes. Cream shortening, brown sugar, and white sugar. Add eggs. Then add flour, cinnamon, soda, and salt. Pour into greased 9x13-inch pan.

CRUMB TOPPING:

2 tablespoons soft butter
3 tablespoons brown sugar
3 tablespoons white sugar

4–6 chopped Heath candy bars
3 chopped Hershey bars
½ cup nuts

Crumble together butter, brown sugar, sugar, Heath bars, Hershey bars, and nuts. Sprinkle on top of cake mixture. Bake cake and topping for 30 minutes at 350°.

Favorite Recipes of Lester Park & Rockridge Schools (Minnesota)

The Best Peanut Butter Cake

2 cups all-purpose flour
¼ cup whole-wheat flour
2 cups packed brown sugar
1 cup peanut butter
½ cup butter or margarine,
  softened

1 teaspoon baking powder
½ teaspoon baking soda
1 cup low-fat milk
1 teaspoon vanilla
3 eggs
1 cup chocolate or carob chips

Heat oven to 350°. Grease bottom only of 9x13-inch pan. Combine flours, brown sugar, peanut butter, and butter in large mixer bowl; mix at low speed until crumbly. Reserve one cup. To remaining mixture in bowl, add baking powder, soda, milk, vanilla, and eggs; blend at low speed until moistened. Beat for 3 minutes at medium speed. Spread batter in pan; sprinkle with reserved crumbs, then chocolate chips. Bake for 35–40 minutes. Makes 18 servings.

Minnesota Heritage Cookbook II (Minnesota)

Amaretto Fudge Cake

1¾ cups flour
1½ cups sugar
¾ cup cocoa
1½ teaspoons baking soda
1½ teaspoons baking powder
½ teaspoon salt
2 eggs

⅔ cup skim milk
½ cup plus 2 tablespoons
  amaretto
½ cup applesauce,
  unsweetened
2 teaspoons vanilla
½ cup boiling water

Spray a 9-inch springform pan with nonstick vegetable cooking spray. Combine all ingredients and beat 2 minutes (batter is thin). Bake at 325° for 12 minutes.

TOPPING:
¼ cup miniature chocolate
  chips

¼ cup almond slices

Combine and sprinkle on cake. Continue baking for 40–45 minutes (total of 50–60 minutes). Cool 30 minutes; loosen sides and remove. Makes 12–15 servings. Cover the cake (it keeps well and is better the second day).

Vaer saa god Cookbook (Minnesota)

Tapawingo's Molten Chocolate Cakes with Cherries

1 (16-ounce) bag frozen pitted dark sweet cherries, halved, thawed, undrained
¾ cup sugar, divided
¼ cup Kirsch (clear cherry brandy) or regular brandy
¼ teaspoon ground cinnamon
2 tablespoons unsweetened cocoa powder
½ stick unsalted butter, cut into small pieces
2 ounces bittersweet (not unsweetened) or semisweet chocolate, chopped
2 large egg yolks
1 large egg
2 teaspoons all-purpose flour
Powdered sugar
Fresh mint

Combine cherries with juice, ¹/₂ cup sugar, Kirsch, and cinnamon in heavy medium saucepan. Stir over medium heat until sugar dissolves. Simmer until sauce thickens and is slightly reduced, about 10 minutes. Using slotted spoon, remove ¹/₄ cup cherries from sauce; drain well. Transfer to work surface and chop coarsely; reserve chopped cherries for cakes. Set aside cherry sauce.

Butter 2 (³/₄-cup) ramekins or custard cups. Whisk cocoa and remaining ¹/₄ cup sugar in small bowl to blend. Stir butter and chocolate in heavy small saucepan over low heat until chocolate melts. Remove from heat; whisk in cocoa mixture. Whisk in egg yolks, then whole egg and flour. Fold in reserved ¹/₄ cup chopped cherries. Divide batter between prepared ramekins. (Sauce and cake batter can be made 1 day ahead. Cover separately; chill.)

Preheat oven to 350°. Bake cakes uncovered until edges are set but center is still shiny and tester inserted into center comes out with some wet batter attached, about 22 minutes. Warm sauce over low heat. Cut around cakes to loosen; turn out onto plates. Spoon sauce alongside. Sift powdered sugar over; garnish with mint. Makes 2 servings.

Cherry Home Companion (Michigan)

Apple Cider Pound Cake

3 cups sugar
3 sticks butter or margarine,
   softened
6 eggs
3 cups all-purpose flour
½ teaspoon salt
½ teaspoon baking powder

1 teaspoon cinnamon
½ teaspoon allspice
½ teaspoon nutmeg
¼ teaspoon ground cloves
1 cup apple cider
1 teaspoon vanilla extract

Cream sugar and butter in a large mixing bowl until light and fluffy. Add eggs 1 at a time, beating well after each addition. Combine flour, salt, baking powder, cinnamon, allspice, nutmeg, and cloves. Set aside. Combine cider and vanilla. Add dry ingredients alternately with the cider to the creamed mixture, mixing well after each addition. Spoon into a greased and floured 10-inch tube pan or Bundt pan. Bake at 325° for 1½ hours or until cake tests done. Cool cake in pan; invert onto a serving plate. Drizzle Buttermilk Icing over each cake slice just before serving. Serves 12–16.

BUTTERMILK ICING:
½ cup sugar
½ stick butter or margarine
¼ cup buttermilk

½ teaspoon vanilla extract
¼ teaspoon baking soda

Combine sugar, butter, buttermilk, vanilla, and baking soda in a saucepan. Bring to a boil. Reduce heat and simmer for 10 minutes.

Between the Lakes (Michigan)

Easy Brandy Alexander Cheesecakes

CAKES:

½ cup softened butter
2 (8-ounce) packages cream
  cheese
2 eggs
¾ cup sugar
¼ cup flour

2 teaspoons creme de cocoa or
  Kahlúa
2 teaspoons brandy
1 cup whipping cream
15 chocolate sandwich cookies
  (Oreos)

Cream butter and cream cheese. Beat in eggs. Add sugar, flour, creme de cocoa, brandy, and whipping cream. Beat until well mixed. Line cupcake tins with 30 paper liners. Twist cookies apart and place half in each of the liners. Fill with batter until liners are almost full. Bake at 350° for 25–30 minutes or until lightly browned; cool.

TOPPING:

1 cup whipping cream
¼–½ teaspoon instant coffee
  powder
1 teaspoon brandy
1 teaspoon creme de cocoa or
  Kahlúa

2 teaspoons sugar
Freshly grated nutmeg, for
  garnish

Combine all topping ingredients. Stir and store in refrigerator for 10 minutes or longer. Remove from refrigerator and beat until soft peaks form. Frost the cheesecakes with this mixture and sprinkle with nutmeg. Store in refrigerator.

Cardinal Country Cooking (Wisconsin)

Turtle Cheesecake

1½ cups graham cracker crumbs

½ cup chopped pecans

6 tablespoons butter or margarine, softened

¼ cup plus ⅓ cup heavy cream, divided

25 caramels, unwrapped

4 (8-ounce) packages cream cheese, softened

1½ cups dark brown sugar

1 cup sour cream

4 eggs

2 egg yolks

1½ teaspoons vanilla

4 ounces semisweet chocolate

Double wrap springform pan with foil. Mix together graham cracker crumbs, pecans, and butter. Put into springform pan; bake at 350° for 10 minutes. Melt ¼ cup heavy cream with caramels. Pour into bottom of crust. Beat cream cheese 4 minutes. Beat in brown sugar 4 minutes. Beat in sour cream, eggs, egg yolks, and vanilla. Beat together until increased in volume. Pour into crust; put pan in roasting pan with half water (roasting pan is best if not taller than springform pan and an inch clearance from sides). Bake at 350° for 1 hour 15 minutes, until center jiggles slightly. Remove from roasting pan; remove foil. Let cool 2 hours. Refrigerate 8 hours or overnight.

Melt remaining ⅓ cup heavy cream and chocolate. Pour over cheesecake.

Variation: Melt additional caramel and cream and drizzle over chocolate. Beat remaining cream with sugar and dollop over chocolate (before drizzling caramel). Top with turtle candies.

Sharing Our Best (Michigan)

Brownie Swirl Cheesecake

1 (8-ounce) package
  brownie mix
2 (8-ounce) packages cream
  cheese
½ cup sugar
1 teaspoon vanilla

2 eggs
1 cup milk chocolate chips,
  melted
Whipped cream
Cherries for garnish

Grease bottom of 9-inch springform pan. Prepare basic brownie mix as directed on package; pour batter evenly into springform pan. Bake at 350° for 15 minutes. Combine cream cheese, sugar, and vanilla, mixing at medium speed on electric mixer until well blended. Add eggs one at a time, mixing well after each addition. Pour over brownie mix layer. Spoon melted chocolate over cream cheese mixture; cut through batter with knife several times for marble effect. Bake at 350° for 35 minutes. Loosen cake from rim of pan; cool before removing rim of pan. Garnish with whipped cream and cherries.

A Collection of Recipes (Wisconsin)

Pretzel Cheesecake

3 cups crushed pretzels
1 stick butter or margarine,
  softened
3 tablespoons sugar
2 (8-ounce) packages cream
  cheese, softened
1 cup powdered sugar

1 (8-ounce) carton Cool Whip,
  thawed
2 (3-ounce) packages
  strawberry Jell-O
2 cups boiling water
2 (10-ounce) boxes frozen
  sliced strawberries

Mix first 3 ingredients and press into bottom of an ungreased 9x13-inch pan. Bake in 350° oven 7 minutes. Cool. Mix cream cheese, powdered sugar, and Cool Whip and spread over pretzels. Mix Jell-O, water, and strawberries. Pour over cream cheese mixture and refrigerate. Serves 8–10.

Michigan Magazine Family and Friends Cookbook (Michigan)

Apple Cheesecake

Easy to prepare and tastes fabulous, this is a nice fall dessert.

½ cup butter, melted
1 cup sugar, divided
1 cup all-purpose flour
¾ teaspoon vanilla, divided
1 (8-ounce) package cream
  cheese, softened

1 egg
3 cups thinly sliced apples
1 teaspoon cinnamon
Sliced almonds to taste (optional)

Mix butter, $1/3$ cup sugar, flour, and $1/4$ teaspoon vanilla in bowl. Press mixture over bottom and one inch up the side of a 9-inch springform pan.

Mix cream cheese, $1/3$ cup sugar, egg, and $1/2$ teaspoon vanilla in a bowl. Pour mixture over prepared layer.

Toss apples with remaining $1/3$ cup sugar and cinnamon in a bowl. Spoon apple mixture over cream cheese mixture. Sprinkle with almonds. Bake at 450° for 10 minutes. Reduce temperature to 400°. Bake 25 minutes longer. Cool in pan. Yields 16 servings.

Dawn to Dusk (Michigan)

The Great Lakes region has long held a legacy of fresh, clean water and renowned sport fishing. In winter, ice returns to the lakes and streams providing a cherished tradition for residents and a time-honored opportunity to visitors—ice fishing. Ice anglers may sit on a stool in the open on a frozen lake, or in a heated cabin on the ice, some with bunks and amenities. Ice shanties can be quite cozy and offer a contrast to the open lakes of summer. Many people argue the fish taste even better coming out of the cold water. Recommended thickness of the ice is 4–6 inches for foot travel, 6–10 inches for Snowmobiles, 10–16 for light cars, and 16 or more inches for full-size trucks.

Caramel-Apple Sundae Cheesecake

⅓ cup butter or margarine
1 cup sugar, divided
4 eggs
1¼ cups flour
2 (8-ounce) packages cream
   cheese, softened
2 tablespoons flour

½ cup sour cream
1 cup apples, peeled and
   chopped
¾ teaspoon cinnamon
½ cup caramel topping (for
   ice cream)
¼ cup chopped pecans

Combine butter and ⅓ cup sugar until light and fluffy. Blend in one egg. Add 1¼ cups flour; mix well. Spread dough onto bottom and sides of 9-inch springform pan. Bake at 450° for 10 minutes.

Combine cream cheese, ⅓ cup sugar, and 2 tablespoons flour, mixing at medium speed until well blended. Add 3 eggs, one at a time, mixing well after each addition. Blend in sour cream. Toss apples in remaining sugar and cinnamon. Stir topping into cream cheese mixture. Pour over crust. Swirl ¼ cup caramel topping into cream cheese mixture. Bake at 350° for one hour. Loosen cake from rim of pan; cool before removing rim of pan. Chill. Top cheesecake with remaining topping and pecans. Makes 10–12 servings.

Centennial Cookbook (Minnesota)

Cookies and Candies

© TRAVEL MICHIGAN

Windmill Island is a municipal park located in the city of Holland, Michigan. It is home to the 245-year-old windmill De Zwaan, the only authentic, working Dutch windmill in the United States. Holland was founded by Dutch Americans, and is in an area that has a large percentage of citizens of Dutch American heritage.

The Parish House Inn Chocolate Chip Cookies

You can make the dough ahead and freeze it in smaller batches for freshly baked cookies anytime.

3 cups all-purpose flour
2 teaspoons baking soda
2 teaspoons ground cinnamon
1 pound butter, softened
2 cups firmly packed brown
** sugar**
1 cup granulated sugar

2 large eggs
1 teaspoon vanilla
3 cups old-fashioned rolled oats
1 cup semisweet chocolate chips
½ cup white chocolate chips
½ cup butterscotch chips

Mix together flour, baking soda, and cinnamon. Beat together butter, brown sugar, and granulated sugar on medium speed until light and fluffy. Beat in eggs and vanilla. At low speed, beat in flour mixture until blended. Fold in oats, chocolate chips, and butterscotch chips. Form into 3 rolls; wrap in plastic wrap. Refrigerate overnight.

Preheat oven to 350°. Coat cookie sheets with cooking spray. Slice into ⅛-inch slices and place on cookie sheet. Bake cookies until lightly brown around edges, 10–12 minutes. Transfer to wire racks to cool completely. Yields 6 dozen cookies.

Best of Breakfast Menus & Recipes (Michigan)

Wisconsin Whoppers

These are great high energy cookies for trips or after skiing, skating or other fun winter activities.

1¼ cups light brown sugar, packed
¾ cup granulated sugar
⅔ cup butter
1½ cups chunky peanut butter
3 eggs
6 cups rolled oats (not quick cooking)
2 teaspoons baking soda
1½ cups raisins or craisins (optional)
1 cup semi-sweet chocolate chips
4 ounces semi-sweet chocolate squares
½ teaspoon vanilla

With a mixer, cream sugars and butters about 3 minutes. Add eggs, one at a time. Beat one minute more. Add oats and baking soda. Mix in optional raisins and chips. Shred the chocolate squares with a knife and mix into cookie batter. Add vanilla. Drop by ¼ measuring cup (or any desired size) onto cookie sheets. Flatten cookies with bottom of a glass tumbler that is dipped frequently in water. Bake at 350° about 15 minutes.

A Collection of Recipes (Wisconsin)

Polka Dot Cookies

⅓ cup butter
¼ cup sugar
½ cup brown sugar
1 egg
1 teaspoon vanilla
1 teaspoon baking powder
¼ teaspoon soda
¼ teaspoon salt
2 cups all-purpose flour
¼ cup milk
1 (6-ounce) package chocolate chips
½ cup cherries, chopped
½ cup nuts, chopped

Mix butter, sugar, and brown sugar. Add egg and vanilla. Mix in baking powder, soda, and salt. Add flour and milk. Add chips, cherries and nuts. Drop dough on baking sheet. Bake at 375° for 10–12 minutes.

Fifth Avenue Food Fare (Wisconsin)

Chocolate Drop Cookies

1 cup shortening
1 cup brown sugar
¾ cup white sugar
1 teaspoon vanilla
½ teaspoon maple flavoring
4 eggs

4 squares melted unsweetened
   chocolate
3½ cups all-purpose flour
1 teaspoon soda
½ teaspoon salt
¾ cup milk

Cream together shortening, brown sugar, white sugar, vanilla, and maple flavoring. Add eggs and chocolate. Mix flour, soda, and salt. Add dry ingredients alternately with milk to cream mixture. You may add nutmeats, if desired. Drop by teaspoonful onto cookie sheet and bake at 350° for 12–15 minutes.

Cardinal Country Cooking (Wisconsin)

Cherry Chocolate Cookies

1 cup powdered sugar
1 cup butter, softened
2 teaspoons maraschino
   cherry liquid
½ teaspoon almond extract

2¼ cups all-purpose flour
½ teaspoon salt
½ cup chopped maraschino
   cherries, drained
½ cup semisweet chocolate chips

Heat oven to 350°. In large bowl, combine powdered sugar, butter, cherry liquid, and almond extract; blend well. Add flour and salt; mix well. Stir in cherries. Shape dough into 1-inch balls. Place 2 inches apart on ungreased cookie sheets. Bake 10–12 minutes or until edges are light golden brown. Let cookies cool thoroughly. Melt chocolate chips in strong plastic sandwich bag in microwave. Snip corner of bag and drizzle chocolate over cookies. Makes 4 dozen cookies.

Sweet Traditions (Michigan)

Festive Gingerbread Cookies

¾ cup firmly packed brown
  sugar
½ cup butter or margarine,
  softened
2 eggs
¼ cup molasses
3¼ cups all-purpose flour

2 teaspoons ginger
1½ teaspoons baking soda
½ teaspoon allspice
½ teaspoon cinnamon
½ teaspoon nutmeg
½ teaspoon salt

In a large bowl, beat sugar and butter until well blended. Add eggs and molasses. Combine remaining dry ingredients. Cover and chill 1 hour.

Roll dough on well-floured board until $1/8$ inch thick. Cut into shapes. Place on greased baking sheet. Bake 10 minutes in 350° oven. Cool on rack. Decorate with sugar icing, if desired. Makes 24 cookies.

Michigan Magazine Family and Friends Cookbook (Michigan)

Whipped Shortbread

1½ cups butter (no sub)
¾ cup sifted powdered sugar
¾ cup cornstarch

2¼ cups all-purpose flour
Sprinkles

Beat butter 30 seconds or until softened. Add powdered sugar and cornstarch; beat well. Add flour; beat until well combined. Using about 1 tablespoon for each, shape dough into $1^1/4$-inch balls. Roll in sprinkles. Place on ungreased cookie sheet about 2 inches apart and flatten slightly. Bake at 350° for 10–12 minutes or until bottoms just start to brown and centers are set. Remove and cool on wire rack. Makes 4 dozen.

Sweet Traditions (Michigan)

Walnut Crescents

½ cup butter or margarine,
  softened
½ cup shortening
⅓ cup sugar
2 teaspoons water

2 teaspoons vanilla extract
2 cups all-purpose flour
½ cup chopped black walnuts
Confectioners' sugar to taste

Beat butter in a mixer bowl until creamy. Add shortening and sugar, beating until light and fluffy. Add water and vanilla; mix well. Beat in flour. Stir in walnuts. Chill, covered, 3–4 hours. Shape dough into ½-inch-thick ropes; cut into 3-inch lengths. Shape into crescents on an ungreased cookie sheet. Bake at 325° for 15 minutes; do not brown. Cool slightly on wire rack. Coat with confectioners' sugar. Yields 4 dozen crescents.

The Flavors of Mackinac (Michigan)

Swedish Farmer Cookies

1 cup sugar
1 cup butter
1 egg, beaten
¼ teaspoon salt
1 teaspoon vanilla

½ teaspoon coconut
  flavoring
2 cups all-purpose flour
1 teaspoon soda

Mix well in order given. Shape into 2 rolls. Wrap in waxed paper. Chill for several hours. Cut into ¼-inch slices. Bake at 350° until edge of cookies begin to brown.

One Hundred Years of Sharing (Minnesota)

Minnesota has the largest public radio membership support anywhere. Garrison Keillor's popular "Prairie Home Companion" (now called "American Radio Company") is one of its innovative programs.

Snowball Cookies

1 cup butter or margarine
½ cup powdered sugar
1 teaspoon vanilla
2¼ cups all-purpose flour
½ cup walnuts, chopped fine

Cream butter or margarine until light. Add powdered sugar and continue creaming. Add vanilla and mix. Add flour and blend. Stir in walnuts. Shape into small balls. Place on ungreased cookie sheet. Bake about 15 minutes at 350°. While still warm, roll in additional powdered sugar. Cool on a rack and then roll again in powdered sugar.

Recipes from St. Michael's (Minnesota)

Crunchy Round-Trip Cookies

Still just as crisp on the way home.

1 cup granulated sugar
1 cup packed brown sugar
1 cup margarine, softened
1 cup vegetable oil
2 eggs
1 teaspoon vanilla
3½ cups all-purpose flour
1 teaspoon cream of tartar
1 teaspoon baking soda
1 teaspoon salt
½ cup chopped nuts
1 cup flaked or shredded coconut
1 cup rolled oats
1 cup Rice Krispies

Blend sugars, margarine, oil, eggs, and vanilla. In separate bowl, stir dry ingredients together; add to first mixture and blend well. Stir in nuts, coconut, oats, and cereal. Chill dough. Heat oven to 350°. Drop by teaspoonfuls onto ungreased cookie sheets. Press down with a fork until very thin. If dough is sticky, chill fork in ice water and wipe dry. Bake 10–12 minutes. Makes 7 dozen.

From Minnesota: More Than a Cookbook (Minnesota)

Molasses Crinkles

¾ cup shortening
1 egg, beaten
2¼ cups all-purpose flour
¼ teaspoon salt
1 teaspoon ginger
½ teaspoon nutmeg

1 cup brown sugar
¼ cup molasses
2 teaspoons soda
1 teaspoon cinnamon
½ teaspoon cloves

Mix thoroughly. Chill well or overnight. Shape in balls. Dip one side in sugar. Place sugared side up on pan. Bake at 350°. Makes 3 dozen big cookies. Good to put chocolate kisses on some.

From the Recipe File of Agnes Gaffaney (Minnesota)

Apple Spice Cookies

½ cup butter, softened
1⅓ cups brown sugar
1 egg
¼ cup milk
2 cups sifted all-purpose flour
1 teaspoon baking soda

1 teaspoon salt
1 teaspoon cinnamon
1 teaspoon cloves
1 teaspoon nutmeg
1 cup chopped apples
1 cup chopped nuts

Cream butter and sugar till light. Add egg and milk, beating till smooth. Sift dry ingredients together and stir into butter mixture with the apples and nuts. Drop by teaspoonfuls on greased cookie sheet. Bake at 375° for 10 minutes. Cool and frost. Yields 4 dozen.

FROSTING:

1 tablespoon butter, softened
1½ cups confectioners' sugar

3 tablespoons milk
¼ teaspoon vanilla

Combine all ingredients well.

The Junior League of Grand Rapids Cookbook I (Michigan)

Lemonade Cookies

Very refreshing.

1 cup margarine or butter
1 cup sugar
2 eggs
3 cups all-purpose flour
1 teaspoon baking soda

1 (6-ounce) can frozen
   lemonade concentrate,
   thawed
Sugar

Cream butter and one cup sugar. Add eggs; beat until fluffy. Sift flour and baking soda. Add alternately to cream mix with $1/2$ cup of lemonade concentrate. Drop from a teaspoon, $2^1/2$ inches apart, on ungreased cookie sheet. Bake in hot oven (400°) 8 minutes, or until lightly browned around the edges. Brush hot cookies with remaining lemonade concentrate. Sprinkle with sugar. Remove to cooling racks. Makes 4 dozen small cookies.

This is a soft cookie. Best stored in a flat pan—only a double layer.

Our Favorite Recipes (Minnesota)

Lemon Thyme Cookies

An unusual and tasty cookie from an herb lady in Northern Michigan.

2½ cups unbleached flour
1 teaspoon cream of tartar
1 cup unsalted butter, softened
1½ cups sugar

2 eggs
3 tablespoons fresh lemon
   thyme, finely chopped

Sift together flour and cream of tartar. Cream butter with sugar, add eggs, and mix well. Work in flour mixture till well blended. Stir in lemon thyme. Chill several hours. Roll into balls the size of small walnuts. Bake on greased cookie sheet 10 minutes in a preheated 350° oven.

Historically Delicious (Michigan)

Apricot Lilies
(A Butter Cookie)

¼ cup sugar
1 cup sweet, unsalted
  butter, softened
1 (3-ounce) package
  cream cheese, softened
1 teaspoon vanilla

2 cups all-purpose flour
¼ teaspoon salt
Approximately ½ cup apricot
  jam (or another fruit jam)
Powdered sugar

Combine sugar, butter, cream cheese, and vanilla. Beat at medium speed until well mixed (about one minute). Reduce speed to low; add flour and salt. Continue beating until well mixed (about 1½–2 minutes). Divide dough into 4 parts. Wrap in plastic food wrap. Refrigerate until firm (at least 2 hours).

On lightly floured surface, roll out dough (¼ at a time) to ⅛-inch thickness. Keep remaining dough refrigerated. Cut with 2-inch round cookie cutter. Place on cookie sheets (½ inch apart). With thin spatula, fold dough over jam to form a lily shape. Gently press narrow end to seal. Jam will show on top of cone-shaped cookie. Heat oven to 375°. Bake 7–11 minutes or until edges are lightly browned. Cool completely. Sprinkle lightly with powdered sugar. Makes approximately 8 dozen cookies.

St. Mary's Family Cookbook (Wisconsin)

Cinnamon Tea Cookies

Not only are these good at "tea-time," but a favorite on the Christmas tray.

1 cup butter, softened
¾ cup sugar
1 egg, separated
1 teaspoon vanilla

2 cups all-purpose flour
4 teaspoons cinnamon
½ cup ground pecans or walnuts

Preheat oven to 350°. In large mixing bowl, cream together butter and sugar. Beat in egg yolk and vanilla. Combine flour and cinnamon, then blend in with a wooden spoon. Form into balls, using a ½ teaspoon measure.

Beat egg white only till frothy. Dip ½ of each ball in egg white then ground nuts. Place, dipped-side up on ungreased cookie sheet, one inch apart. Bake 12 minutes. Yields 8 dozen.

Hollyhocks & Radishes (Michigan)

Cereal Bars

5 cups cereal (Special K, flakes or Chex)
1 cup sugar
1 cup white syrup

1½ cups peanut butter
½ cup chocolate chips
½ cup butterscotch or peanut butter chips

Put cereal in large bowl. Bring to boil the sugar and syrup; remove from heat when it starts to boil. Add peanut butter and mix with cereal. Put in 9x13-inch pan. Melt chips together and frost bars.

Clinton's 110th Cookbook (Minnesota)

Peanut Squares

CRUST:

1½ cups all-purpose flour
⅔ packed brown sugar
½ teaspoon baking powder
½ teaspoon salt
¼ teaspoon baking soda

½ cup margarine
1 teaspoon vanilla
2 egg yolks
3 cups mini-marshmallows

Heat oven to 350°. Combine all crust ingredients except marshmallows. Press firmly in bottom of ungreased 9x13-inch pan. Bake at 350° for 12–15 minutes or until light golden brown; remove from oven. Immediately sprinkle with marshmallows. Return to oven for 1–2 minutes or until marshmallows just begin to puff. Cool while preparing topping.

TOPPING:

⅔ cup corn syrup
½ cup margarine
2 teaspoons vanilla
1 (12-ounce) package peanut
   butter chips (2 cups)

2 cups crisp rice cereal
2 cups salted peanuts

In large saucepan, heat corn syrup, margarine, vanilla, and peanut butter chips until chips are melted and mixture is smooth; stir constantly. Remove from heat, stir in cereal and peanuts. Immediately spoon warm topping over marshmallows; spread to cover. Refrigerate until firm. Cut into bars.

Centennial Cookbook (Wisconsin)

Salted Peanut Bars

3 cups self-rising flour
¾ cup brown sugar

1 cup margarine
½ teaspoon salt

Mix like pie crust and pat in a cookie sheet. Bake 10 minutes at 350°.

TOPPING:

1 (12-ounce) package
   butterscotch chips
3 tablespoons butter

3 tablespoons water
½ cup white syrup
3 cups peanuts or mixed nuts

Combine chips, butter, water, and syrup and melt over hot water. When melted add peanuts or mixed nuts and spread over crust. Return to oven for 8 minutes longer. Cool and cut into bars.

The Queen of Angels Anniversary Cookbook (Minnesota)

Pumpkin Bars

4 eggs
1 cup salad oil
2 cups sugar
1 (15-ounce) can pumpkin
2 cups all-purpose flour
2 teaspoons baking powder

1 teaspoon baking soda
½ teaspoon nutmeg
½ teaspoon salt
2 teaspoons cinnamon
½ teaspoon ginger
½ teaspoon cloves

Preheat oven to 350°. Mix first 4 ingredients together well and add the others. Mix well; pour into a greased 12x8-inch pan. Bake at 350° for 25–30 minutes. Cool and frost.

FROSTING:

1 (8-ounce) package cream
   cheese, softened
¾ stick butter

1 tablespoon cream or milk
1 teaspoon vanilla
4 cups powdered sugar

Mix all ingredients and frost bars.

Old Westbrook Evangelical Lutheran Church Cookbook (Minnesota)

Little Debbie Bars

Prepare one devil's food cake mix as directed on package. Divide into 2 jellyroll pans ($10^1/_2$ x $15^1/_2$ x 1) and bake 20 minutes at 350°.

FILLING:

5 tablespoons self-rising flour

1 cup milk

½ teaspoon salt

1 cup sugar

½ cup Crisco

½ cup margarine

1 teaspoon vanilla

Blend flour, milk, and salt. Cook until thick, then cool. Cream at high speed the sugar, Crisco, and margarine. Gradually add cooled mixture and vanilla. Beat 7 minutes at high speed. Put filling on one cake; put other cake on top.

FROSTING:

1⅓ cups sugar

6 tablespoons margarine

⅓ cup milk

½ cup chocolate chips

Boil sugar, margarine, and milk for one minute. Take off heat and stir in chocolate chips until melted. Let cool for 15 minutes. Stir often. Frost cake on top only. Keep in refrigerator; it is best cooled.

Variation: Twinkie Bars—substitute yellow cake mix for devil's food: then serve with or without frosting.

The Queen of Angels Anniversary Cookbook (Minnesota)

Minneapolis, sometimes called the "City of Lakes," is abundantly rich in water with over twenty lakes and wetlands, the Mississippi river, creeks and water-falls, many connected by parkways. The city lies on both banks of the Mississippi River, just north of the river's confluence with the Minnesota River, and ad-joins Saint Paul, the state's capital.

Mystery Bars

3 eggs
2 cups sugar
1 cup cooking oil
2 cups unpeeled zucchini,
  coarsely grated and packed
2 cups all-purpose flour

1 tablespoon cinnamon
2 teaspoons soda
¼ teaspoon baking powder
1 tablespoon (yes) vanilla
½ cup nuts (optional)
½ cup raisins (optional)

Beat eggs; add sugar, oil, and zucchini. Sift in flour, cinnamon, soda, and baking powder. Add vanilla, nuts, and raisins. Bake in greased and floured jellyroll pan or 9x13-inch pan at 350° for 20–35 minutes. Cool. Frost with Cream Cheese Frosting.

CREAM CHEESE FROSTING:
4 tablespoons melted butter
  or margarine
6 ounces cream cheese,
  softened

3 cups powdered sugar
1 teaspoon vanilla

Mix well. Frost bars.

Kitchen Keepsakes (Minnesota)

Frosted Apple Bars

2½ cups self-rising flour
1 tablespoon sugar
1 teaspoon salt
1 cup shortening
2 egg yolks (add milk to make
  ⅔ cup liquid)
2 egg whites

1½ cups crumbled cornflakes
8–10 pared apples, sliced thin
1½ cups granulated sugar
1¼ teaspoons cinnamon
1 cup powdered sugar
3 or 4 teaspoons water

Sift flour, sugar, and salt together. Cut in shortening. Add egg yolks and milk. Chill and then roll out ½ of dough to fit a 12x15-inch jellyroll pan. Sprinkle cornflakes over dough. Add apples. Mix sugar and cinnamon and sprinkle over apples. Roll out other ½ of dough and place on top of apples. Pinch edges together. Beat egg whites until frothy and spread over crust. Bake at 350° for one hour. Remove from oven. Mix powdered sugar and water together, and drizzle over hot crust.

Anoka County 4H Cook Book (Minnesota)

Sour Cream Apple Squares

Sour Cream Apple Squares are amazingly easy to prepare, especially for last-minute company, since they are best served the day they are made. Top them off with whipped cream or ice cream.

2 cups all-purpose flour
2 cups firmly packed brown
  sugar
1 stick butter or margarine,
  softened
1 cup chopped walnuts or
  pecans
1 cup sour cream

1 egg
1 teaspoon baking soda
2 teaspoons cinnamon
½ teaspoon salt
1 teaspoon vanilla extract
2 medium Ida Red apples, peeled,
  finely chopped (or 2 cups)

Preheat oven to 350°. Mix flour and brown sugar in a mixer bowl. Blend in butter at low speed until mixture is crumbly. Stir in walnuts. Press 2¾ cups mixture into a greased 9x13-inch baking pan. Add sour cream, egg, baking soda, cinnamon, salt, and vanilla to remaining crumb mixture; mix well. Stir in apples. Spread evenly in prepared pan. Bake at 350° for 25–35 minutes or until a tester inserted in center comes out clean. Cut into squares to serve. Serves 12–15.

The Dexter Cider Mill Apple Cookbook (Michigan)

Apricot Bars

¾ cup butter
1 cup sugar
2 cups all-purpose flour

½ teaspoon salt
½ teaspoon baking soda

Cream butter, sugar, flour, salt, and baking soda together. Spread 3 cups into a 10x15-inch pan. Bake 10 minutes at 400°.

FILLING:
1 small jar apricot jam
½ cup chopped walnuts

1½ cups oatmeal

Spread over first mixture. Sprinkle remaining crumbs over the apricot filling. Bake at 400° for 15–20 minutes.

Kompelien Family Cookbook (Minnesota)

Hungarian Fruit Pastry Bars

5 cups all-purpose flour
1 cup plus 3 tablespoons sugar, divided
4 teaspoons baking powder
2 teaspoons baking soda
⅛ teaspoon salt
1¼ cups shortening
4 egg yolks
½ cup sour cream
¼ cup water
1 teaspoon vanilla
2½ cups chopped walnuts, divided
1 (18-ounce) jar strawberry or apricot jam

In a large bowl, combine flour, 1 cup sugar, baking powder, baking soda, and salt. Cut in shortening until it resembles coarse crumbs. In a bowl, whisk egg yolks, sour cream, water, and vanilla. Add to crumb mixture. Form dough into ball. Divide into thirds. Chill 30 minutes.

Roll one portion of dough into 10x15x1-inch rectangle; sprinkle with 1¼ cups walnuts and 2 tablespoons sugar. Roll out next portion same size as first. Place over walnuts. Spread with jam; sprinkle with remaining walnuts and sugar. Roll out third portion; cut into strips. Arrange in a crisscross pattern over filling. Bake at 350° for 30 minutes, or until golden brown. Cool. Cut into bars.

Tasteful Garden Treasures (Michigan)

Ishpeming, located in Michigan's Upper Peninsula, is known as "the birthplace of organized skiing in America." The sport was introduced here by Scandinavian iron miners. The miners' Norden Ski Club, formed in 1887, held the first ski jumping contests, and in 1905 its successor, the Ishpeming Ski Club, met with other ski clubs to establish the National Ski Association, now known as the U.S. Ski & Snowboard Association. To draw attention to Ishpeming's hallowed role in the sport, the local ski club started the U.S. National Ski and Snowboard Hall of Fame and Museum in 1954.

Cheesy Rhubarb Bars

CRUST:

1 cup all-purpose flour
½ cup butter

5 tablespoons sugar

Mix together and press into 9x13-inch pan.

FILLING:

2 eggs, slightly beaten
⅛ teaspoon salt
1½ cups sugar
¼ cup flour

1 (8-ounce) package cream
cheese
2 cups rhubarb, peeled
and finely cut

Bake at 350° for 10 minutes. Mix together and pour over crust.

TOPPING:

¼ cup butter
½ cup flour

2½ tablespoons powdered
sugar

Mix and crumble on top of filling. Bake at 350° for 40–45 minutes or until set.

A Taste of Home (Wisconsin)

Cherry Nut Bars

2 cups all-purpose flour
2 cups quick cooking oats
1½ cups sugar
½ cup pecans or walnuts,
chopped
1 teaspoon baking soda

1 cup butter, melted (may use
margarine)
1 (21-ounce) can cherry pie
filling
1 cup miniature marsh-
mallows

Combine flour, oats, sugar, nuts, soda, and butter. Mix at low speed until crumbly consistency. Set aside 1½ cups for topping. Press remaining into a 9x13-inch pan. Bake at 350° for 12–15 minutes or until lightly browned at edges. Carefully spread pie filling over crust; sprinkle with marshmallows and remaining crumb mixture. Bake for 25–30 minutes more or until lightly browned. Cool. Yields 4 dozen small bars.

St. John Evangelical Lutheran Church (Wisconsin)

Chocolate-Cherry Squares

1¼ cups chocolate wafer
  cookie crumbs
2 tablespoons sugar
¼ cup margarine, melted
3 squares semisweet chocolate

¼ cup water
½ (8-ounce) package cream
  cheese, softened
2 cups chocolate Cool Whip
1 (21-ounce) can cherry pie filling

Mix crumbs, sugar, and margarine in a 9-inch square pan. Press firmly into bottom of pan. Refrigerate 10 minutes. Microwave chocolate and water 1–2 minutes, or till chocolate is almost melted, stirring halfway through heating time. Stir till chocolate is completely melted. Beat cream cheese till smooth and fluffy. Gradually beat in chocolate mixture. Gently stir in 2 cups Cool Whip. Spread evenly over crumb crust. Spoon pie filling over chocolate layer. Refrigerate 3 hours, or till set. Cut into squares. Store leftovers in refrigerator.

Trendfully Cookin' (Michigan)

Cherry Cheese Brownie Bars

1 (16-ounce) package fudge
  brownie mix
2 teaspoons vanilla
1 egg
1 (14-ounce) can sweetened
  condensed milk

1 (8-ounce) package cream
  cheese, softened
1 (21-ounce) can cherry pie
  filling

Prepare brownie mix as directed on package, except bake only 20 minutes. Beat vanilla, egg, milk, and cream cheese until smooth and pour over partially baked brownie mix. Bake until topping is set, about 25 minutes. Cool. Spread cherry pie filling on top.

Serving from the Heart (Michigan)

Café Brownies

1 cup sugar	4 eggs, beaten
1 stick margarine, melted	1 cup chocolate syrup
1 teaspoon baking powder	1 cup all-purpose flour

Mix brownie ingredients, and bake at 350° in 9x13-inch pan until edges begin to pull away from pan.

FROSTING:

1 cup sugar	½ cup mini-marshmallows
¼ cup milk	½ cup chocolate chips
¼ cup margarine	

Stir sugar, margarine and milk together in small saucepan, until it comes to a boil. Add marshmallows and boil for no more than one minute. Remove from heat, and add chocolate chips. Stir briskly until marshmallows and chips are melted. Pour over brownies and let cool before cutting.

Wannaska Centennial (Minnesota)

Date Roll

4 cups sugar	1 cup nutmeats
2 cups milk	1 teaspoon vanilla
1 pound chopped dates	Powdered sugar

Boil sugar and milk until it forms a soft ball in cold water. Do not stir. After it forms a soft ball, add dates and cook until they are dissolved, stirring all the time to keep it from sticking. Remove from fire and add nutmeats and vanilla. Stir until cool enough that when put on a clean wet cloth, it will not stick. Roll up in the cloth and allow to stand in a cool place for a while before removing from cloth. Slice in small slices and roll in powdered sugar.

Sharing Our Best (Michigan)

Crispy Nests

1 (7-ounce) jar marshmallow crème
¼ cup creamy peanut butter
2 tablespoons butter or margarine, melted
1 (5-ounce) can chow mein noodles
1 cup chopped holidays plain M&M's
1 cup holidays peanut M&M's

Combine marshmallow crème, peanut butter, and butter; mix until well blended. Add noodles and plain M&M's; mix well. Drop by ¹/₃ cupfuls onto greased cookie sheet. Shape with greased fingers to form nests. Let stand until firm. Dust bottom of nests lightly with confectioners' sugar, if desired. Fill with holidays peanut M&M's before serving. Makes 10–12 nests.

Dell & Barry's Holiday Delights for All Seasons (Michigan)

Nature's Candy Kisses

A great way to pop some natural ingredients into their mouths.

1¼ cups peanut butter
¾ cup honey
1½ teaspoons vanilla
1¼ cups instant non-fat dry milk
1¼ cups quick cooking oats
½ cup graham cracker crumbs
¼ cup wheat germ
1 cup powdered sugar

In large bowl, blend peanut butter, honey, and vanilla. Add dry milk, oats, graham cracker crumbs, and wheat germ; mix well. Refrigerate 1–2 hours. Place powdered sugar in a small bowl. Roll peanut butter mixture into balls, using 1 heaping teaspoon of mixture per ball. Shape each ball into a "kiss" (a pyramid with a round base). Roll each kiss through the powdered sugar. Refrigerate several hours or overnight.

Smart Snacks (Michigan)

Chocolate Amaretto Truffles

2 ounces unsweetened baking chocolate, coarsely chopped
2 tablespoons butter
1 (8-ounce) package cream cheese, softened
⅔ cup granulated Splenda
½ teaspoon vanilla extract
½ teaspoon almond flavoring
2 tablespoons amaretto liqueur
⅔ cup finely chopped walnuts

Melt chocolate pieces and butter (about 2 minutes on defrost setting in microwave); add to cream cheese and mix. Add sweetener and flavorings and mix until thoroughly combined. Chill until firm enough to handle, about 1 hour. Use a melon baller dipped in hot water to make small rounds and roll in chopped nuts. (Or work with 2 teaspoons—dip $1/2$ teaspoon batter with one spoon, then push batter into nuts with other spoon. Use spoons to roll candy in nuts.) Place each candy in a small truffle wrapper or mini-muffin cup. Store in single layer in an airtight container in refrigerator. Makes about 30 (1-inch) candies.

Recipes from Joan's Kitchen (Michigan)

Chocolate Golf Balls

2 sticks margarine, melted
2 cups crushed graham crackers
1 cup peanut butter
½ cup ground nuts
1 pound powdered sugar
1 (6-ounce) package chocolate chips
1 (6-ounce) package peanut butter or butterscotch chips
⅛ block paraffin

Mix together first 5 ingredients and form into balls. Refrigerate until firm. Melt chocolate chips, peanut butter or butterscotch chips, and paraffin wax in medium saucepan. Dip balls into mixture. Lift out with fork. Place on wax paper and refrigerate. Makes 40–50 balls.

Generations of Treasured Recipes! (Michigan)

Peanut Butter Christmas Mice

1 cup creamy peanut butter
½ cup butter, softened
½ cup sugar
½ cup packed brown sugar
1 egg
1 teaspoon vanilla extract
1½ cups all-purpose flour
½ teaspoon baking soda
½ cup peanut halves
2 tablespoons green and red M&M's miniature baking bits
4 teaspoons mini semisweet chocolate chips
Cake decorator holly leaf and berry candies
60–66 (2-inch) pieces red shoestring licorice

In large mixing bowl, cream peanut butter, butter, sugar, and brown sugar. Beat in egg and vanilla. Combine flour and baking soda; gradually add to creamed mixture. Refrigerate 1 hour or until easy to handle.

Roll into 1-inch balls. Place 2 inches apart on ungreased baking sheets. Pinch each ball at one end to taper. Insert 2 peanut halves in center of each ball for ears. Add one M&M's baking bit for nose and 2 chocolate chips for eyes. Arrange holly and berry candies in front of one ear. Bake at 350° for 8–10 minutes or until set. Gently insert 1 licorice piece into each warm cookie for tail. Remove to wire racks to cool completely. Makes 5 dozen mice.

Sweet Traditions (Michigan)

Peanut Butter Logs

2 cups peanut butter
½ cup butter
1 (1-pound) box powdered sugar, sifted
3 cups Rice Krispies
1 (6-ounce) package semisweet chocolate chips

In saucepan, melt peanut butter and butter. In large bowl, combine powdered sugar and cereal. Pour peanut butter mixture over cereal mixture; blend with hands. Roll into ½-inch balls. Chill till firm. Melt chocolate in double boiler. Dip candies in this and swirl top with back of spoon. Place on wax paper in cookie sheet; chill. Makes 100 candies.

From Our Home to Yours (Michigan)

Tumbledowns

½ cup sugar
½ cup brown sugar, firmly
   packed
½ cup shortening or butter
½ cup peanut butter
2 tablespoons milk
1 teaspoon vanilla
1 egg

1 (6-ounce) package chocolate
   chips
1 (6-ounce) package Heath bits
1½ cups miniature
   marshmallows
1¾ cups all-purpose flour
1 teaspoon baking soda
½ teaspoon salt

In a large bowl, combine sugar, brown sugar, shortening, peanut butter, milk, vanilla, and egg. Blend at medium speed until smooth. Stir in flour, soda, and salt. Mix well. Add the chocolate chips, Heath bits, and marshmallows and mix.

Using a teaspoon, drop 2 inches apart on ungreased cookie sheet. Bake at 375° for 8–12 minutes until light golden brown. Let cool slightly before removing from pan. Makes 36 cookies.

Winning Recipes from Wisconsin with Love (Wisconsin)

Butter Toffee

1 cup sugar
½ teaspoon salt
¼ cup water

½ cup butter
½ cup walnuts (optional)
1 cup chocolate chips

Combine first 4 ingredients and cook to 285° (hard crack) stirring constantly. Add ½ cup chopped walnuts, if desired. Pour onto well-greased cookie sheet. Sprinkle one cup chocolate chips over immediately. Allow a few minutes to melt and spread, using back of teaspoon. Cool and break.

A Collection of Recipes (Wisconsin)

Michigan Nut and Berry Bark

1 pound bittersweet chocolate, finely chopped
1½ cups chopped nuts, (such as almonds, walnuts, or macadamia) toasted, divided
1½ cups dried cranberries, apricots, or cherries, divided
½ cup flaked coconut, toasted, divided
4 ounces white chocolate, melted

Melt bittersweet chocolate in top of a double boiler over simmering water. Stir in 1 cup nuts, 1 cup dried cranberries, and ¼ cup coconut. Pour onto a parchment- or foil-lined 10x15-inch baking pan. Spread chocolate mixture over parchment to a 10x14-inch rectangle with a rubber spatula. Sprinkle with remaining ½ cup dried cranberries, ½ cup nuts, and ¼ cup coconut. Cover with plastic wrap and gently pat down. Remove plastic wrap and drizzle with white chocolate. Chill, covered, until bark is hard. Break into large pieces. Store in an airtight container for a week or freeze in sealable plastic bags. Serves 14.

Between the Lakes (Michigan)

Tiger Butter

1 pound white chocolate, chopped
¼ cup semisweet chocolate chips
⅓ cup crunchy peanut butter
½ cup crispy rice cereal

Line a 9x9-inch pan with wax paper. Combine white chocolate, chocolate chips, and peanut butter in a 2-quart microwave-safe dish and microwave on low for 1 minute. Stir until smooth. Stir in rice cereal and spread into prepared pan. Let cool completely before cutting into squares.

Red Flannel Town Recipes (Michigan)

Heath Candy

1 cup pecans, crushed
¾ cup brown sugar

½ cup butter
½ cup semisweet chocolate chips

Sprinkle pecans onto the bottom of a greased 9-inch pan. Combine sugar and butter in a saucepan and bring to a boil, stirring for 7 minutes. Remove from heat and spread over nuts. Sprinkle chocolate pieces on top. Cover pan so heat will melt chocolate pieces, then spread them over the top. Cut into squares and refrigerate to set.

Favorite Recipes of the Wisconsin NFO

Creamy Maple Fudge

3 cups brown sugar
⅓ cup Wisconsin pure
maple syrup
⅓ cup milk

2 tablespoons butter
Salt
½ teaspoon vanilla
½ cup chopped nuts

Combine all ingredients except vanilla and nuts. Stir gently over low heat until dissolved. Do not stir, but boil to soft-ball stage. Cool. Beat until thick and creamy. Add flavoring and nuts. Pour into greased pan, and cut before mixture cools and hardens.

Wisconsin Pure Maple Syrup Cookbook (Wisconsin)

Pies and Other Desserts

WWW.WIKIPEDIA.ORG

In addition to being Hormel's corporate headquarters, Austin, Minnesota, is also home to the Spam Museum, and the plant that produces Spam for most of North America and Europe.

Killer Peanut Butter and Fudge Ripple Pie

1 (8-ounce) package cream
  cheese, softened
¾ cup powdered sugar
¼ cup peanut butter
1 teaspoon vanilla
2 eggs

1 pre-made chocolate crumb
  pie crust
1 cup whipping cream, whipped
½ cup semisweet chocolate
  chips, melted

Combine cream cheese, powdered sugar, peanut butter, and vanilla; beat at medium speed till smooth and well blended. Add eggs, one at a time, beating well after each addition. Fold in whipped cream. Spoon into crust. Spoon melted chocolate randomly over filling. Gently pull knife through chocolate to marble. Freeze. When ready to serve, let stand at room temperature about 15 minutes before serving. Serves 8–10.

Note: To pasteurize raw eggs: Place eggs in simmering water for 1 – 2 minutes, then submerge in ice water. You may also break eggs into a small glass bowl and microwave on HIGH 15 seconds; this will slightly cook the eggs, yet they will still have a runny consistency.

What's Cookin' (Michigan)

Peanut Butter Cream Cheese Pie

6 ounces cream cheese,
  softened
¾ cup sifted powdered sugar
½ cup peanut butter

2 tablespoons milk
2 cups Cool Whip
1 (8-inch) graham cracker pie
  crust

Beat cheese and sugar till light and fluffy. Add peanut butter and milk. Beat till smooth and creamy. Fold in Cool Whip and turn into crust. Chill 5–6 hours or overnight.

Maple Hill Cookbook (Minnesota)

Wisconsin Cheese Pie with Apple Cider Marmalade

12 ounces cottage cheese
  (or ricotta)
16 ounces softened
  cream cheese
1½ cups sugar
1 teaspoon vanilla

1 lemon, seeds removed,
  quartered
4 eggs, slightly beaten
1 unbaked 9-inch pie shell
Whipped cream for garnish
Fresh strawberries for garnish

Preheat oven to 350°. Combine all pie ingredients except eggs. Blend in food processor until smooth. Fold in eggs. Pour into pie shell. Bake at 350° for 30 minutes. Cool completely before serving. Garnish, and serve slices in plate with Apple Cider Marmalade.

APPLE CIDER MARMALADE:

5 cups firm apples, cored
  and slivered (unpeeled)
1 cup apple cider
½ cup orange juice
  concentrate

½ cup grated orange rind
½ cup grated lemon rind
1 (1¾-ounce) package pectin
7 cups sugar

Place apples, cider, orange juice concentrate, rinds, and pectin in a large saucepan or jelly kettle. Bring the mixture to a rolling boil. Add sugar and stir until completely dissolved. Bring to a rolling boil again. Boil 65 seconds, stirring constantly. Remove the mixture from heat. Cool for 3 minutes. Skim off any foam with a slotted spoon. Ladle into sterilized jars, seal and process in a water bath according to manufacturer's instructions. Yields 7 cups.

Note: Many varieties of firm apples will work, but we prefer Cortlands.

Recipe from Old Rittenhouse Inn, Bayfield. Innkeepers Mary and Jerry Phillips
Wisconsin Cooks with Wisconsin Public Television (Wisconsin)

Grasshopper Pie

20 large marshmallows
½ cup milk
18 chocolate cookies, crushed
¼ cup melted butter

1 cup whipping cream, whipped
1 ounce (¼ cup) cream de cocoa
1 ounce (¼ cup) cream de menthe

Melt marshmallows in milk and let cool. Mix cookie crumbs with butter and press into pie tin. Stir liqueurs into whipped cream, then add marshmallow mixture. Pour into crust and let set overnight in refrigerator.

From the Recipe File of Agnes Gaffaney (Minnesota)

Bits 'O Brickle Ice Cream Pie

PIE:
Prepared 9-inch graham cracker pie shell
½ gallon vanilla ice cream, softened

½ (7.8-ounce) bag brickle bits, divided

Spoon ½ of ice cream into prepared pie shell. Sprinkle bits (½ bag) on top. Heap with remaining ice cream. Freeze.

SAUCE:
1½ cups sugar
1 cup evaporated milk
¼ cup butter

¼ cup Karo (light)
Dash of salt
Remaining ½ bag bits

Combine sugar, milk, butter, syrup, and salt. Bring to boil over low heat; boil one minute. Remove from heat and stir in remaining bits. Cool. Stir occasionally. Chill. Stir sauce well before serving, spoon over pie. Keep remaining sauce. Good! Enjoy!

Favorite Recipes of Lester Park & Rockridge Schools (Minnesota)

Maple Pecan Pie

1 pie shell, unbaked
¼ cup butter
⅔ cup firmly packed brown
   sugar
⅛ teaspoon salt

¼ cup maple syrup
3 eggs, beaten until light
1 cup broken pecans
1 teaspoon vanilla

Cream butter, brown sugar, and salt. Stir in other ingredients. Turn into lined pie pan. Bake for 10 minutes at 450° and then turn heat down to 350°. Bake for 30–35 minutes longer. Serve with whipped cream.

Wisconsin Pure Maple Syrup Cookbook (Wisconsin)

Mom Miller's Old Fashioned Pumpkin Pie

3 tablespoons butter, softened
⅓ cup firmly packed brown
   sugar
⅓ cup chopped pecans
1 unbaked pie shell
2 cups pumpkin, no spices
   added

1 cup sugar
½ teaspoon salt
1 teaspoon cinnamon
½ teaspoon ginger
¼ teaspoon nutmeg
1 cup undiluted evaporated milk

Mix together butter, brown sugar, and pecans. Smooth into bottom of unbaked pie shell and bake at 450° for 10 minutes. Cool on wire rack 10 minutes. While hot, prick any bubbles with a fork tine. Reduce heat to 350°. Beat remaining ingredients till smooth; pour into shell over pecan bottom. Bake 45–50 minutes.

From Our Home to Yours (Michigan)

Fresh Berry Berry Pie

Blueberries smothered in blueberries, then raspberries topping all, will give you one of the best desserts of many a summer eve.

4 cups fresh blueberries,
  divided
½ cup sugar
2 tablespoons cornstarch
6 tablespoons water
1 tablespoon lemon juice

3–4 ounces cream cheese,
  well softened
1 (9-inch) pie shell, baked,
  cooled
1 cup fresh raspberries
Whipped cream

In a medium saucepan, combine 2 cups blueberries with sugar, cornstarch, and water. Bring to a boil and cook slowly until thickened, stirring constantly, about 2 minutes. Remove from heat, stir in lemon juice, then set aside to cool.

Gently spread cream cheese on bottom of cooled pie crust. Stir 1½ more cups blueberries into cooled berry mixture. Pour into prepared crust. Sprinkle raspberries over top, then remaining ½-cup blueberries. Chill completely (at least 2 hours). To serve, garnish with dollops of whipped cream. Serves 8–10.

Note: This recipe is ideal for individual tarts. For tart or pie shells, for best appearance and least amount of shrinkage, prick pastry with a table fork across bottom and along sides, then bake at 425° for 10–12 minutes . . . just until golden brown.

Hollyhocks & Radishes (Michigan)

Peaches and Cream Pie

CRUST:

½ cup shortening
1½ cups all-purpose flour
¼ teaspoon baking powder
¼ teaspoon salt

½ egg, beaten
2½ tablespoons water
½ tablespoon vinegar

Blend shortening into flour, baking powder, and salt. Mix together egg, water, and vinegar; add to flour mixture. Press into bottom of pie pan.

FILLING:

4 cups sliced peaches
½ cup sugar
½ teaspoon cinnamon

2 eggs
4 tablespoons cream

Mix together peaches, sugar, and cinnamon. Beat eggs with cream and pour over peaches. Pour peach mixture on top of Crust.

CRUMB TOPPING:

¼ + 2 tablespoons butter
¾ cup brown sugar

¾ cup all-purpose flour

Mix butter and brown sugar; cut in flour and sprinkle over pie. Bake at 425° for 35–45 minutes.

From Our Home to Yours (Michigan)

WWW.WIKIPEDIA.ORG

Gerald R. Ford grew up in Grand Rapids, Michigan. He was the first person appointed to the vice presidency under the terms of the 25th Amendment, and became president upon Richard Nixon's resignation on August 9, 1974. Ford was the fifth U.S. president never to have been elected to that position, and the only one never to have won a national election.

The Gerald R. Ford Museum, opened in Grand Rapids, Michigan, in 1981. The Gerald R. Ford Presidential Library is located in Ann Arbor, Michigan, on the campus of the University of Michigan, Ford's alma mater.

Apple Sour Cream Pie

This is the best thing I make!

PIE:

2 tablespoons flour
¾ cup sugar
¾ teaspoon cinnamon
⅛ teaspoon salt
1 egg

½ teaspoon vanilla
1 cup (½ pint) sour cream
6 medium apples, peeled,
  pared and sliced
1 (9-inch) graham cracker crust

Preheat oven to 400°. Combine all pie ingredients except apples and crust. Add the apples and pour mixture into crust. Bake for 15 minutes, reduce heat to 350° and bake for 30 minutes.

TOPPING:

⅓ cup sugar
⅓ cup flour

¾ teaspoon cinnamon
¼ cup butter, creamed

Combine Topping ingredients and crumble over pie. Bake at 400° for 10 minutes. Serve warm or cold.

Good Cooking, Good Curling (Wisconsin)

Michigan Four Seasons Pie

CRUST:

½ cup butter
1½ cups all-purpose flour

1 tablespoon water

Melt butter in a 9-inch pie pan. Add flour and water. Mix with fork and press into bottom and sides of pan. Bake at 425° for 15 minutes.

SYRUP:

1 cup sugar
1 tablespoon cornstarch
1 cup water

¼ cup dry flavored gelatin
  powder
4 cups sliced fresh Michigan fruit

Combine sugar, cornstarch, and water. Boil 1 minute or till clear. Stir gelatin into syrup; cool. Pour mixture over fresh fruit which has been placed in the baked Crust. Serves 6–8.

Variations: Use strawberry gelatin for strawberry pie; peach for peach pie; lemon for blueberry pie; raspberry for raspberry pie.

Some Enchanted Eating (Michigan)

Lazy Cherry Cobbler

Sure to be a family favorite.

**2 (21-ounce) cans cherry pie
   filling**
½ (21-ounce) can water
½ teaspoon almond extract

1½ cups self-rising flour
1 cup sugar
1 cup skim milk

Preheat oven to 375°. Combine cherries, water, and almond extract;
mix well. Place in ungreased 9x13-inch baking pan. In a mixing bowl,
combine dry ingredients; mix well. Add milk and stir till well mixed.
Pour evenly over cherries; run a knife through the mixture as if mar-
bleizing. Bake 25–40 minutes till golden brown. Serves 12.

"Life Tastes Better Than Steak" Cookbook (Michigan)

Hemingway's Fresh Fruit Cobbler

1 cup all-purpose flour
1 cup sugar
1 teaspoon baking soda
1 egg
⅔ cup milk
2 teaspoons lemon juice
1 teaspoon vanilla

1 tablespoon butter
¼ cup cinnamon sugar
**1½ cups chopped fresh fruit
   (pears, pineapple, strawberries,
   blueberries, raspberries,
   bananas)**

Mix flour, sugar, and baking soda together in medium bowl. Mix egg,
milk, vanilla, and lemon juice in another bowl; pour into flour mixture.
Mix till blended.

   Chop fruit into raspberry-size pieces. Grease small glass casserole
dish or 9-inch smooth pie pan with 1 tablespoon butter; add cinnamon sugar to pan, swirl out excess butter. Add chopped fruit except
bananas; cover fruit with batter. Put sliced bananas on top of batter;
sprinkle with cinnamon sugar.

   Bake in 325° oven 20–25 minutes, or till done. Use toothpick to test
for doneness. Let rest 5 minutes before serving. Makes 4 generous
servings.

Note: The fruit can be chopped and mixed ahead of time, though do not mix
strawberries, raspberries, or blueberries till the last minute.

Four Seasons Cookbook (Michigan)

Keith Famie's Michigan Apple and Cherry Cobbler

1½ pounds butter
1½ cups brown sugar
2 cinnamon sticks
8 Granny Smith apples, peeled, cored, diced
1½ cups dried cherries

½ cup brandy
3 sheets pie dough or puff pastry
1 egg, beaten lightly for egg wash
Whipped cream for topping

Preheat oven to 400°. In a sauté pan, melt butter with brown sugar and cinnamon. Stir in apples, cherries, and brandy. Cook over medium heat for 10 minutes, stirring occasionally until apples are soft. Remove mixture from heat and cool to room temperature. Remove cinnamon sticks. This can be made a day ahead and refrigerated.

Fill 4 individual dishes or 9x9-inch glass or ceramic dish to top with apple mixture. Place pie dough on top, being sure that you cover all the mixture. Brush lightly with egg wash. Bake 15–20 minutes or until top is golden brown. Serve with freshly whipped cream. Serves 4.

Cherry Home Companion (Michigan)

Rhubarb Dream

1 cup flour
5 tablespoons powdered sugar
½ cup butter or margarine
2 eggs

1½ cups sugar
¼ cup flour
¾ teaspoon salt
2 cups rhubarb

Blend flour, powdered sugar, and butter. Press in ungreased 11x7½-inch pan. Bake for 15 minutes at 350°. Beat eggs. Sift sugar, flour, and salt. Mix with eggs. Add to this mixture, rhubarb, finely cut. Pour over crust and bake for 35 minutes at 350°.

Recipes from St. Michael's (Minnesota)

Danish Puff Pastry

1 cup flour
½ cup margarine

2 tablespoons water

Blend flour, margarine, and water. Roll into a ball. Divide in half. Spread the 2 halves on a large cookie sheet to 4x12 inches each.

TOPPING:

1 cup water
½ cup margarine
1 teaspoon almond extract

1 cup flour
3 eggs

Boil water and margarine. Remove from heat and add almond extract and flour. Mix until in a ball. Add eggs and beat in by hand, one at a time. Spread evenly on crust to edges. Bake at 350° for one hour or less until golden.

ICING:

1½ cups confectioners' sugar
2 tablespoons margarine

1 teaspoon vanilla
1–2 teaspoons warm water

Cream ingredients together and spread on pastry. Top with chopped nuts.

Cooking with the Lioness Club (Wisconsin)

Old-Fashioned Strawberry Shortcake

Pinch of salt
2 cups all-purpose flour
4 teaspoons baking powder
1 tablespoon sugar
4 tablespoons shortening
⅔–¾ cup milk

Butter
1 (10-ounce) box frozen strawberries, thawed
Sugar to taste
Heavy cream

Mix dry ingredients together. Work in shortening with fingertips. Add milk and mix to a soft dough. Pat out on a slightly floured board. Cut with a large round cutter. Bake in 425° oven for 10–15 minutes. Split open while hot and spread on a lot of butter. Pour crushed sweetened strawberries between layers and on top. Serve while warm with heavy cream.

Great Lakes Cookery (Michigan)

Cream Puff Dessert

1 cup water
½ cup margarine
1 cup all-purpose flour
4 eggs
2½ cups milk
1 (8-ounce) package cream
  cheese, softened

2 (3-ounce) packages vanilla
  instant pudding mix
1 (12-ounce) carton frozen
  whipped topping, thawed
Chocolate curls or chocolate
  syrup

Preheat oven to 400°. Grease a 10x15-inch jellyroll pan. In a saucepan over high heat, bring water and margarine to a boil. Reduce heat. Stir in flour until mixture forms a ball. Remove from heat. By hand, beat in eggs, one at a time. Beat well after each addition, until smooth. Spread mixture evenly over bottom of prepared pan. Bake 25 minutes. (Surface of pastry will be uneven.) Cool completely in pan on wire rack.

In large bowl, with electric mixer, beaters set on low speed, gradually blend milk into cream cheese, beating until smooth. Then add pudding mix. Beat on low speed until slightly thickened. Pour over crust. Spread thawed whipped topping over pudding mixture. Sprinkle with chocolate curls or drizzle chocolate syrup over top. Refrigerate until serving. To serve, cut into squares. Makes 24 (2½-inch) squares.

Recipes from Our Home to Yours (Michigan)

Cream Puff Dessert

CRUST:

1 cup flour
½ cup margarine

1 cup boiling water
4 eggs, unbeaten

Boil margarine in water. Add flour into steadily boiling water. Cook and stir constantly until mixture leaves sides of pan and is in smooth compact mass. Remove from heat and add one egg at a time. Beat well after each egg added, by hand. Spread dough in jellyroll pan and bake in hot oven (400°) for 15 minutes. Reduce heat to 350° and bake for 10–15 minutes more.

FILLING:

1 (8-ounce) package cream cheese
2 (3-ounce) packages instant vanilla pudding

3 cups milk
1 large carton Cool Whip
Hershey's Chocolate Syrup

Beat cream cheese, pudding, and milk together and pour over crust. Spread Cool Whip over pudding. Drizzle syrup on Cool Whip and may add chopped peanuts. Refrigerate.

Kompelien Family Cookbook (Minnesota)

Romme Grot

(Scandinavian Cream Pudding)

1 quart whipping cream (at least 24 hours old)
1 cup flour
1 quart milk (boiled)

1 teaspoon salt
1 tablespoon sugar
Butter
Sugar and cinnamon

Use heavy kettle, boil cream 10–15 minutes. Add flour slowly using a wire whip to keep mixture smooth, keep boiling on lower heat and stirring until butter appears. Add boiled milk and boil and stir to right consistency. Add sugar and salt. Put into bowl and pour butter over. Sprinkle with sugar and cinnamon. Serve lukewarm.

Bethany Lutheran Church Celebrating 110 Years (Minnesota)

Rice Pudding

½ cup rice (not Minute)
½ teaspoon salt
3 cups milk
1 package Knox gelatin

3 tablespoons water
1 cup whipping cream,
 whipped
1½ cups sugar

Cook rice, salt, and milk in a covered, double boiler until done, or about 1½–2 hours. Stir occasionally. Soak gelatin in water and add to the cooked rice. Stir gently and chill. Add whipped cream and sugar to the cooked, cooled rice. Put the pudding in an oiled ring mold.

SAUCE:

2 packages of frozen
 raspberries or strawberries
2½ tablespoons cornstarch

½ cup sugar
1 tablespoon lemon juice

Thaw berries (reserve 1 cup of juice). Add cornstarch and sugar to the juice and cook until thick. Add lemon juice after the mixture has cooked. Pour the mixture over the thawed fruit and cool.

Unmold the rice and serve the sauce in a dish placed in the middle of the rice ring.

Our Beloved Sweden: Food, Faith, Flowers & Festivals (Minnesota)

Baked Lemon Pudding

This baked pudding is very easy to make and can be served warm or cold. Be sure to use fresh lemon juice for best flavor. While pudding is baking, it separates into a thin bottom layer of lemon sauce with a fluffy cake-like layer on top.

¾ cup sugar, divided
5 tablespoons flour
¼ teaspoon baking powder
⅛ teaspoon salt
2 eggs, separated

3 tablespoons fresh lemon juice
Grated rind of 1 lemon
1½ tablespoons butter, melted
1 cup milk

Preheat oven to 375°. Combine ½ cup sugar with flour, baking powder, and salt. Beat egg yolks until light; add lemon juice, rind, butter, and milk. Beat well with a spoon. Stir in dry ingredients until smooth. Beat egg whites until foamy; gradually beat in remaining ¼ cup sugar until stiff but not dry. Fold into flour mixture.

Transfer mixture to 1-quart baking dish. Put baking dish in a larger pan filled with warm water. Bake at 375° for 40–45 minutes until top is firm and nicely browned. Makes 6 servings.

50 Years of Regal Recipes (Wisconsin)

The Green Bay Packers have been NFL champions 12 times (more than any other team in the NFL) and captured the first two Super Bowl titles and another one in 1997. The team was founded in 1919 by former high-school football rivals Earl "Curly" Lambeau and George Whitney Calhoun. Lambeau solicited funds for uniforms from his employer, the Indian Packing Company. He was given $500 for uniforms and equipment, on the condition that the team be named for its sponsor. Today "Green Bay Packers" is the oldest team name still in use in the NFL. The Packers are the only publicly owned, non-profit corporation major league professional sports team in the United States.

Bread Pudding with Lemon Sauce

2½ cups bread cubes
4 cups scalded milk
¾ cup sugar
2 tablespoons butter

¼ teaspoon salt
4 eggs, slightly beaten
1 teaspoon vanilla
Raisins as desired

Soak bread in milk 5 minutes. Add sugar, butter, and salt; pour slowly over beaten eggs. Add vanilla and raisins, if desired, and mix well. Pour into greased baking dish. Bake in pan of hot water at 350° till firm, about 50 minutes. Serve warm with Lemon Sauce.

LEMON SAUCE:
1 tablespoon cornstarch
½ cup sugar
½ teaspoon salt
1 cup boiling water

2 tablespoons butter
1½ tablespoons lemon juice
A little nutmeg

Mix cornstarch, sugar, and salt; gradually add boiling water, and cook over low heat till thick and clear. Add butter, lemon juice, and nutmeg; blend.

Home Cookin': First Congregational United Church of Christ (Michigan)

Pineapple Kugel

1 (12-ounce) package
   yolkless noodles
½ cup applesauce
1 (8-ounce) carton nonfat sour
   cream or yogurt
1 (12-ounce) carton nonfat
   cottage cheese
1 teaspoon vanilla

1 (8-ounce) can crushed
   pineapple
½ cup sugar
½ cup dried cherries
Cinnamon to taste
3 egg whites
Crushed cornflake crumbs with
   cinnamon (optional topping)

Cook and drain noodles; set aside. In a large bowl, mix together everything except egg whites and crumbs. Beat egg whites and fold into mixture; add cooked noodles. Spray Pam on 9x13-inch pan; pour in mixture. Add cornflake crumbs for topping, if desired. Bake at 350° for 35–45 minutes.

The Fruit of Her Hands (Michigan)

Lori's Easy Magic Shell Ice Cream Dessert

12 ice cream sandwiches
2 (8-ounce) containers Cool Whip, thawed
1 large jar marshmallow fluff
2 boxes Heath Klondike Ice Cream Bars

2 bottles Magic Shell chocolate or fudge topping
Chopped nuts, M&M's, or toffee chips for topping

In a 9x13-inch pan, place ice cream sandwiches, cutting to fit edges (probably won't use them all). Mix Cool Whip and marshmallow fluff together. Cover sandwiches with half the mixture. Put layer of Heath Klondike Bars on top and cover with remaining Cool Whip mixture. Shake Magic Shell and pour over Cool Whip layer. Sprinkle nuts or whatever topping you prefer over top quickly before shell hardens. Place in freezer for several hours before serving. Serves 10–12.

Favorite Recipes from Our Kitchens to Yours (Michigan)

Apple-Crisp Parfait

Unbelievably fantastic!

2 cups quick-cook rolled oats
½ cup butter or margarine, melted
½ cup brown sugar, firmly packed

1 (21-ounce) can apple pie filling
½ teaspoon cinnamon
Vanilla ice cream

Preheat oven to 300°. Use one ungreased 11x15-inch cookie sheet. Combine oats, butter, and brown sugar in bowl; mix well. Bake 20 minutes using cookie sheet. Cool completely. (Oatcrisp will harden as it cools.)

Break oatcrisp into small pieces. If not making parfait immediately, this can be stored in an airtight container. Mix pie filling and cinnamon in small bowl; chill.

In 6 parfait glasses layer a scoop of ice cream, 2 tablespoons pie filling and 2 tablespoons oatcrisp mixture. Repeat layers again until glasses are filled; finish with oatcrisp mixture. Serve immediately. Makes 6 servings.

Kinder Bakker (Michigan)

Buster Bar Dessert

½ cup melted butter
1 pound sandwich cookies
½ gallon vanilla ice cream
2 cups Spanish peanuts (or
  more to suit taste)

2 cups powdered sugar
⅔ cup chocolate chips
1½ cups evaporated milk
½ cup butter
1 teaspoon vanilla

Mix together melted butter and crushed sandwich cookies. Place in a 9x13-inch pan; refrigerate until firm.

Place ice cream (softened) on top of crust, then peanuts. Mix together powdered sugar, chocolate chips, evaporated milk and butter. Boil this mixture for 8 minutes, then stir and add vanilla. Cool and pour on top layer; freeze.

Salem Cook Book II (Minnesota)

©TODD MURRAY, WWW.WIKIPEDIA.ORG

Declared the world's largest flour mill after its completion in 1880, the structure housing Mill City Museum is a National Historic Landmark. Known as the Washburn A Mill, it was nearly destroyed by fire in 1991. After the City of Minneapolis cleaned up the rubble and fortified the mill's charred walls, the Minnesota Historical Society constructed a milling museum and education center within the ruins. Located on the historic Mississippi Riverfront, visitors of all ages learn about the intertwined histories of the flour industry, the river, and the city of Minneapolis.

For nearly 50 years, the Washburn A Mill was the most technologically advanced and the largest mill in the world. At the peak of its production, it could grind over 100 boxcars of wheat into almost 2,000,000 pounds of flour per day. After World War I, flour production in Minneapolis began to decline as flour milling technology no longer depended on water power. The mill was shut down in 1965, along with eight other of the oldest mills.

Cherry Breeze

⅓ cup butter
1 cup corn flake crumbs
½ cup lemon juice
1 (8-ounce) package cream
  cheese, softened

1 (14-ounce) can sweetened
  condensed milk
1 teaspoon vanilla
1 can cherry pie filling

Melt butter. Stir in corn flake crumbs. Pat into 8x8-inch pan. Chill. In a bowl, mix lemon juice, cream cheese, sweetened condensed milk and vanilla. Pour over corn flake mixture. Chill. Top with cherry pie filling. Keep refrigerated until served.

Camp Hope Cookbook (Wisconsin)

Lace-Crusted Apples

5 tart cooking apples
3 tablespoons raisins
1 tablespoon lemon juice
Water
1½ teaspoons grated lemon
  peel
1 tablespoon lemon juice

½ teaspoon cinnamon
1½ cups brown sugar, firmly
  packed
½ cup finely chopped walnuts
½ cup melted butter
Vanilla ice cream

Peel and core apples. Cut into ⅓-inch thick lengthwise slices. Place in saucepan with raisins, lemon juice, and water to cover halfway. Cover; bring to a boil. Simmer until tender, about 5 minutes. Drain well. Turn into a 10-inch oven glassware pie plate. Sprinkle with lemon peel, lemon juice, and cinnamon. Combine brown sugar, walnuts, and melted butter; sprinkle over fruits. Broil about 6 inches from heat until sugar is melted and golden brown. Cool slightly. Tap crust to break and top with ice cream. Makes 6 servings.

Country Heart Cooking (Wisconsin)

Cherry Soup

Some people say they come to Pommerntag just for this wonderful fruit soup!

4 cups water
1¾ cups sugar

3 cups fresh pitted sour cherries

Boil water with sugar, add cherries and cook to soften. Check sweetness and add more sugar if necessary. Bring to a good boil.

DUMPLING MIXTURE:

1 egg, beaten
½ teaspoon baking powder
4 tablespoons flour, heaping

¾ cup milk
Pinch of salt

Mix together. It will look like cake batter. Continue cooking soup while dribbling in (pouring in slowly) the dumpling mixture. Remove from heat. Eat warm or cold.

Favorite Recipes of Pommern Cooks (Wisconsin)

Contributing Cookbooks

The Dells of the Wisconsin River is a five-mile gorge on the Wisconsin River in southern Wisconsin noted for its scenic beauty, in particular for its unique sandstone rock formations and canyons. The cliffs, some over 100 feet high, and side canyons are closed to the public to protect sensitive ecological features. Viewing of the area by water is a popular attraction. The nearby city of Wisconsin Dells is the center of summer tourist activity.

Listed below are the cookbooks that have contributed recipes to this book, along with copyright, author, publisher, city, and state.

a-MAIZE-ing Tailgating ©1997 by Suzanna Wangler, Troy, MI

A-Peeling Apple Recipes, Friends of Retzer Nature Center, Waukesha, WI

All in Good Taste I & II ©1979–1989 Service League, Inc., Fond du Lac, WI

Allen Park Garden Club Recipe Book, Allen Park, MI

Anoka County 4H Cook Book, Anoka, MN

Apples, Brie & Chocolate ©1996 by Nell Stehr, Amherst Press, Amherst, WI

The Bell Tower Cookbook ©1995 Catholic Community of St. Andrew Church, Rochester, MI

The Best Cranberry Recipes, Eagle River Cranberry Fest, Eagle River, WI

The Best of Breakfast Menus & Recipes, Parish House Inn, Ypsilanti, MI

Bethany Lutheran Church Celebrating 110 Years, Lydia Circle, Bethany Lutheran Church, Windom, MN

Bethany Lutheran Church Celebrating 125 Years, Bethany WELCA, Jackson, MN

Between the Lakes ©2005 Junior League of Saginaw Valley, Saginaw, MI

Blessed Be the Cook, St. Anne's Altar Society, Camp Douglas, WI

Blissfield Preschool Cookbook, Blissfield Preschool Co-op, Blissfield, MI

The Bountiful Arbor ©1994 The Junior League of Ann Arbor, MI

Bringing Grand Tastes to Grand Traverse ©1994 Newcomers Club of Grand Traverse, MI

Camp Hope Cookbook, Camp Hope, Stevens Point, WI

Cardinal Country Cooking, School District of Brodhead Playground, Brodhead, WI

Celebrating 150 Years of Faith and Food, Christ Lutheran Church Women, DeForest, WI

Celebrating 300 Years of Detroit Cooking ©2001, Detroit Historical Society Guild, Detroit, MI

Celebration of Grace, Our Savior's Lutheran Church, Oconomowoc, WI

Centennial Cookbook, Second Presbyterian Church, Racine, WI

Centennial Cookbook, Welcome Corners United Methodist Church, Hastings, MI

The Centennial Society Cookbook, Centennial Society Union Congregational Church, Elk River, MN

A Century of Recipes Through the Windows of Time, East Congregational United Church of Christ, Grand Rapids, MI

Cherry Berries on a Cloud and More, Trinity Pilgrim United Methodist Women, Brookfield, WI

Cherry Home Companion ©2002 by Patty LaNoue Sterns, Arbutus Press, Traverse City, MI

Chickadee Cottage Cookbook, by Donna Hawkins, Mahtomedi, MN

Clinton's 110th Cookbook, Clinton Ladies Civic Club, Clinton, MN

The Clovia Recipe Collection ©1996 Alumnae Assn. Beta of Clovia, Bloomington, MN

A Collection of Recipes, St. Joseph's Home and School Assn., Stratford, WI

Come and Discover Special Appetites, Capital Area Down Syndrome Assn., Mason, MI

Cook Book: The Best of Michigan ©1994 June Harding, Ferndale, MI

Cooking with Friends, by Dorothy Jean Bixel Aschenbrenner, Pinckney, MI

Cooking with Grace, St. Bernard Parish, Wauwatosa, WI

Cooking with the Lioness Club, Brown Deer, WI

Cooks Extraordinaries ©1993 Service League of Green Bay, Inc., Green Bay, WI

Country Cookbook, Marilla Historical Society, Copemish, MI

Country Heart Cooking, by Lois A. Johnson, Plainfield, WI

Country Life: Vegetarian Cookbook ©1990 Family Health Publications, Hope, MI

Cranbrook Reflections ©1991 Cranbrook House and Gardens Auxiliary, Bloomfield Hills, MI

Create, Share, Enjoy!, St. Joseph's Christian Women's Society, Brookfield, WI

Crooked Lake Volunteer Fire Department Cookbook, Ladies Auxiliary, Crivitz, WI

Crystal Clear Cooking ©1995 by Judy Brouwer, Beulah, MI

Dad's Cook Book, by C. G. Oplinger, Sliverwood, MI

Dawn to Dusk ©1996 Holland Junior Welfare League, Holland, MI

Dell & Barry's Holiday Delights for All Seasons, by Dell Vaugh and Barry Stutesman, Rose City, MI

The Dexter Cider Mill Apple Cookbook ©1995 by Katherine Merkel Koziski, Chelsea, MI

Dorthy Rickers Cookbook: Mixing & Musing, by Dorthy Rickers, Worthington, MN

Dr. Martin Luther Church 100th Anniversary Cookbook, Dr. Martin Luther Church, Oconomowoc, WI

Drink Your Beer & Eat It Too ©1995 Amherst Press, Amherst, WI

Duluth Woman's Club 70th Anniversary Cookbook, Duluth, MN

Eet Smakelijk ©1976 Holland Junior Welfare League, Holland, MI

Encore Wisconsin ©1992 Amherst Press, Amherst, WI

Family Fare, by Arieth Erickson, Grantsburg, WI

Favorite Recipes of Lester Park & Rockridge Schools, Duluth, MN

Favorite Recipes from Our Kitchens to Yours, Women's Ministries of Michiana Christian Embassy, Niles, MI

Favorite Recipes of the Wisconsin NFO, Sauk City, WI

Feeding the Flock, Maple Grove Evangelical Free Church, Maple Grove, MN

Ferndale Friends Cook Book, by June Harding, Ferndale, MI

Fifth Avenue Food Fare, Fifth Avenue United Methodist Church, West Bend, WI

Fifty Nifty . . . Cool Summer Recipes, by Angie Wazny, Saginaw, MI

50 Years of Regal Recipes ©1995 Amherst Press, Amherst, WI

Finn Creek Museum Cookbook, Minnesota Finnish American Historical Society, New York Mills, MN

Fish & Game Menu Cookbook ©1987 by Kay L. Richey, Grawn, MI

The Flavors of Mackinac ©1997 Mackinac Island Medical Center, Mackinac Island, MI

Flavors of Washington County, Washington County Historical Society, Inc., West Bend, WI

Four Seasons Cookbook ©1993 by Bea Smith, Avery Color Studios, Gwinn, MI

Four Seasons at Hawks Inn, Hawks Inn Historical Society, Inc., Delafield, WI

Foxy Ladies ©1981 by Ellen Kort, Appleton, WI

Fresh Market Wisconsin by Terese Allen ©1993 Amherst Press, Amherst, WI

From Minnesota: More Than a Cookbook ©1985 Laurie and Debra Gluesing, Shoreview, MN

From Our Home to Yours, United Home Health Services, Inc., Canton, MI

From the Recipe File of Agnes Gaffaney, by Cindy Stamness, Mora, MN

The Fruit of Her Hands, Temple Israel Sisterhood, West Bloomfield, MI

Generations of Treasured Recipes!, NAHCA, Powers, MI

Good Food from Michigan ©1995 by Laurie Woody, Johnston, IA

Grandmothers of Greenbush ©1996 Amherst Press, Amherst, WI

Great Cooks of Zion Church, Zion United Church of Christ, Le Sueur, MN

Great Lakes Cookery ©1991 by Bea Smith, Avery Color Studios, Gwinn, MI

Green Thumbs in the Kitchen ©1996 Green Thumb, Inc., Wisconsin Program, Neillsville, WI

Growing & Using Herbs by Rosemary Divock ©1996 Amherst Press, Amherst, WI

Have Breakfast with Us II ©1993 Wisconsin Bed and Breakfast Homes and Historic Inns Assn., Sheboygan, WI

Have Breakfast with Us . . . Again ©1995 Amherst Press, Amherst, WI

Heart Smart Cookbook II ©1996 Detroit Free Press / Henry Ford Health System, Detroit, MI

Heart Smart Kids Cookbook ©2000 Detroit Free Press / Henry Ford Health System, Detroit, MI

Heavenly Helpings, Friends of Hospice, Owosso, MI

Herbs in a Minnesota Kitchen, by Jan Benskin and Bonnie Dehn, Ramsey, MN

Here's to Your Heart: Cooking Smart, The Heart Care Center, Waukesha, WI

High Fit–Low Fat Vegetarian ©1996 The University of Michigan Medical Center, Ann Arbor, MI

Historically Delicious ©1994 Tri-Cities Historical Society, Grand Haven, MI

History from the Hearth ©1997 by Sally Eustice, Mackinaw City, MI

Hollyhocks & Radishes ©1989 by Bonnie Stewart Mickelson, Belleview, WA

Home Cookin', Almont Elementary PTA, Almont, MI

Home Cookin': First Congregational United Church of Christ, Morenci, MI

In the Dough ©1994 The J. B. Dough Company, St. Joseph, MI

The Junior League of Grand Rapids Cookbook I ©1976 Junior League of Grand Rapids, MI

Just Inn Time for Breakfast ©1992 by Tracy and Phyllis Winters, Winters Publishing, Greensburg, IN

Kinder Bakker ©1983 Holland Junior Welfare League, Holland, MI

Kitchen Keepsakes, The Houselog Family, Ellsworth, MN

Kompelien Family Cookbook, by Janeen Kompelien, Cottonwood, MN

Life Tastes Better Than Steak Cookbook, Avery Color Studios, Gwinn, MI

Look What's Cookin' at Wal-Mart, Children's Miracle Network, Black River Falls, WI

Look What's Cooking at C.A.M.D.E.N, C.A.M.D.E.N. Foundation, Inc., Milton, WI

The Madison Herb Society Cookbook ©1995 The Madison Herb Society, Madison, WI

The Manor Cookbook, Jonesville, MI

Maple Hill Cookbook, Maple Hill Senior Citizens Club, Hibbing, MN

Marketplace Recipes Volume I, Action Advertising, Inc., Fond du Lac, WI

Marquette University High School Mother's Guild Cookbook, Milwaukee, WI

Martha Chapter #132 OES Cookbook, Order of Eastern Star, Anoka, MN

McManus Family Recipes Volumes 2 and 3, by Theresa Neville, Manistique, MI

Michigan Gourmet Cookbook ©1996 Michigan Gourmet Television, Lansing, MI

Michigan Magazine Family and Friends Cookbook II, Michigan Magazine, Rose City, MI

Minnesota Heritage Cookbook II ©1985 American Cancer Society, MN Division

Mt. Carmel's "Cooking with the Oldies," Mount Carmel Medical and Rehabilitation Center, Burlington, WI

Mrs. Boone's Wild Game Cookbook ©1992 Momentum Books, Troy, MI

Mucky Duck Mustard Cookbook ©1991 by Michele Marshall, Mucky Duck Mustard Co., Bloomfield Hills, MI

Northcountry Kitchens Cookbook ©1980, Sion Lutheran Church, Gwinn, MI

The Oke Family Cookbook ©1994 by Barbara and Deborah Oke, Minneapolis, MN

Old Westbrook Evangelical Lutheran Church Cookbook, Old Westbrook WELCA, Lamberton, MN

Old World Swiss Family Recipes, Monroe Swiss Singers of Monroe, WI

One Hundred Years of Sharing, Calvary Covenant Women, Evansville, MN

Opaa! Greek Cooking Detroit Style ©1993 by George Gekas, Bonus Books, Chicago, IL

Our Beloved Sweden: Food, Faith, Flowers & Festivals ©1996 by Janet Letnes Martin and Ilene Letnes Lorenz, Hastings, MN

Our Best Cookbook 2 ©1993 Amherst Press, Amherst, WI

Our Best Home Cooking, Keep Michigan Beautiful, Inc., Farmington, MI

Our Favorite Recipes, Aurdal Lutheran Church, Underwood, MN

The Ovens of Brittany Cookbook, by Terese Allen ©1991 Amherst Press, Amherst, WI

The Palmyra Heritage Cookbook, Palmyra Historical Society, Palmyra, WI

People Pleasers, by Goldie Pope Lohse, Fairmont, MN

Pleasures from the Good Earth, Heritage Circle of RLDS Church, St. John, MI

Potluck Volume II, Minnesota Catholic Daughters of the Americas, Medford, MN

Queen of Angels Anniversary Cookbook, The Queen of Angels Women's Council, Austin, MN

Recipes from the Flock, Tonseth Lutheran Church, Erhard, MN

Recipes from Joan's Kitchen, by Joan Kitiuk, Rock, MI

Recipes and Memories, Romeo Monday Club, Romeo, MI

Recipes from Minnesota with Love ©1981 by Betty Malisow, Strawberry Point, Inc., Prior Lake, MN

Recipes from St. Michael's, St. Michael's Cookbook Committee, Bloomington, MN

Recipes of Note for Entertaining, Rochester Civic Music Guild, Rochester, MN

Recipes & Remembrances II, Rockwood Area Historical Society, Rockwood, MI

Red Flannel Town Recipes, Red Flannel Festival, Cedar Springs, MI

Red Oak Grove Lutheran Church Family Cookbook, Women of the Evangelical Lutheran of America, Austin, MN

Renaissance Cuisine ©1981 Fontbonne Auxiliary of St. John Hospital & Medical Center, Detroit, MI

The Rustic Gourmet ©2007 by Marie Lapointe Hanis, Williamsburg, MI

Sacred Heart Centennial Cookbook, Sacred Heart Altar Society, Mondovi, WI

Salem Cook Book II, Salem Lutheran Church Women, Montevideo, MN

Seasoned Cooks II, Isabella County Commission on Aging, Mt. Pleasant, MI

Seasoned with Love, Trinity Unity United Church of Christ, Brookfield, WI

Seasons of a Farm Family ©1996 JDK Productions, Amherst Press, Amherst, WI

Serving from the Heart, Our Redeemer Lutheran Church Choir, Ramsay, MI

Sharing Our Best, Berger Lutheran Church, Montevideo, MN

Sharing Our Best, Home of the Good Shepherd, St. Paul, MN

Sharing Our Best, Michigan State Grange, Haslett, MI

Sharing Our Best, St. Joseph Parish, Stevens Point, WI

Sharing Our Best Volume II, Harrietta Area Civic Club, Harrietta, MI

Sharing Our Best to Help the Rest, United Way of the Saint Paul Area, St. Paul, MN

Ships of the Great Lakes Cookbook ©2001 Creative Characters Publishing Group, Central Lake, MI

The Simply Great Cookbook I & II ©1992 C. A. Muer Corporation, Troy, MI

Simply Sensational, Our Lady Queen of Apostles Parish, Hamtramck, MI

Smart Snacks ©1994 by Betsy Rhein and Sandy Drummond, Holland, MI

Some Enchanted Eating ©1986 Friends of the Symphony, Muskegon, MI

Something Special, by Sharon Zubosky Breyer, Traverse City, MI

Soul Food, Ascension Lutheran Church, East Lansing, MI

Sparks from the Kitchen, by Syd and Florence Herman, Manitowoc, WI

Spice of Life Cookbook ©1995 by Triva Davis, Dousman, WI

The Spice of Life Cookbook ©1997 by Jeffrey C. Leeds, Troy, MI

St. Charles Parish Cookbook, St. Charles Parish, Cassville, WI

St. Frederick Parish Centennial Recipe Collection, Cudahy, WI

St. John Evangelical Lutheran Church, St. John Ladies Aid, Stratford, WI

St. Mark's Lutheran Church Cookbook, Sarah Circle, St. Mark's, Manawa, WI

St. Mary's Family Cookbook, St. Mary's Council of Catholic Women, Bloomington, WI

The Sunday Cook Collection ©1993 by Grace Howaniec, Amherst Press, Amherst, WI

Sunflowers & Samovars, St. Nicholas Orthodox Church, Kenosha, WI

Sweet Traditions, The Cookie Connection, Hamtramck, MI

Taste and See, St. Philip Neri Catholic Church, Milwaukee, WI

Taste of Clarkston: Tried & True Recipes, Clarkston Area Chamber of Commerce, Clarkston, MI

A Taste of Home, South Wood County YMCA Woman's Auxiliary, Port Edwards, WI

Taste of Kennedy Cook Book, Kennedy Elementary PTSA, Willmar, MN

Tasteful Art ©1995 Working Women Artists, Lansing, MI

Tasteful Garden Treasures, by Nancy Smith, Taylor Garden Club, Taylor, MI

Thank Heaven for Home Made Cooks, First Congregational U.C.C., Oconomowoc, WI

A Thyme for All Seasons ©1982 Junior League of Duluth, MN

Treasured Recipes of Chippewa County, Chippewa County Historical Society, Montevideo, MN

Treasured Recipes from Treasured Friends, by Colleen Beal, Faribault, MN

Treasures from Heaven, Countryside U. B. Church, Breckenridge, MI

Trendfully Cookin', Trendway Corporation, Holland, MI

The Ultimate Potato Cookbook, Williams Community Commercial Assn., Williams, MN

Vaer saa god Cookbook, WELCA St. John's Lutheran Church, Springfield, MN

Vegetarian International Cuisine ©1996 The Cheese Factory Cookbook, LLC., Wisconsin Dells, WI

Wannaska Centennial, Riverside Lutheran Church, Wannaska, MN

What's Cooking at St. Stephens, Street Ann's Alter Society, Port Huron, MI

What's Cookin', by Jeanne E. Briggs, Rockford, MI

What's Cook'n?, Manitou Girl Scout Council, Sheboygan, WI

What's on the Agenda?, The Woman's Club of DePere, WI

When Friends Cook, Friends of the Minneapolis Institute of Arts, Minneapolis, MN

Wild Game Recipes from the Heart of the U.P., P-S Recreation Club, Powers, MI

Winnehaha's Favorite Recipes, Winnehaha's of Minnesota, Circle Pines, MN

Winning Recipes from Wisconsin with Love, by The Cooks of Wisconsin, Prior Lake, MN

Wisconsin Cooks with Wisconsin Public Television ©1996 Friends of WHA-TV, Inc., Madison, WI

Wisconsin Pure Maple Syrup Cookbook, Wisconsin Maple Syrup Producers, Holcombe, WI

Wisconsin's Best, Women's Auxiliary WAPHCC, Waukesha, WI

Woman's National Farm and Garden Association–Rochester Cookbook Volume II, Troy, MI

Zingerman's Guide to Good Eating ©2003 by Ari Weinzwig, Ann Arbor, MI

Index

© TRAVEL MICHIGAN

Michigan's Mackinac Island's population grows from roughly 550 people year-round to 15,000 visitors during the summer. The island is located in Lake Huron, between the state's Upper and Lower Peninsulas and can only be reached by boat, small aircraft, and, in the winter, by snowmobile. The entire island is listed as a National Historic Landmark.

INDEX